AF761817

Resolving Conflicts between Human Rights

Under the influence of the global spread of human rights, legal disputes are increasingly framed in human rights terms. Parties to a legal dispute can often invoke human rights norms in support of their competing claims. Yet, when confronted with cases in which human rights conflict, judges face a dilemma. They have to make difficult choices between superior norms that deserve equal respect. In this high-level book, the author sets out how judges the world over could resolve conflicts between human rights. He presents an innovative legal theoretical account of such conflicts, questioning the relevance of the influential proportionality test to their resolution. Instead, the author develops a novel resolution framework, specifically designed to tackle human rights conflicts. The book combines concerted normative theory with profound practical analysis, firmly rooting its theoretical arguments in human rights practice. Although the analysis draws primarily on the case law of the European Court of Human Rights, the book's core arguments are applicable to judicial practice in general. As such, the book should be of great interest to academics, postgraduate students and legal practitioners in Europe and beyond. The book is particularly suited for use in advanced courses on legal theory, human rights law and jurisprudence.

Stijn Smet is Postdoctoral Fellow at the Law School of Ghent University. His research interests are human rights, legal theory and political theory. He has published on human rights conflicts in *Human Rights Law Review*, *American University International Law Review* and *Religion & Human Rights*.

Routledge Research in Human Rights Law

Available titles in this series include:

Care, Migration and Human Rights
Law and Practice
Siobhán Mullally

The Protection of Vulnerable Groups under International Human Rights Law
Ingrid Nifosi-Sutton

Human Dignity and Degrading Treatment in the European Convention on Human Rights
The Ends of Article 3 of the European Convention on Human Right
Elaine Webster

The Istanbul Convention, Domestic Violence and Human Rights
Ronagh McQuigg

The Right to Truth in International Law
Victims' Rights in Human Rights and International Criminal Law
Edited by Melanie Klinkner and Howard Davis

Children's Rights Law in the Global Human Rights Landscape
Isolation, inspiration, integration?
Edited by Eva Brems, Ellen Desmet and Wouter Vandenhole

Human Rights in the Media
Fear and Fetish
Edited by Michelle Farrell, Edel Hughes and Eleanor Drywood

Freedom of Expression and Religious Hate Speech
You Can't Say That!
Erica Howard

The Right to Food
From Sovereignty to Security
Kirsteen Shields

Resolving Conflicts between Human Rights
The judge's dilemma

Stijn Smet

Routledge
Taylor & Francis Group
LONDON AND NEW YORK

First published 2017 by Routledge

2 Park Square, Milton Park, Abingdon, Oxfordshire OX14 4RN
52 Vanderbilt Avenue, New York, NY 10017

Routledge is an imprint of the Taylor & Francis Group, an informa business

First issued in paperback 2018

Copyright © 2017 Stijn Smet

The right of Stijn Smet to be identified as author of this work has been asserted by him in accordance with sections 77 and 78 of the Copyright, Designs and Patents Act 1988.

All rights reserved. No part of this book may be reprinted or reproduced or utilised in any form or by any electronic, mechanical, or other means, now known or hereafter invented, including photocopying and recording, or in any information storage or retrieval system, without permission in writing from the publishers.

Notice:
Product or corporate names may be trademarks or registered trademarks, and are used only for identification and explanation without intent to infringe.

British Library Cataloguing in Publication Data
A catalogue record for this book is available from the British Library

Library of Congress Cataloging in Publication Data
Names: Smet, Stijn, author.
Title: Resolving conflicts between human rights : the judge's dilemma / Stijn Smet.
Description: Abingdon, Oxon [UK] ; New York : Routledge, 2017. | Series: Routledge research in human rights law | Includes bibliographical references and index.
Identifiers: LCCN 2016029868| ISBN 9781138658011 (hbk) | ISBN 9781315621012 (ebk)
Subjects: LCSH: Human rights. | Civil rights.
Classification: LCC K3240 .S5485 2017 | DDC 342.08/5—dc23
LC record available at https://lccn.loc.gov/2016029868

ISBN: 978-1-138-65801-1 (hbk)
ISBN: 978-0-367-07566-8 (pbk)

Typeset in Galliard
By Keystroke, Neville Lodge, Tettenhall, Wolverhampton

Contents

Acknowledgements

This book is based on my Ph.D. dissertation, entitled 'Resolving Conflicts between Human Rights: A Legal Theoretical Analysis in the Context of the ECHR', which I defended at Ghent University on 2 April 2014. I am exceedingly grateful and deeply indebted, first and foremost, to the supervisor of my doctoral research, Eva Brems. In my dissertation, and in this book, I further develop a framework for the resolution of human rights conflicts she first sketched in her work. Without Eva's sincere encouragement to build upon her work, and without her invaluable support and ever critical eye, this book would never have seen the light of day.

I also wish to extend my profound thanks to the members of the guidance committee of my doctoral research, Françoise Tulkens and Sébastien Van Drooghenbroeck, for their insightful comments, probing questions and eagerness to think with me throughout the research process. I am particularly indebted to Françoise Tulkens for believing in the value of the research presented in this book, not only as an academic, but also as (then) Judge and Vice-President of the European Court of Human Rights. I am, finally, extremely grateful to the remaining evaluators of my Ph.D. dissertation: Janneke Gerards, Lorenzo Zucca, Dirk Voorhoof, Mark Van Hoecke, Eduard Somers and Johan Erauw. Their critical remarks on my dissertation, and positive responses thereto, were of immeasurable value in convincing me of the salience of this book.

I owe a special thank you to my colleagues at the Human Rights Centre of Ghent University's Law School, for providing a stimulating (and often fun) research environment, as well as for their thoughtful – and thought provoking – feedback on parts of the research presented in this book. I am exceedingly grateful, in particular, to the four persons with whom I commenced my Ph.D. research as part of a European Research Council project: Lourdes Peroni, Maris Burbergs, Alexandra Timmer and Saïla Ouald Chaib. To Lourdes especially: I could absolutely not have done this without you! I am also deeply grateful for the important feedback I received from countless participants at numerous conferences, seminars and workshops at which I presented parts of my research. I finally wish to extend my profound thanks to Routledge for believing in the value of this book, to two anonymous referees for their critical comments and invaluable suggestions for improvement of the book's argument and structure, and to Katie Carpenter, Olivia Manley, Sue Cope and Sarahjayne Smith for their impeccable editorial support throughout the publication process.

The research presented in this book was made possible thanks to funding provided by the European Research Council and the Special Research Fund of Ghent University (*Bijzonder Onderzoeksfonds*).

Introduction

Under the influence of the global spread of human rights, legal disputes across the globe are increasingly framed in human rights terms. In a myriad of court cases the world over, opposing parties can invoke human rights norms in support of their competing claims. Take, for instance, a labour dispute in which a church invokes its religious freedom to shield it from the complaint of a lay employee, who claims that his dismissal for having engaged in an extramarital relationship has violated his right to privacy. Or take the case of a politician who sues a newspaper for defamation, claiming that a corruption story on the newspaper's front page has breached her right to reputation. Or the case of an adopted person who seeks a court order for the disclosure of information related to her origins, against the express wishes of her biological mother, who had given birth to her anonymously.

When confronted with such cases in which human rights conflict, judges face a dilemma. In 'traditional' human rights cases, in which human rights are opposed by the public interest, the former arguably function as 'trumps' over or 'shields' against the latter. Human rights, in other words, hold special normative force over the public interest invoked to justify their infringement. In 'traditional' human rights cases, the scales of justice are thus loaded in favour of human rights. When human rights conflict with each other, however, there are no 'trumps' to be played or 'shields' to be wielded. Instead, often difficult choices have to be made between superior norms that deserve principled equal respect. I do not mean to imply, here, that 'traditional' human rights cases are always easy to resolve, nor that conflicts between human rights invariably make for complex cases. But human rights conflicts do pose particular challenges for adjudication. Those challenges are identified and tackled throughout this book.

The central argument of this book is that human rights conflicts are uniquely problematic, in that they are special kinds of hard cases that require a distinct resolution framework. The need for such a distinct framework flows directly from the special normative force of human rights, as 'trumps' over or 'shields' against the public interest. Taking the special normative force of human rights seriously, I posit, necessitates a departure from the proportionality test in the specific domain of human rights conflicts. Throughout this book, I question the relevance of the proportionality test, ubiquitous in human rights reasoning, to conflicts between human rights. Instead, I propose an alternative (or refined) framework, specifically designed to tackle the hard cases in which human rights collide.

In presenting a legal theoretical argument on the adjudication of human rights conflicts, this book pursues three core aims: (1) to debunk the scholarly argument that human rights conflicts do not pose distinct challenges for adjudication; (2) to propose a theoretically sound and practically useful framework for judicial practice, which currently struggles to adequately conceptualise and resolve human rights conflicts; and (3) to develop an alternative to – or refined account of – the proportionality test in the specific domain of conflicts between human rights.

Structure and content

This book on human rights conflicts is composed of three parts. Part I identifies the special nature of conflicts between human rights, provides a definition of human rights conflicts, introduces a framework for their resolution and discusses the first and second steps of the framework (defusing conflicts and reaching compromises, respectively). Parts II and III focus on the third and final step of the framework: balancing of human rights. Part II deals with theoretical challenges against and practical obstacles to balancing. Part III, conversely, aims to make balancing work for conflicts between human rights by proposing a structured balancing test, evaluating it against alternative tests and exploring its limits.

In more detailed terms, the book's argument proceeds as follows. In Chapter 1, I make the case for special treatment of human rights conflicts as a distinct category of hard cases in law. I first dispel the 'specificationist' argument that human rights conflicts do not exist. The specificationist argument insists that, once properly defined, human rights are absolute norms that cannot conflict with each other. Contrary to the specificationist argument, I submit that human rights function as principles. As *pro tanto* rights, I posit, they can and do conflict with each other in concrete cases. Having dispelled the specificationist argument that human rights conflicts do not exist, I move on to consider the proportionality argument that, although real, human rights conflicts are not special. On the proportionality argument, human rights conflicts do not pose distinct challenges for adjudication. Instead, they are to be resolved like all other conflicts of principles: through application of the proportionality test. Contrary to the proportionality argument, I posit that taking the special normative force of human rights seriously requires the development of a distinct framework for their resolution. The framework, which I introduce in Chapter 1 and elaborate in Chapters 3 and 6, is composed of three consecutive steps: (1) defusing human rights conflicts, (2) reaching a compromise between human rights in conflict, and (3) balancing human rights.

Before detailing the different steps of the framework, I first define conflicts between human rights. In Chapter 2, I argue that the need to unmask human rights rhetoric, counteract aggregation of interests and elude speculation warrants a rather narrow definition of human rights conflicts. The narrow definition I propose aims to erect a barrier between 'traditional' human rights cases, in which human rights are opposed by the public interest, and genuine human rights conflicts. I define genuine conflicts with reference to incompatible duties of the state towards human rights that are actually and sufficiently at stake. To operationalise the definition for judicial practice, I propose a double test that may assist judges in identifying genuine human rights conflicts in concrete cases.

To tackle purported human rights conflicts, I develop a distinct resolution framework throughout the book. In Chapter 3, I detail the first and second steps of the framework. These steps are concerned, respectively, with defusing conflicts between human rights and reaching a compromise between human rights in conflict. I present defusing as the optimal approach to human rights conflicts, since it allows judges to remove conflicts themselves while keeping the human rights within them intact. Whenever a conflict cannot be avoided, I posit, the impact of its resolution should at least be minimised. I argue that such minimisation is best achieved by reaching a compromise between human rights in conflict, wherever feasible. Most human rights conflicts, however, will resist defusing and elude compromises. In most cases, balancing between human rights will prove inevitable. Given the centrality of balancing to the resolution of human rights conflicts, I dedicate the remaining chapters of the book to making balancing work.

In Chapters 4 and 5, respectively, I discuss theoretical challenges against and practical obstacles to balancing. In Chapter 4, I identify incommensurability as the primary theoretical challenge against balancing human rights. Incommensurability of human rights – *i.e.* the absence of a common metric through which the relationship between human rights can be adequately expressed – precludes balancing, insofar as balancing is understood along the scales metaphor. Human rights do not have weight. They can therefore not be weighed against each other in the manner suggested by the scales metaphor of balancing. To overcome the challenge from incommensurability, I propose to abandon the scales metaphor of balancing and the concomitant idea of weight altogether. Although both offer the benefit of painting a visual image of balancing in the eye of the beholder, they ultimately do more to obscure balancing than to elucidate it. Instead, I favour Kai Möller's conception of 'balancing as reasoning',[1] a mode of practical reasoning that I develop to enable comparative judgments on the strength of reasons in favour of – and against – human rights in conflict. To operationalise such 'balancing as reasoning', I outline the skeleton of a structured balancing test in Chapter 4 (I develop the test in full in Chapter 6).

In Chapter 5, I turn from *theoretical* challenges against balancing to *practical* obstacles to balancing in judicial practice. I identify and discuss four practical obstacles to balancing: subjectivity in open ended balancing; overzealous reliance on intuitions by judges in balancing; lack of coherence within and across balancing decisions; and 'preferential framing' – or skewing – of judicial balancing exercises. Throughout Chapter 5, I argue that the structured balancing

1 Kai Möller, *The Global Model of Constitutional Rights* (Oxford University Press, 2012), 25 and 137–139.

test of Chapters 4 and 6 goes a long way towards tackling these four practical obstacles to balancing. By imposing structure on judicial balancing exercises and by enabling comparative judgments on the strength of reasons in favour of – and against – human rights in conflict, the test aims to minimise the influence of subjective preferences, nudge judges towards quasirationality, increase the coherence of judicial reasoning and eliminate preferential framing effects. I conclude that, although the structured balancing test is an imperfect solution, it is arguably the best we can aim for in the adjudication of human rights conflicts, on which reasonable disagreement often persists and which often confront judges with the dilemma of deciding which human right should prevail over the other.

In Chapter 6, I develop the structured balancing test first introduced in Chapter 4. The test aims to bring structure to balancing in two ways. First, it limits the criteria with reference to which judicial balancing exercises are to be constructed, thereby avoiding the pitfalls of open-ended balancing. The test is, in particular, comprised of a limited set of seven balancing criteria: a value criterion, impact criterion, core-periphery criterion, additional rights criterion, general interest criterion, purpose criterion and responsibility criterion. Second, the test enables comparative judgments on the strength of reasons in favour of – and against – human rights in conflict. Such comparative judgments are generally absent in judicial balancing decisions, rendering outcomes incoherent and fuelling impressions of subjectivity. To enable the rendering of comparative judgments on human rights in conflict, the structured balancing test invites the construction of nets of arguments, into which reasons in favour of human rights are woven. Comparison of the strength of these nets of arguments should enable judges to decide, with some measure of rational confidence, which human right should prevail under the concrete circumstances of a given conflict. For the moment, this inevitably remains rather abstract. But much will become clear, I trust, in Chapter 6, where I explicate the structured balancing test and illustrate its practical potential by applying it to a concrete case.

Cognisant of the existence of alternative balancing tests, as well as alternatives *to* balancing, I go on to evaluate the structured balancing test of Chapter 6 against available alternatives. In Chapter 7, I first clarify that the structured balancing test is – upon reflection – compatible with Lorenzo Zucca's purported non-balancing approach to 'constitutional dilemmas'.[2] I show that any disagreement I have with Zucca is located at the conceptual level. Zucca and I rely on different conceptions of human rights and, concomitantly, favour distinct definitions of conflicts between them. Whereas Zucca conceives of balancing as *avoiding* human rights conflicts, I envisage balancing to *resolve* such conflicts. But the largest part of Chapter 7 is dedicated not to evaluating purported alternatives to balancing, but

2 Lorenzo Zucca, *Constitutional Dilemmas – Conflicts of Fundamental Legal Rights in Europe and the USA* (Oxford University Press, 2007).

to scrutinising alternative balancing tests. I focus, in particular, on evaluating theories of balancing proposed by Robert Alexy, Kai Möller and Aharon Barak.[3] Whereas I am rather critical of Alexy's Weight Formula balancing test (while retaining some of its core elements), I prove more receptive to the approaches of Möller and Barak (while disagreeing with some of their core assumptions). In evaluating existing balancing tests, I suggest that the structured balancing test of Chapter 6 may well prove superior.

I conclude the book by exploring the limits of the structured balancing test. In Chapter 8, I explain that the test is able to overcome the challenge from weak incommensurability, but is powerless in the face of strong incommensurability. Since strong incommensurability implies incomparability, the core aim of the structured balancing test cannot be achieved. No comparative judgment on human rights in conflict can be rendered where strong incommensurability is in play. Yet, such strong incommensurability will only rarely obtain. Throughout Chapter 8, I argue that the structured balancing test should be able to resolve most human rights conflicts. It only fails to provide a solution to human rights *dilemmas*: particularly intense conflicts that are marked by an element of tragedy and in which strong incommensurability obtains. Such genuine dilemmas, I posit, cannot be resolved with even the semblance of rationality. Instead, they can only be tackled by making an *arational* choice. I conclude Chapter 8 by arguing that, given the inevitable subjectivity involved in arational choices, they are best left to the legislator.

What this book is about (and what it is not about)

Human rights conflicts and 'traditional' human rights cases

This book is about conflicts between human rights. It does not deal with 'traditional' human rights cases, in which human rights are opposed by the public interest (or private interests that are not protected by way of human rights). Throughout the book, I remain largely agnostic about how such 'traditional' human rights cases should be adjudicated. I do defend, however, a particular conception of human rights, which has a direct bearing on judicial practice in 'traditional' human rights cases. In Chapter 1, I favour a conception of human rights as strong entitlements, which hold special normative force over non-rights considerations. I go on to critique certain conceptions of proportionality, such as those defended by Kai Möller and David Beatty, for disregarding the special normative force of human rights.[4]

3 Robert Alexy, *A Theory of Constitutional Rights* (Oxford University Press, 2002); Robert Alexy, 'On Balancing and Subsumption. A Structural Comparison', 16 *Ratio Juris* (2003), 433–449; Robert Alexy, 'The Construction of Constitutional Rights', 4 *Law & Ethics of Human Rights* (2010), 20–32; Möller, *supra* note 1; Aharon Barak, *Proportionality – Constitutional Rights and Their Limitations* (Cambridge University Press, 2012).

4 Möller, *supra* note 1; David Beatty, *The Ultimate Rule of Law* (Oxford University Press, 2004).

Other conceptions of proportionality, however, are perfectly consonant with the conception of human rights I favour in this book. Frederick Schauer's 'rule of weight' model of proportionality, in particular, relies on a similar conception of human rights as strong, but defeasible entitlements.[5] Matthias Klatt and Moritz Meister's 'weak trumping' model of proportionality also incorporates the special normative force of human rights.[6] These and other versions of what Luc Tremblay has termed the 'priority of rights' model of proportionality thus align with the core conception of human rights defended in this book.[7]

This does not imply, however, that proportionality analysis would be the only mode of human rights adjudication available in 'traditional' human rights cases. Reason-blocking models of human rights adjudication, such as defended by George Letsas (inspired by the work of Ronald Dworkin),[8] are equally founded on the special normative force of human rights and their concomitant counter-majoritarian function.[9] Throughout this book, I remain agnostic about which model of human rights adjudication – the reason-blocking model, the 'priority of rights' model of proportionality or yet another model – best serves the special normative force of human rights. Answering that question in earnest would require a separate book-length study. The answer moreover depends, I venture, on the specific context in which human rights adjudication takes place.[10]

Absolute and relative human rights

Within the realm of human rights conflicts, this book is primarily concerned with conflicts between *relative* human rights. It is less concerned with conflicts that involve *absolute* human rights. Relative human rights are rights that can justifiably be overridden. In human rights instruments, relative rights come with an (explicit or implicit) limitation clause, which details the conditions under which they can

5 Frederick Schauer, 'Proportionality and the Question of Weight', in Grant Huscroft *et al.* (eds), *Proportionality and the Rule of Law: Rights, Justification, Reasoning* (Cambridge University Press, 2014), 173–185.

6 Matthias Klatt and Moritz Meister, *The Constitutional Structure of Proportionality* (Oxford University Press, 2012).

7 Luc B. Tremblay, 'An Egalitarian Defense of Proportionality-based Balancing', 12 *International Journal of Constitutional Law* (2014), 866 and 868.

8 Ronald Dworkin, *Taking Rights Seriously* (Harvard University Press, 1977).

9 George Letsas, *A Theory of Interpretation of the European Convention on Human Rights* (Oxford University Press, 2007); George Letsas, 'Rescuing Proportionality', in Rowan Cruft *et al.* (eds), *Philosophical Foundations of Human Rights* (Oxford University Press, 2015), 316–340.

10 In the context of the European Convention on Human Rights system, for instance, the reason-blocking model of human rights adjudication appears particularly suited to tackle non-discrimination cases, which often centre on determining whether or not certain motives can justify differential treatment. The 'priority-of-rights' model of proportionality, conversely, seems more suitable to deal with those cases, such as privacy cases, in which the central question is whether the public interest pursued by the state can justify the human rights restriction at issue. For discussion, see Letsas, 'Rescuing Proportionality', *supra* note 9.

justifiably be infringed. Absolute human rights, conversely, do not come with a limitation clause. Absolute rights are violated as soon as they suffer damage. No countervailing considerations can ever justify their infringement.

In human rights practice, conflicts between relative human rights make up the vast bulk of human rights conflicts. From the perspective of human rights theory, they moreover raise more interesting questions than conflicts involving absolute human rights. Conflicts between two absolute human rights, in particular, belong to the realm of the theoretically impossible. Since absolute human rights function as rules, only one can apply to a given set of circumstances. Other absolute rights, which might *appear* to clash with the first, are per definition inapplicable to the situation at hand. Conflicts between an absolute and a relative human right, conversely, are easily resolved: the absolute right 'trumps' the relative right by its very nature. Since absolute rights cannot be overridden by other considerations, including relative rights, they automatically prevail when in conflict with the latter.

Since conflicts involving absolute human rights are either theoretically impossible or easily resolved, I do not engage with them in detail throughout this book. For detailed discussion, I instead refer the reader to my earlier work, in which I have dealt with conflicts between absolute human rights,[11] and conflicts between absolute and relative human rights.[12] In this book, I briefly touch upon conflicts involving absolute rights in Chapter 1, where I elaborate on the above categorisation of different types of human rights conflicts. Certain steps of the framework I develop throughout the book are, moreover, of immediate salience to conflicts involving absolute rights. The first step of the framework – defusing conflicts between human rights – in particular, can be applied to conflicts between absolute and relative human rights. Since defusing aims to remove the conflict itself, while keeping the human rights within intact, it not only provides the optimal approach to conflicts between relative human rights, it also offers the optimal 'solution' to purported conflicts between absolute and relative human rights.

Courts and legislators

Human rights conflicts pose challenges to a myriad of actors, ranging from local authorities such as the police and municipalities, over national governments and legislative bodies, to the highest judicial authorities, including constitutional courts and regional human rights courts. Importantly, conflicts between human rights play out differently in front of these diverse actors, which face distinct

11 Stijn Smet, 'Conflicts between Human Rights: A Reply to Steven Greer', 13 *Human Rights Law Review* (2013), 469–498.

12 Stijn Smet, 'Freedom of Religion V. Freedom from Religion: Putting Religious Dictates of Conscience (Back) on the Map', in Jeroen Temperman (ed.), *The Lautsi Papers: Multidisciplinary Reflections on Religious Symbols in the Public School Classroom* (Martinus Nijhoff, 2012), 113–142.

challenges in tackling them. The roles of the legislator and the courts, in particular, are arguably quite different. Whereas the legislator's primary concern is to tackle any *potential* conflict in the *abstract* and thus *ex ante*, courts have to determine – *ex post* – whether they are confronted with a *genuine* conflict in a *concrete* case and, if so, resolve it.

While courts are thus concerned with resolving concrete conflicts between identified right holders, legislators are preoccupied by preventing, minimising and/or resolving abstract conflicts between undetermined right holders. Yet, both levels – the legislative and the judicial – patently do *not* deal with human rights conflicts in a vacuum. On the contrary, they influence each other. Courts may, for instance, let their assessment of a concrete human rights conflict be informed by the aims pursued by the relevant legislation, which deals with the conflict in the abstract. Legislators, conversely, may (have to) adapt their legislative framework to conform to court judgments in concrete cases on human rights conflicts.

This book elects to focus on just one of the abovementioned actors: courts. The framework developed throughout the book is designed for judicial practice. It is intended to tackle concrete human rights conflicts between identified right holders. It is not concerned with the more abstract questions that confront the legislator: how to prevent, minimise or resolve human rights conflicts through a legislative framework. This becomes particularly clear in the last step of the framework: balancing of human rights. To make such balancing work for human rights conflicts, I propose an *ad hoc* structured balancing test. That test only makes sense when applied to the particular circumstances of a given human rights conflict. It is patently not designed to assist in the development of legislative frameworks to deal with human rights conflicts in the abstract (*e.g.* through defamation legislation).

Yet, the first two steps of the framework – defusing conflicts between human rights and reaching compromises between human rights in conflict – *do* carry the potential to prove relevant to the legislative tackling of human rights conflicts. As I explain in Chapter 3, both steps require legal creativity in finding ways to render states' duties towards right holders either entirely compatible (defusing conflicts) or as compatible as possible (reaching compromises). Such legal creativity may need to be undertaken at a more abstract level and could thus be of immediate salience to locating appropriate legislative responses to (purported) human rights conflicts. In Chapter 3, I discuss a number of examples. For instance, I argue that conflicts between doctors' freedom of conscience and women's right to an abortion could be defused by having the state adopt a legislative and regulatory framework on which doctors are granted an exemption, while health services are *simultaneously* set up to ensure women's access to abortion (for instance by requiring a steady roster of doctors who do not conscientiously object to performing abortions). As an example of compromise, I discuss counter-demonstrations. I argue that the state should take legislative and regulatory measures that allow counter-demonstrations to take place, instead of barring them. Although the requisite measures, including physical separation of demonstrations, have a marginal impact on demonstrators' freedom of movement, they succeed in securing a viable compromise between the human rights in conflict. In relation to these and other situations, the framework proposed in this book *does* provide insight into how legislators and other non-judicial state actors could tackle human rights conflicts.

Judicial practice, specific and general

The framework I propose in this book is developed against the analytical backdrop of the case law of the European Court of Human Rights (ECtHR) on human rights conflicts.[13] The ECtHR is the world's most influential human rights court. Its case law is binding on the 47 member states of the Council of Europe, which include all European Union countries and large states like Russia and Turkey. Judgments rendered in Strasbourg, the seat of the ECtHR, have the potential to influence the lives and legal position of hundreds of millions of human rights holders throughout Europe. The Court's case law is, moreover, a direct source of inspiration and authority for human rights and constitutional courts across the globe.

The ECtHR is, however, struggling to come to grips with the intricacies – and occasionally even the very possibility of – human rights conflicts (see Chapters 1, 2 and 5). At the same time, the Court's case law contains a plethora of elements that are of immediate salience to the development of a framework for the resolution of human rights conflicts. The framework proposed in this book finds direct inspiration in the ECtHR's existing case law. The book's theoretical arguments are, in other words, firmly embedded in judicial practice.

Despite its analytical focus on the case law of the ECtHR, the book aims to propose a framework that is of immediate salience to judicial practice in general. Most of the book's arguments – and its framework, in particular – are of direct value to judicial practice the world over. Arguably the most important limiting factor is the conception of human rights that underlies the book's core arguments. In this book, I conceive of (relative) human rights as *pro tanto* rights that hold special normative force over the public interest. The book's core arguments are built on this founding premise. As a result, they are of immediate salience to jurisdictions that favour – as the ECtHR does – a 'priority to human rights' model of adjudication. This arguably encompasses a variety of human rights and constitutional courts across the globe, including the Inter-American Court of Human Rights, the African Court on Human and Peoples' Rights, the Supreme Court of Israel and the Constitutional Court of South Africa.

13 The focus on the case law of the ECtHR stems from the origins of this book as a Ph.D. dissertation on human rights conflicts at the ECtHR (Stijn Smet, 'Resolving Conflicts between Human Rights: A Legal Theoretical Analysis in the Context of the ECHR' (Ph.D. dissertation, Ghent University, 2014)). The dissertation was written in the context of a European Research Council-funded project on the case law of the ECtHR ('Strengthening the European Court of Human Rights: More Accountability through Better Legal Reasoning' (2009–2014)).

But the framework I propose in this book is also of value to constitutional courts, such as the Constitutional Court of Germany, that do *not* adopt a conception of human rights as strong entitlements. The structured balancing test of Chapter 6, in particular, can be applied directly in such jurisdictions as well, given that it operationalises the idea that competing rights deserve equal respect in balancing. If the framework were to be adopted by the ECtHR, moreover, it could 'spread' to national jurisdictions across Europe. National courts, including constitutional and supreme courts, are bound – *per* established case law of the ECtHR – by the Court's standards on the adjudication of human rights conflicts.[14] As such, the framework could prove relevant, via the case law of the ECtHR, to the Italian Constitutional Court, the United Kingdom Supreme Court, the Russian Constitutional Court and other highest courts (and lower courts, for that matter) across Europe.

Given its reliance on a conception of human rights *qua* principles, the book's framework is perhaps least suited to immediate application in US constitutional law. This, however, is arguably only true insofar as constitutional rights – such as free speech – are conceived of in absolute terms in US constitutional law. In relation to other rights, such as the right to privacy, the framework may well prove relevant to the constitutional adjudication of human rights conflicts in the United States as well.

One final preliminary clarification is in order. Because this book aims to develop a general framework for the resolution of human rights conflicts in judicial practice, it purposively avoids getting bogged down in discussions on particular features of human rights adjudication at the ECtHR. The book especially eschews debates on the ECtHR's margin of appreciation doctrine and the concomitant 'procedural turn' in the Court's adjudication of human rights conflicts. The Court's margin of appreciation doctrine is directly linked to the subsidiary nature of its human rights review. As a regional court, the ECtHR is acutely aware of both its limitations in assessing local/national circumstances and its need for legitimacy in the eyes of states. The subsidiary nature of the Court's human rights review implies that states hold the primary responsibility for enforcing and protecting human rights. To give practical effect to this subsidiarity principle, the Court utilises the margin of appreciation as a tool to either adopt a deferential stance towards states or engage in a thorough scrutiny of rights-restrictive measures taken by states. The Court grants states a so-called wide margin of appreciation where, for instance, socio-economic issues are concerned.[15] But in relation to discrimination on the basis of race or ethnicity, for instance, the Court strictly scrutinises rights-restrictive measures.[16]

14 See, for instance, *Axel Springer AG v Germany* [2012] ECHR 227, para 88.
15 See, for instance, *Hatton and Others v the United Kingdom* [2003] ECHR 338, para 100.
16 See, for instance, *Sejdić and Finci v Bosnia and Herzegovina* [2009] ECHR 2122, paras 43–44.

In its recent case law, the Court has tended to grant a *wide* margin of appreciation to states in the resolution of human rights conflicts.[17] This, in turn, has led to a 'procedural turn' in the Court's adjudication of such conflicts, whereby the Court in principle – but certainly not consistently – evaluates whether or not the national authorities have resolved the conflict in line with the Court's established principles (instead of engaging in substantive reasoning of its own).[18] In this book, I largely steer clear of the margin of appreciation and other *procedural* aspects of the ECtHR's case law on human rights conflicts.[19] Instead, I focus on developing a framework for the *substantive* resolution of such conflicts in judicial practice. Implementation of the framework in specific legal systems – including that of the ECtHR – may well require adaptation to, among others, procedural aspects of adjudication within those systems. The need for such adaptation to suit particular circumstances does not, however, detract from the normative and analytical validity of the framework as such.

17 See, for instance, *Eweida v the United Kingdom* [2013] ECHR 37, para 106; *MGN Limited v the United Kingdom* [2011] ECHR 66, para 142; *Fernández Martínez v Spain* [2014] ECHR 615, para 123.

18 See, for instance, *MGN Limited, supra* note 17 at para 150; *Axel Springer, supra* note 14 at para 88; *Delfi AS v Estonia* [2015] ECHR 586, para 139.

19 But see Chapter 5, footnote 130 and 'Preferential Framing in Human Rights Practice?' for limited discussion. For detailed discussion, see Stijn Smet, 'When Human Rights Clash in "The Age of Subsidiarity": What Role for the Margin of Appreciation?', in Petr Agha (ed.), *Human Rights between Law and Politics: The Margin of Appreciation in Post-National Contexts* (Hart Publishing, forthcoming 2017; manuscript on file with the author).

Part I

Identifying conflicts between human rights

1 Conflicts between human rights: it does really make a difference[1]

Two shipwreck victims are holding on for life to the same plank of wood, which cannot support their combined weight.[2] A woman in search of her origins seeks information about her biological mother, who gave birth to her anonymously.[3] A hiker caught in a blizzard breaks into someone else's cabin to save her life.[4] And a newspaper publishes photographs of a celebrity (Naomi Campbell) leaving a Narcotics Anonymous meeting.[5] In all these cases – some real, others imagined – the human rights of different persons appear to conflict. In the Plank Case, the rights to life of both shipwreck victims appear irreconcilable. In the Anonymous Birth Case, the daughter's right to identity appears to clash with her mother's right to privacy. In the Cabin Case, the hiker's right to life appears incompatible with the cabin owner's right to property. And in the Celebrity Case, the newspaper's freedom of expression appears to conflict with the celebrity's right to privacy.

Although human rights law scholarship has recently taken an increased interest in these and other purported conflicts between human rights, debates on the *existence* of such conflicts remain situated at the fringes of the discipline. The handful of human rights law scholars who have substantively engaged with human rights conflicts tend to move straight to their categorisation and resolution, glossing over the prior question of their existence.[6] Yet, we should not forego the

1 The title is inspired by Janneke Gerards, 'Fundamental Rights and Other Interests: Should It Really Make a Difference?', in Eva Brems (ed.), *Conflicts between Fundamental Rights* (Intersentia, 2008), 655–690.

2 Claire Oakes Finkelstein, 'Two Men and a Plank', 7 *Legal Theory* (2001), 279–306.

3 *Odièvre v France* [2003] ECHR 86.

4 Joel Feinberg, 'Voluntary Euthanasia and the Inalienable Right to Life', 7 *Philosophy and Public Affairs* (1978), 102.

5 *MGN Limited v the United Kingdom* [2008] ECHR 1255.

6 Eva Brems (ed.), *Conflicts between Fundamental Rights* (Intersentia, 2008); Lorenzo Zucca, *Constitutional Dilemmas – Conflicts of Fundamental Legal Rights in Europe and the USA* (Oxford University Press, 2007); Peggy Ducoulombier, *Les conflits de droits fondamentaux devant la Cour européenne des droits de l'homme* (Bruylant, 2011); Sébastien Van Drooghenbroeck, 'Conflits entre droits fondamentaux, pondération des intérêts: fausses pistes(?) et vrais problèmes', in Jean-Louis Renchon (ed.), *Les droits de la personnalité* (Bruylant, 2009), 299–346.

prior question: can human rights really conflict, in the sense of being incompatible with one another? And if so, are such human rights conflicts special? Do they differ from 'traditional' human rights cases?[7]

In this chapter, I will answer these questions in the affirmative. I will first dispel the 'specificationist argument' according to which human rights co-exist harmoniously and can therefore not conflict. I will submit that the *pro tanto* model of human rights, coupled with a conception that distinguishes a right's interference from its violation, is superior to the specificationist conception, both in theoretical terms and when assessed in light of actual human rights practice. Crucially, the superior conception of human rights acknowledges, rather than denies, the reality of human rights conflicts. We should thus have no qualms about accepting that conflicts between human rights are real, not imagined. Having established as much, I will proceed to tackle the 'proportionality argument', which insists that human rights conflicts – although real – are not special. On the proportionality argument, conflicts between human rights do not pose distinct challenges in terms of their resolution. Instead, they are to be tackled in identical fashion to 'traditional' human rights cases: through proportionality analysis. In countering the proportionality argument, I will argue that taking the special normative force of human rights seriously requires the development of a distinct framework for the resolution of conflicts between them.

The existence of conflicts between human rights

Although the Plank Case, Anonymous Birth Case, Cabin Case, Celebrity Case – and a myriad of other cases[8] – *appear* to involve a conflict between human rights, some scholars dismiss this as mere fantasy. Upon closer examination, they submit, the purported conflict invariably turns out to be imagined, rather than real. One prominent motivation that drives scholars to deny the possibility of human rights conflicts is the Kantian ideal that each individual's freedom should be part of a system of equal freedom for all.[9] On the Kantian view, acknowledging that the rights of different individuals may conflict threatens to render the underlying rights theory incoherent.[10] To avoid such incoherence, certain scholars deny the possibility of conflicts of rights and emphasise their harmonious compatibility

7 By 'traditional' human rights cases, I mean cases in which a human right is opposed by a public interest or other non-human-rights consideration (*e.g.* a private interest or legal right that does not have human rights status).

8 See the ECtHR cases discussed throughout this book.

9 Jürgen Habermas, *Between Facts and Norms* (Polity Press, 1996), 93; Nigel E. Simmonds, 'Rights at the Cutting Edge', in Matthew H. Kramer *et al.*, *A Debate over Rights* (Oxford University Press, 1998), 135–136 and 138; James Griffin, *On Human Rights* (Oxford University Press, 2008), 58–59 (arguing in favour of the Kantian principle, but adding that, although its acceptance considerably reduces the amount of real conflicts, there nevertheless 'remain conflicts of rights that resist such dissolution').

10 Griffin, *supra* note 9 at 58–59; Zucca, *supra* note 6 at 61.

instead.[11] These scholars thus rely on a conception of human rights that precludes conflicts between them.[12] I will refer to this view as the 'specificationist conception of human rights', and to those who adhere to it as 'specificationists'. I believe the specificationists are mistaken. I aim to show that their conception of human rights not only suffers from important theoretical defects, but is also out of line with human rights practice.

The (mistaken) specificationist conception of human rights

On the specificationist conception of human rights, determining which human rights we have – in abstract philosophical terms as well as in concrete legal terms – involves a process of definition. On the specificationist argument, we do not have a general human right to freedom of expression or right to privacy. Instead, we 'only' have (highly) detailed versions of those rights. The purported upshot is that we do really *have* those detailed rights, because – once properly specified – our human rights are absolute.[13] They cannot be outweighed by the public interest, nor can they conflict with other human rights. On the specificationist view, when human rights *appear* to conflict, a process of specification determines which right applies to the situation at hand.[14] The other right – once specified – is by definition inapplicable to the circumstances. Thus, it turns out, there is no *actual* conflict between both human rights; nor can there ever be.[15]

Confronted with the Cabin Case, for example, specificationists insist that either (A) the right to life does not entail the right to break into someone else's cabin to save one's life when caught in a blizzard, or (B) the right to property does not entail the right to have one's cabin safeguarded against someone who, caught in a blizzard, breaks into it to save her life. Specificationists are most likely to pursue

11 See most notably Hillel Steiner, *An Essay on Rights* (Blackwell, 1994), 2–3 and 80 (presenting his views on a set of 'compossible' rights).

12 See, for instance, John Hasnas, 'From Cannibalism to Caesareans: Two Conceptions of Fundamental Rights', 89 *Northwestern University Law Review* (1995), 921–922 and 940–941; Alexander Green, 'An Absolute Theory of Convention Rights: Why the ECHR Gives Rise to Legal Rights that Cannot Conflict with Each Other', 16 *UCL Jurisprudence Review* (2010), 75–93.

13 Grégoire Webber, 'On the Loss of Rights', in Grant Huscroft *et al.* (eds), *Proportionality and the Rule of Law: Rights, Justification, Reasoning* (Cambridge University Press, 2014), 130; Green, *supra* note 12 at 77.

14 See, for instance, Thomas M. Scanlon, 'Adjusting Rights and Balancing Values', 72 *Fordham Law Review* (2004), 1478–1479; Carl Wellman, *Real Rights* (Oxford University Press, 1995), 224; Christopher H. Wellman, 'On Conflicts between Rights', 14 *Law and Philosophy* (1995), 277; John Oberdiek, 'Lost in Moral Space: On the Infringing/Violating Distinction and Its Place in the Theory of Rights', 23 *Law and Philosophy* (2004), 325–346.

15 Wellman (Carl), *supra* note 14 at 210 and 215; Wellman (Christopher), *supra* note 14 at 273–274, 277 and 279; Daniel Shapiro, 'Conflicts and Rights', 55 *Philosophical Studies* (1989), 269; Green, *supra* note 12.

strategy (B),[16] given that it is the least radical one, but the salient point is that both strategies have the same objective: they aim to deny the existence of a real human rights conflict in the Cabin Case. On the specificationist conception of the right to life and the right to property, these two rights can never conflict. And the same goes for all other human rights.

Admittedly, specificationism is not entirely alien to human rights practice, including under the European Convention of Human Rights (ECHR). Article 11 ECHR, for instance, only grants 'the right to freedom of *peaceful* assembly'. Violent assemblies are, by definition, excluded from the scope of Article 11.[17] Although this circumscribes the content of the human right to freedom of assembly to some extent, it falls short of what specificationists seek: a series of narrowly tailored human rights that are fully specified. It should, however, come as no surprise that fully specified rights do not feature in human rights instruments like the ECHR, which aim to do no more – and no less – than list our human rights in general terms. To locate true markers of the success (or failure) of the specificationist strategy, we must turn to human rights adjudication.

To that end, let us take a closer look at how the ECtHR deals with human rights conflicts. The relevant case law of the ECtHR oscillates between two key principles. On the one hand, the Court explicitly recognises the inevitability of human rights conflicts: '[i]t is precisely [the] constant search for a balance between the fundamental rights of each individual which constitutes the foundation of a "democratic society"'.[18] Yet, on the other hand the Court also conceptualises the ECHR as a 'Convention [that] must … be read as a whole, and interpreted in such a way as to promote internal consistency and harmony between its various provisions'.[19] Here, we encounter the idea(l) of harmonious co-existence of norms pursued by specificationists. Presumably inspired by this idea(l), the ECtHR has at times walked the specificationist path, denying the possibility of human rights conflicts to avoid principled problems of human rights adjudication.

Instances in which the Court outright denies the possibility of human rights conflicts are, however, extremely rare. Only two can be found in the entire, voluminous case law of the ECtHR.[20] The first is a leading defamation judgment, in which a Chamber of the Court held that

16 See, for instance, Oberdiek, *supra* note 14 at 342; Grégoire Webber, *The Negotiable Constitution: On the Limitation of Rights* (Cambridge University Press, 2009), 129 and 131.

17 *Kudrevičius and Others v Lithuania* [2013] ECHR 1178, para 92.

18 *Chassagnou and Others v France* [1999] ECHR 22, para 113.

19 See, for instance, *Otto-Preminger-Institut v Austria* [1994] ECHR 26, para 47; *Pretty v the United Kingdom* [2002] ECHR 427, para 54.

20 For another example, but restricted to *obiter dictum*, see *Fernández Martínez v Spain* [2014] ECHR 615, para 128 ('Article 9 of the Convention does not enshrine a right of dissent within a religious community; in the event of any doctrinal or organisational disagreement between a religious community and one of its members, the individual's freedom of religion [conflicting with the religious community's right to religious autonomy] is exercised by the option of freely leaving the community').

> the purported conflict between Articles 8 [the right to private life] and 10 [freedom of expression] of the Convention … in matters of protection of reputation, is one of appearance only [since] the inherent logic of Article 10 … precludes the possibility of conflict with Article 8.[21]

The second is a leading freedom of expression judgment, in which the Grand Chamber of the Court ruled that a professor did not have 'a "negative" right within the meaning of Article 10 to refuse to make … research material belonging to his public employer available',[22] since

> finding that [he] had such a right … would run counter to the property rights of [his University]. It would also impinge on [other researchers'] rights under Article 10 … to receive information in the form of access to the public documents concerned.[23]

Lending further credence to the specificationist conception of human rights implicit in these two judgments, the former President of the ECtHR – Dean Spielmann – has argued, in his extra-judicial writings, that the conflict-avoidance stance of the Court

> can be explained by the Court's adoption of a particular theory of rights guaranteed by the Convention that, effectively, interprets such rights as not capable of coming into conflict with each other because by their nature or limits either one or the other is not really at stake in a particular set of circumstances.[24]

Yet, Spielmann's specificationist claim fails to convince. It relies on two rare judgments,[25] dwarfed in numbers by an abundance of cases in which the ECtHR explicitly recognises that it faces a conflict between human rights.[26] The Court's

21 *Karakó v Hungary* [2009] ECHR 712, paras 17 and 25.

22 *Gillberg v Sweden* [2012] ECHR 569, para 94.

23 Ibid. at para 93.

24 Dean Spielmann and Leto Cariolou, 'The Right to Protection of Reputation under the European Convention on Human Rights', in Dean Spielmann *et al.* (eds), *The European Convention on Human Rights, A Living Instrument – Essays in Honour of Christos L. Rozakis* (Bruylant, 2011), 584.

25 In reality, Spielmann's claim rests on only one judgment (*Karakó*), given that his claim predates the *Gillberg* judgment. He would, however, surely have found support for his claim in *Gillberg*.

26 See, among many examples, *Axel Springer AG v Germany* [2012] ECHR 227, para 84 ('the Court may be required to verify whether the domestic authorities struck a fair balance when protecting two values guaranteed by the Convention which may come into conflict with each other in certain cases, namely, on the one hand, freedom of expression protected by Article 10 and, on the other, the right to respect for private life enshrined in Article 8'); *Von Hannover v Germany (No. 2)* [2012] ECHR 228, para 106 ('In cases such as the present one, which

own case law simply does not support Spielmann's claim that the Court relies on a theory of rights in which human rights cannot conflict. But neither does it support a claim to the contrary. Instead, what can be gleaned from the Court's case law is ambivalence and uncertainty. The Court oscillates between acceptance and rejection. It generally accepts, rather uncritically, the 'reality' that human rights can and do conflict. Occasionally, however, it rebels and questions the very possibility of human rights conflicts. The picture that emerges is of a Court struggling to come to grips with the intricacies of conflicts between human rights. The Court appears deeply unsure how to fit purported human rights conflicts in its conception of the ECHR.

Against this backdrop of uncertainty, I intend to show that the specificationist conception of human rights – and its strategy to deny the possibility of human rights conflicts – fails to convince. I submit that an alternative conception of human rights, based on the *pro tanto* view of rights and the distinction between a right's interference and its violation, is superior to the specificationist conception, both in theoretical terms and when assessed in light of human rights practice.[27] Given its superiority, I posit, this alternative conception of human rights should be favoured.

The superiority of the pro tanto *model of human rights*

The specificationist conception of human rights fails to convince for three theoretical reasons, independent from the specific context in which human rights operate, and one practical reason, directly related to how human rights function under the ECHR system. First, the specificationist conception of human rights leads to counterintuitive and troubling results when applied to some of the proto-typical human rights 'conflicts' we considered at the start of this chapter. In tackling the Plank Case, in particular, specificationists can only hope to deny the existence of a human rights conflict by arguing that *neither* shipwreck victim has a right to life. Indeed, since both victims rely on exactly the same right, it is not possible to define one of the rights away without simultaneously defining away

require the right to respect for private life to be balanced against the right to freedom of expression…'); *Fernández Martínez*, *supra* note 20 at para 123 ('The Court reiterates that when it is called upon to rule on a conflict between two rights that are equally protected by the Convention, it must weigh up the interests at stake … In the present case, this balancing exercise concerns the applicant's right to his private and family life, on the one hand, and the right of religious organisations to autonomy, on the other"); *Otto-Preminger-Institut*, *supra* note 19 at para 55 ('The issue before the Court involves weighing up the conflicting interests of the exercise of two fundamental freedoms guaranteed under the Convention, namely the right of the applicant association to impart to the public controversial views … on the one hand, and the right of other persons to proper respect for their freedom of thought, conscience and religion, on the other hand').

27 I develop the argument more fully in Stijn Smet, 'On the Existence and Nature of Conflicts between Human Rights at the European Court of Human Rights', *Human Rights Law Review* (forthcoming).

the other. Thus, on the specificationist conception of human rights, no rights are in play in the Plank Case. That is a counterintuitive and embarrassing result. Conceptions of human rights that manage to avoid it could claim superiority over the specificationist conception.

Second, as demonstrated by Joel Feinberg, the specificationist conception of human rights fails to explain the existence of moral residue in certain hard cases, such as the Cabin Case.[28] If the specificationist would be correct in arguing that the hiker in the Cabin Case has the right to break into the cabin to save her life, while the cabin owner does not have a right to see his cabin safeguarded against the break-in, there would be no reason to grant the cabin owner compensation or offer him an apology. Yet, as Feinberg convincingly argues, our intuition tells us that the hiker *should* compensate the cabin owner for the forced door, broken window and/or wood, food and water she consumed during the blizzard.[29] At the very least, she should apologise for the damage caused. Yet, the specificationist conception of human rights does not leave any room for such moral residue. This, as well, is a counterintuitive and embarrassing result. Once more, if an alternative conception of human rights would avoid this result, it could claim superiority over the specificationist conception.

Third, and arguably most important, specificationists cannot possibly live up to their own ideal of fully specifying – *i.e.* defining – each and every human right in order to determine which applies to any given situation. Given the countless situations that might arise, and myriads of minute details that might affect the purported content of our human rights, full specification enters the scene as a Herculean task, unfit for mortal judges.[30] This renders the specificationist conception of human rights not only practically useless, but also normatively objectionable. What good is it to have a conception of human rights that no one can truly apply? Indeed, as Joel Feinberg argues, specification comes at the great cost of 'admitting that we do not really know, and cannot agree, which rights exactly [there] are'.[31]

True enough, there are situations in which specificationists tease us with 'easy' answers, such as 'there is no right to falsely shout "Fire!" in a crowded theatre'.[32] But most cases – especially hard cases – cannot be brought under the specificationist umbrella as swiftly. The ease (in a single sentence!) with which the Crowded Theatre Case is resolved should moreover not blind us to the availability of alternative explanations. Specificationists might be able to point towards a simple rule to resolve the Crowded Theatre Case, but they have thereby patently not

28 Joel Feinberg, 'Voluntary Euthanasia and the Inalienable Right to Life', 7 *Philosophy and Public Affairs* (1978), 102.

29 Ibid.

30 James Nickel, *Making Sense of Human Rights: Philosophical Reflections on the Universal Declaration of Human Rights* (University of California Press, 1987), 43.

31 Feinberg, *supra* note 28 at 101.

32 Paraphrased from *Schenck v United States* 249 U.S. 47 (1919) ('The most stringent protection of free speech would not protect a man in falsely shouting fire in a theater and causing a panic').

explained *how* that rule came to exist; nor how different situations should be resolved. If we abandon the specificationist track and turn our gaze towards alternative conceptions of human rights, we might yet learn more.

The *pro tanto* conception of human rights – which views rights as supplying reasons for action that carry normative weight, but may nevertheless be outweighed by other considerations – is particularly promising.[33] On the *pro tanto* conception, we can reformulate the Crowded Theatre Case in terms of a conflict between two *pro tanto* rights: the freedom of expression of the person who wishes to falsely shout 'Fire!', let us call her Jane, and the rights to life and physical integrity of the theatregoers, who risk being trampled in the panic that would ensue if Jane really were to shout 'Fire!'.[34] When we posit those rights against each other – balance them, if you will – it seems undeniable that the rights of the theatregoers should prevail over Jane's rights. The complete lack of ambiguity explains why we are able to formulate such a simple rule to resolve the conflict. There is simply no room for reasonable disagreement here.

The great advantage of the *pro tanto* conception of human rights, however, is that it can deal just as swiftly with varying circumstances, for instance those in which there actually *is* a fire or in which the theatre is virtually empty. In both cases, suddenly Jane might very well have a right to shout 'Fire!', given that her *pro tanto* right is either in line with that of the other theatregoers (when there really is a fire) or because it is no longer outweighed by the rights to life and physical integrity of the few other theatregoers (given that they no longer risk being trampled).

The *pro tanto* conception of human rights has further benefits. Most importantly, it avoids some of the counterintuitive and embarrassing results to which the specificationist conception is vulnerable. Under the *pro tanto* conception of human rights, there is no reason to insist that neither victim in the Plank Case can claim a right to life. Instead, we can 'safely' acknowledge that *both* victims have a right to life, thereby doing full justice to the true dilemma inherent in the Plank Case. The *pro tanto* model also sits comfortably with a conception of human rights that distinguishes a right's interference from its violation. Such a conception has been put forth by Judith Jarvis Thomson and Joel Feinberg as an alternative to the specificationist conception.[35] Feinberg has convincingly shown how the

33 Jonathan Crowe, 'Explaining Natural Rights: Ontological Freedom and the Foundations of Political Discourse', 4 *New York University Journal of Law & Liberty* (2009), 87; George Letsas, 'The Scope and Balancing of Rights: Diagnostic or Constitutive?', in Eva Brems and Janneke Gerards (eds), *Shaping Rights in the ECHR: The Role of the European Court of Human Rights in Determining the Scope of Human Rights* (Cambridge University Press, 2013), 47.

34 *Contra* Letsas, *supra* note 33 at 48 (arguing that the Crowded Theatre Case entails a *prima facie* right to free speech that, upon closer scrutiny, turns out not to exist under the circumstances – 'it wasn't really a right *at all*' (emphasis in original) – and therefore never reaches the level of a *pro tanto* right).

35 Judith Jarvis Thomson, *The Realm of Rights* (Harvard University Press, 1990), 118–120; Feinberg, *supra* note 28 at 98. See also James Nickel, 'Are Human Rights Utopian?', 11 *Philosophy & Public Affairs* (1982), 248.

interference/violation distinction successfully explains the existence of moral residue in the Cabin Case.[36] Indeed, the cabin owner's right might not have been violated, but it has still been interfered with. This interference creates a hook onto which the moral residue can be latched.[37] These additional benefits confirm the *theoretical* superiority of the *pro tanto* model of human rights over the specificationist model. But also in relation to human rights *practice*, the former fares better than the latter.

The pro tanto *model and the case law of the ECtHR*

In arguing for the superiority of the *pro tanto* model of human rights, coupled with a conception that distinguishes a right's interference from its violation, we have arrived at an important practical objection to the specificationist conception of human rights: it is dramatically out of line with actual human rights practice (at least under the ECHR). The *pro tanto* model, conversely, is fully consonant with how human rights function in the ECHR system.

In resolving a given case, the ECtHR does not – in principle – narrowly tailor the relevant right to the particular circumstances to determine whether or not it applies. Instead, the Court generally starts off by acknowledging that a broadly formulated human right (*e.g.* freedom of expression) applies, before determining whether or not it has been violated.[38] The Court is driven to this dual-track reasoning by the structure of many of the ECHR's human rights provisions, particularly Articles 8–11 and Article 1 of Protocol 1.[39] In relation to the key human rights enumerated in these provisions – the right to private life, freedom of expression, freedom of religion, freedom of assembly and association and the right to property – the ECHR creates a distinction between the right's scope, set out in the first paragraph of the relevant article, and the so-called limitation clause, set out in the second paragraph. When examining a human rights claim under the relevant provisions, the Court first determines whether or not the complaint falls within the scope of the relevant human right. If the Court accepts that it does,

36 Feinberg, *supra* note 28 at 102. See also Finkelstein, *supra* note 2 at 304–305.

37 Letsas, *supra* note 33 at 48 ('When *pro tanto* rights are justifiably overridden they always leave behind a residue of obligation: one has a duty to feel regret, to apologise and possibly to make amends'). *Contra* Frederick Schauer, 'A Comment on the Structure of Rights', 27 *Georgia Law Review* (1993), 127–128 ('it seems plausible to speculate that when a genuine right is overridden ... we as a society do not feel obliged to provide the right-holder ... with even an apology, let alone compensation'). For an example of an ECtHR case that arguably involves moral residue, see *Evans v the United Kingdom* [2006] ECHR 264, paras 73 and 90.

38 Gerhard van der Schyff, *Limitation of Rights – A Study of the European Convention and the South African Bill of Rights* (Wolf Legal Publishers, 2005). For criticism of this approach, see Webber, *supra* note 16 at 5–6.

39 As noted *infra* (notes 57–58 and accompanying text), the specificationist conception of human rights may successfully explain the relevant practice as far as purported conflicts between absolute rights are concerned. The salient point, however, is that it fails to explain the bulk of the practice, which involves relative human rights.

and finds that the applicant has suffered a detriment, it establishes that there has been an interference with the human right at issue. The Court then proceeds, in the second stage of its analysis, to examine whether or not that interference can be justified under the limitation clause of the relevant article. If it cannot be justified, the human right has been violated. If it can, the right has been interfered with, but not violated.

The distinction between a right's interference and violation is thus crucial to a proper understanding of human rights adjudication by the ECtHR.[40] As a result, the specificationist conception of human rights is effectively disqualified as a potential candidate to explain the Court's practice. The superior *pro tanto* conception of human rights, which is not only theoretically more sound, but also consonant with the human rights practice of the ECtHR, should be favoured instead. Crucially, since *pro tanto* rights leave room for other considerations,[41] which may or may not outweigh them, there is no longer a reason to deny the existence of human rights conflict.[42] Instead, we can proceed to tackle those conflicts head on, asking in the first place: do they really matter; are they actually special?

The special nature of conflicts between human rights

In defending the superiority of the *pro tanto* model of human rights, I have not (yet) made any claims about the nature of human rights, nor of conflicts between them. On one particularly prominent view of human rights, they are not inherently special. And neither are human rights conflicts. This is the proportionality conception of rights. Here, I will counter the proportionality argument, to the extent that it denies the special normative force of human rights. I will explain why human rights *are* special. Taking the special normative force of human rights seriously, I will posit, mandates the development of a distinct framework to resolve conflicts between them.

40 Janneke Gerards and Hanneke Senden, 'The Structure of Fundamental Rights and the European Court of Human Rights', 7 *International Journal of Constitutional Law* (2009), 619–653.

41 Note that Ronald Dworkin appears to defend a third model, which lies somewhere in between the specificationist and the *pro tanto* conception of (human) rights. Dworkin distinguishes abstract rights from concrete rights and insists that, while abstract rights (such as the right to free speech and the right to privacy) can conflict, concrete rights (*i.e.* more precisely defined versions of the abstract rights that more definitively express their weight) cannot. See Ronald Dworkin, *Law's Empire* (Harvard University Press, 1986), 293.

42 See, for instance, *Karaahmed v Bulgaria* [2015] ECHR 217, paras 91–92 ('At the heart of this case is the exercise of two sets of competing fundamental rights: ... freedom of expression and freedom of peaceful assembly [of] Articles 10 and 11 [on the one hand] ... freedom of religion [of] Article 9 [on the other]. None are absolute rights: all three Articles provide that the exercise of these rights may be subject to restrictions ... The Convention does not establish any a priori hierarchy between these rights: as a matter of principle, they deserve equal respect. They must therefore be balanced against each other').

The proportionality view: (conflicts between) human rights are not special

The importance of proportionality to contemporary rights reasoning can hardly be underestimated. Proportionality is ubiquitous in constitutional and human rights reasoning the world over, including by the ECtHR. It has been hailed as marking a new era of 'global constitutionalism'[43] and labelled 'the global model of constitutional rights'.[44] But proportionality theory comes with a catch. Its proponents generally deny that human rights hold special normative force over non-rights considerations.[45] Along with other scholars, I consider this to be an objectionable feature of proportionality theory.[46] Not only should human rights carry special normative force as a matter of normative theory, their principled priority over non-rights consideration is actually engrained in human rights practice, including that of the ECtHR. Taking the special nature of human rights seriously moreover requires the development of a distinct framework to deal with human rights conflicts. Or so I will argue. First, however, we require a more thorough understanding of proportionality theory, and how it relates to the human rights system of the ECHR.

At the heart of proportionality theory, as originally formulated by Robert Alexy on the basis of his analysis of the case law of the German Constitutional Court,[47] lies a distinction between rules and principles.[48] Building on the work of Ronald Dworkin,[49] Alexy posits that rules and principles are logically distinct types of norms that operate in radically different ways.[50] Rules, Alexy posits, are 'definitive commands' that operate through subsumption: '[i]f a rule is valid and applicable, it is definitively required that exactly what it demands be done'.[51] In other words, rules apply in an all-or-nothing fashion.[52] Principles, conversely, can be satisfied to

43 Alec Stone Sweet and Jud Mathews, 'Proportionality, Balancing and Global Constitutionalism', 47 *Columbia Journal of Transnational Law* (2008), 73–165.

44 Kai Möller, *The Global Model of Constitutional Rights* (Oxford University Press, 2012).

45 See, for instance, David Beatty, *The Ultimate Rule of Law* (Oxford University Press, 2004), 170–171; Kai Möller, 'Proportionality and Rights Inflation', in Grant Huscroft *et al.* (eds), *Proportionality and the Rule of Law: Rights, Justification, Reasoning* (Cambridge University Press, 2014), 166.

46 Stavros Tsakyrakis, 'Proportionality: An Assault on Human Rights?', 7 *International Journal of Constitutional Law* (2009), 468–493; Webber, *supra* note 16; Habermas, *supra* note 9; George Letsas, 'Rescuing Proportionality', in Rowan Cruft *et al.* (eds), *Philosophical Foundations of Human Rights* (Oxford University Press, 2015), 316–340.

47 Robert Alexy, *A Theory of Constitutional Rights* (Oxford University Press, 2002).

48 Robert Alexy, 'The Construction of Constitutional Rights', 4 *Law & Ethics of Human Rights* (2010), 21.

49 Ronald Dworkin, 'The Model of Rules', 35 *University of Chicago Law Review* (1967), 14–46.

50 *Contra* Joseph Raz, 'Legal Principles and the Limits of Law', 81 *Yale Law Journal* (1972), 823–854.

51 Alexy, *supra* note 48 at 21.

52 Gustavo Zagrebelsky, 'Ronald Dworkin's Principle Based Constitutionalism: An Italian Point of View', 1 *International Journal of Constitutional Law* (2003), 633.

varying degrees.[53] Alexy labels principles 'optimization requirements', 'norms requiring that something be realized to the greatest extent possible, given the factual and legal possibilities at hand'.[54]

According to Alexy and other proportionality scholars, human (and constitutional) rights are principles and, as such, necessarily subject to the proportionality principle. Indeed, a cornerstone of proportionality theory is the 'necessary connection between constitutional rights and proportionality'.[55] On proportionality theory, there is thus no principled difference between so-called absolute and relative human rights. Although certain proportionality scholars have devised strategies to approximate the idea of absolute rights,[56] proportionality theory does not leave room for truly absolute rights, given that all rights are subject to proportionality analysis. This constitutes a first point of tension with the ECHR system of human rights. Although most human rights enumerated in the ECHR and developed in the case law of the ECtHR are relative rights – *i.e.* rights that may justifiably be overridden (or outweighed) by other considerations – a small number of rights are absolute – *i.e.* entirely immune to any and all overriding considerations. The most prominent example of an absolute human right under the ECHR is the prohibition of torture of Article 3 ECHR, which 'does not allow for any exceptions or justifying factors or balancing of interests'.[57]

In the language of Alexy's principles theory, absolute human rights thus do not function as principles under the ECHR. Instead, they function as rules. Relative human rights, conversely, do function as principles under the ECHR, in line with proportionality theory. In terms of potential conflicts between human rights, this translates to three categories of conflict, each with their own logic. For starters, conflicts between absolute human rights do not exist. They are logically impossible.[58] Since absolute human rights function as rules, when they *appear* to conflict only one right can truly apply to the situation at hand. The other right must, by definition, be inapplicable. Interestingly, this actually redeems the specificationist conception of human rights somewhat. But it is a hollow victory, because purported conflicts between absolute human rights belong – for the time being – to the realm of the purely hypothetical.[59] Indeed, the vast case law of the ECtHR does not contain a single instance in which absolute rights allegedly

53 Alexy, *supra* note 48 at 21.
54 Ibid.
55 Ibid. at 24.
56 See, for instance, Mattias Kumm and Alec D. Walen, 'Human Dignity and Proportionality: Deontic Pluralism in Balancing', in Grant Huscroft *et al.* (eds), *Proportionality and the Rule of Law: Rights, Justification, Reasoning* (Cambridge University Press, 2014), 71.
57 *Gäfgen v Germany* [2010] ECHR 759, para 107.
58 Alison L. Young, 'Proportionality is Dead: Long Live Proportionality!', in Grant Huscroft *et al.* (eds), *Proportionality and the Rule of Law: Rights, Justification, Reasoning* (Cambridge University Press, 2014), 47.
59 Stijn Smet, 'Conflicts between Human Rights: A Reply to Steven Greer', 13 *Human Rights Law Review* (2013), 469–498.

collide.[60] Conflicts between an absolute human right and a relative human right *do* exist, but mandate a straightforward solution: if the absolute human right applies, it automatically prevails – by virtue of its nature – over the relative human right. When the absolute human right does not apply, conversely, there never was a conflict to begin with.[61] That leaves us with the third category: conflicts between relative human rights. Here we find the real challenge for human rights theory and practice: how should conflicts between relative human rights be tackled? I posit that no satisfactory answer is currently available, in the literature or the case law. Indeed, the core argument of this book is that a distinct framework should be developed to tackle conflicts between (relative) human rights.

Most – if not all – proportionality theorists would, however, disagree. They would insist that the proportionality principle already provides the answer: since there is nothing inherently special about (relative) human rights, they go into the proportionality test, along with any conflicting principles. Whether the latter are non-rights considerations or other (relative) human rights does not matter. But the full proportionality picture is, fortunately, more nuanced. First off, there are many conceptions of proportionality, not just one.[62] Among the 'range of proportionalities' defended in the literature,[63] some categorically deny that human rights carry special normative force,[64] while others attempt to accommodate the (alleged) special normative force of human rights.[65] A small minority of scholars even insists that the principled, but defeasible, priority of human rights over non-rights considerations is inherent in the very idea of proportionality.[66]

Frederick Schauer is the staunchest defender of the last view. Schauer insists that '[p]roportionality adjudication ... recognizes that rights are worth more than non-rights protected interests'.[67] According to Schauer, there is 'a rule of weight ... implicit in the common structure of proportionality', according to which more weight is given to human rights than to public interests.[68] 'And this is as it should

60 *Contra* Steven Greer, 'Should Police Threats to Torture Suspects Always be Severely Punished? Reflections on the Gäfgen Case', 11 *Human Rights Law Review* (2011), 67–89.

61 For discussion, see Stijn Smet, 'Freedom of Religion v. Freedom from Religion: Putting Religious Dictates of Conscience (Back) on the Map', in Jeroen Temperman (ed.), *The Lautsi Papers: Multidisciplinary Reflections on Religious Symbols in the Public School Classroom* (Martinus Nijhoff, 2012), 113–142.

62 Grant Huscroft *et al.*, 'Introduction', in Grant Huscroft *et al.* (eds), *Proportionality and the Rule of Law: Rights, Justification, Reasoning* (Cambridge University Press, 2014), 3.

63 Ibid. (emphasis removed).

64 Möller, *supra* note 44.

65 Matthias Klatt and Moritz Meister, *The Constitutional Structure of Proportionality* (Oxford University Press, 2012); Matthias Klatt, 'An Egalitarian Defense of Proportionality-based Balancing: A Reply to Luc B. Tremblay', 12 *International Journal of Constitutional Law* (2014), 891–899; Alexy, *supra* note 47.

66 Frederick Schauer, 'Proportionality and the Question of Weight', in Grant Huscroft *et al.* (eds), *Proportionality and the Rule of Law: Rights, Justification, Reasoning* (Cambridge University Press, 2014), 173–185.

67 Ibid. at 177.

68 Ibid. at 178.

be', Schauer claims, 'because this rule of weight is implicit in the very idea of a right.'[69]

The 'middle view', by contrast, emphasises the flexibility of the proportionality test. Its proponents argue that the special normative force of human rights may not be *inherent* in proportionality analysis, but can certainly be *accommodated* within its structure.[70] Matthias Klatt, for instance, insists that within 'the optimization model [of constitutional rights], it is well possible to ... assign higher abstract weights to the class of rights, as opposed to the class of public interests'.[71] What is more, according to Klatt:

> [t]he elaborated version of the optimization model has already included some elements of the priority of rights model in order to reflect the view that some or all rights may have special force in a particular legal system, vis-à-vis public interests.[72]

Here, I do not take immediate issue with either Schauer's or Klatt's conception of proportionality, although I will return to Schauer's views, in particular, later. Instead, I will focus on critiquing those proportionality scholars who categorically deny that human rights hold special normative force over non-rights considerations. David Beatty and Kai Möller are the most ardent proponents of what could be termed the 'strict view' of proportionality theory, on which '[i]t is all and only about proportionality'.[73] Beatty claims that (human) rights hold 'no special status'[74] and Möller affirms: '[we] must abandon the idea that rights hold a special normative force'.[75] For Möller, this conclusion follows irrefutably from the principle of proportionality, 'because proportionality ... denies the special normative force of rights'.[76]

Beatty's and Möller's conception of proportionality is, however, both principally objectionable and empirically inaccurate. Their views are principally objectionable, because human rights should, as a matter of normative theory, carry special normative force over non-rights considerations. Their claims are also empirically inaccurate, since proportionality analysis does not, at least under the ECHR, deny the special normative force of human rights. Instead, the ECtHR arguably employs what Luc Tremblay has termed a 'priority of rights model' of proportionality, as

69 Ibid.

70 Mattias Kumm, 'Political Liberalism and the Structure of Rights: On the Place and Limits of the Proportionality Requirement', in George Pavlakos (ed.), *Law, Rights and Discourse – The Legal Philosophy of Robert Alexy* (Hart Publishing, 2007), 148–149; Robert Alexy, 'Thirteen Replies', in George Pavlakos (ed.), *Law, Rights and Discourse – The Legal Philosophy of Robert Alexy* (Hart Publishing, 2007), 341.

71 Klatt, *supra* note 65 at 893.

72 Ibid. at 894.

73 Beatty, *supra* note 45 at 171.

74 Ibid. at 170.

75 Möller, *supra* note 44 at 73.

76 Möller, *supra* note 45 at 166.

opposed to the 'model of optimization of values in conflict' defended by Beatty and Möller.[77]

Why (conflicts between) human rights are *special*

On Beatty's and Möller's account, conflicts between human rights are no different from conflicts between a human right and a public interest. Since all principles are optimisation requirements – or, in Möller's terms, because everything can and should be expressed in terms of 'autonomy interests'[78] – all conflicts should be treated identically: through application of the proportionality principle.[79] Yet, I posit, this view is mistaken. Beatty's and Möller's claims are deeply at odds with two primary functions of human rights: safeguarding individuals' *fundamental* interests and protecting individuals from abuse of power by the state.

One of the primary functions of human rights, it is often argued, is to protect certain fundamental interests of individuals, related to values such as freedom, autonomy, equality and, many maintain, human dignity.[80] Other interests and preferences are, by contrast, insufficiently fundamental to justify protection by way of human rights. A person's interests in driving a car or having a good dinner, for instance, are generally not accepted as being protected by human rights, certainly not under the ECHR.[81] Yet, if one argues, as Beatty and Möller do, that human rights are no different from (other) 'optimization requirements' or 'autonomy interests', one is condemned to conclude that there is nothing that warrants setting human rights aside as norms that deserve increased protection.[82] This, however, runs contrary to the very idea behind human rights systems. It is precisely

77 Luc B. Tremblay, 'An Egalitarian Defense of Proportionality-based Balancing', 12 *International Journal of Constitutional Law* (2014), 866 and 868. Note that Tremblay favours the 'model of optimization of values in conflict'. Note further that Matthias Klatt has responded to Tremblay's claims by insisting that the 'optimization model' *can* incorporate the idea of rights holding some (weak) sense of priority over the public interest. See Klatt, *supra* note 65.

78 Möller, *supra* note 44.

79 Ibid. at 24.

80 Griffin, *supra* note 9; Nickel, *supra* note 30; Denise Meyerson, 'Why Courts Should Not Balance Rights against the Public Interest', 31 *Melbourne University Law Review* (2007), 873–902.

81 Both interests qualify as autonomy interests under Möller's account and are thus protected by his general right to autonomy (although to Möller 'protected' means no more than that a limitation of a person's autonomy interests triggers a duty of justification under the proportionality principle). See Möller, *supra* note 44 at 73, 87 and 179.

82 Note, however, that Möller concedes that 'a list of rights has the advantage that it can single out particularly important aspects of personal autonomy, thus making it clear that interferences with these particularly important interests will require correspondingly solid justifications. A list thus avoids the misleading impression that all instances of a person's autonomy receive the same level of protection'. It is not entirely clear, to me, how this statement relates to Möller's argument that rights do not hold any special normative force. See Möller, *supra* note 44 at 89.

because human rights protect certain fundamental interests of individuals that they are considered special, in the sense of being a hierarchically superior category of norms.[83]

The view of human rights as strong entitlements is further supported – mandated, even – by another vital function of human rights: their counter-majoritarian role. As George Letsas states: '[t]he purpose of human rights treaties, unlike that of many other international treaties, is to protect the autonomy of individuals against the majoritarian will of their state, rather than to give effect to that will'.[84]

Human rights indeed play a vital role in protecting individuals against abuse of power by states, or majorities within states.[85] They are, in fact, purposively designed to perform that role. As the ECtHR routinely holds, 'it would be incompatible with the underlying values of the Convention if the exercise of Convention rights by a minority group were made conditional on its being accepted by the majority'.[86]

In democratic states with a well-functioning parliamentary process, human rights may often not be of immediate importance to individuals who think and act in line with the views of the ruling majority, since their interests will generally be protected through the political process. But human rights can be vital to those who find themselves out of line with the views of the ruling majority. Indeed, human rights allow individuals to further their own conception of the good life by protecting them against the threat of subordination, through abuse of power, by the majority. In that respect, treating all interests – public and private – on an equal footing with human rights, as Beatty and Möller do, undermines the counter-majoritarian function of human rights. Suddenly, utilitarian considerations threaten to determine the fate of the few, who find themselves out of line with the views of the many. If human rights are not given some sort of special normative force, over and above the public interest, simple aggregation of the preferences and interests of the many will always threaten to outweigh the human rights of the few. It is thus essential, as a matter of normative theory, to grant human rights some sense of priority over non-rights considerations, even if this priority would be defeasible.

83 Tsakyrakis, *supra* note 46 at 479.

84 George Letsas, *A Theory of Interpretation of the European Convention on Human Rights* (Oxford University Press, 2007). See also Aharon Barak, *Proportionality: Constitutional Rights and their Limitations* (Cambridge University Press, 2012), 494 ('[t]he accepted and proper view considers constitutional rights as a shield to protect individuals from tyranny of the majority').

85 As former President of the ECtHR, Judge Sir Nicolas Bratza, stated: '[i]t is in the nature of the protection of fundamental rights and the rule of law that sometimes minority interests have to be secured against the view of the majority'. See Speech of Judge Sir Nicolas Bratza at *High Level Conference on the Future of the European Court of Human Rights*, Brighton, 18–20 April 2012, available at http://hub.coe.int/20120419-nicolas-bratza (last accessed 7 October 2013).

86 *Barankevich v Russia* [2007] ECHR 648, para 31; *Alekseyev v Russia* [2010] ECHR 1562, para 81.

Ultimately, however, everything boils down to normative choices. Beatty and Möller are likely to remain unconvinced by the arguments I have just sketched. Möller, for instance, is fully aware of these arguments, but nevertheless rejects the special normative force of human rights out of sincere conviction that an 'inflation of rights' model, coupled with the imposition on the state of a duty of justification under the proportionality test, is more apt at protecting individuals' 'autonomy interests'.[87] These 'autonomy interests' should, according to Möller, be interpreted extremely broadly to ensure full inclusion.[88] In Möller's view, this *requires* that we abandon the special normative force of human rights.[89] I have defended the opposite normative choice, positing that the moral ideals behind human rights systems mandate that human rights be considered special. This conclusion, I venture, is fully consonant with the manner in which human rights operate under the ECHR system. Beatty's and Möller's views, conversely, are incompatible with the human practice of the ECtHR.

The ECtHR's conception of proportionality: 'priority-to-rights'

Möller's model of 'rights inflation' might be compatible with constitutional rights adjudication by the German Constitutional Court, which has accepted the existence of – among others – a constitutional right to feed pigeons in the park.[90] But his conception of proportionality is much more difficult to reconcile with human rights adjudication under the ECHR. Although the ECtHR has interpreted the right to private life of Article 8 ECHR expansively – including, for instance, the right to give birth at home under its umbrella[91] – the Court is adamant that the ECHR does not include a human right to adopt,[92] to have an abortion[93] or to asylum.[94] Other rights are subject to a threshold requirement before they can claim human rights status under the ECHR. The right to reputation, for example, only enters the scope of Article 8 ECHR if an 'attack on personal honour and reputation [attains] a certain level of gravity ... in a manner causing prejudice to personal enjoyment of the right to respect for private life'.[95] Human rights practice under the ECHR is, thus, far removed from Möller's 'rights inflation' model. Instead, the Court views human rights as hierarchically superior norms that carry special normative force over non-rights considerations. Human rights

87 Möller, *supra* note 45.

88 Möller, *supra* note 44 at 73 (the autonomy interests extend to '*every* autonomy interest, including trivial interests and even autonomy interests in engaging in immoral activities [such as murder]' (emphasis in original)).

89 Möller, *supra* note 45 at 165–166. See also Tremblay, *supra* note 77.

90 BVerfGE 54, 143 (1980); Möller, *supra* note 45.

91 *Ternovszky v Hungary* [2010] ECHR 2028. See also *Dubska and Krejzova v the Czech Republic* [2014] ECHR 1373.

92 *E.B. v France* [2008] ECHR 55, para 41.

93 *A. B. and C. v Ireland* [2010] ECHR 2032, para 214.

94 *Saadi v Italy* [2008] ECHR 179, para 124.

95 *Lavric v Romania* [2014] ECHR 44, para 31 (with further references).

status under the ECHR must be earned. It is not handed out to all 'autonomy interests'.

Nevertheless, human rights ***adjudication*** under the ECHR does take the form of proportionality analysis (at least insofar as relative human rights are concerned). The case law of the ECtHR is thus broadly in line with proportionality theory. Yet, in determining whether or not a human rights restriction is 'necessary in a democratic society', the Court employs its own version of the proportionality test, which deviates somewhat from the 'classic' proportionality test. The 'classic' proportionality test, as deduced by Alexy from the case law of the German Constitutional Court, consists of three stages: suitability, necessity and proportionality *strictu senso* (or balancing).[96] Each stage aims to answer a different question. The suitability stage asks whether the rights-restricting measures are able to realise the aim pursued. The necessity stage asks whether the measures are strictly necessary to realise the aim or whether, conversely, there are equally efficient measures available that would lead to a less invasive restriction of the right. The balancing stage, finally, asks whether the measures have disproportionate effects on the exercise of the right, when balanced against the aim they are meant to achieve.

The ECtHR's proportionality test,[97] conversely, asks three slightly different questions: (1) do the measures meet a pressing social need; (2) are the measures relevant and sufficient to achieve the legitimate aim pursued; and (3) are the measures proportionate to the legitimate aim pursued?[98] The last question is, in practice, equivalent to the last stage of the 'classic' proportionality test, in that it boils down to a balancing exercise. The other two questions, however, do not neatly track the suitability and necessity stages of the 'classic' proportionality test. Nevertheless, the Court's proportionality test is largely – if imperfectly[99] – in line with proportionality theory.[100] Determining the relevance and sufficiency of rights-restrictive measures is, for all intents and purposes, equivalent to determining their suitability. The necessity stage, finally, may seem to be curiously absent from the standard version of the Court's proportionality test. But in its adjudicatory practice, the ECtHR is increasingly employing 'less restrictive means'

96 Alexy, *supra* note 47 at 397–402. See also Barak, *supra* note 84 at 3.

97 In the text, I describe the test in its theoretical form, abstracting from the impact the margin of appreciation has on the ***concrete application*** of the test. As noted in the Introduction, I will not deal with the margin of appreciation in this book. For analysis, see Sébastien Van Drooghenbroeck, *La proportionnalité dans le droit de la convention européenne des droits de l'homme: prendre l'idée simple au sérieux* (Bruylant, 2001), 173 and 190–191.

98 Ibid. at 81.

99 Janneke Gerards, 'How to Improve the Necessity Test of the European Court of Human Rights', 11 *International Journal of Constitutional Law* (2013), 466–490.

100 The difference between the Court's application of proportionality analysis and the 'traditional' proportionality test as it originated in German constitutional law is arguably due, in large part, to the influence of the margin of appreciation on the manner in which the ECtHR conducts its 'European supervision'. See *supra* note 91.

reasoning, which is more or less equivalent to the necessity stage of the 'classic' proportionality test.[101]

Although its human rights reasoning is thus not completely aligned with proportionality theory, the Court is undeniably and utterly convinced of the virtues of the proportionality test. Yet, and this is the salient point, the specific conception of proportionality employed by the ECtHR is closer to the 'rule of weight model' of Schauer than to the 'strict optimization model' of Beatty and Möller. The ECtHR consistently holds that the ECHR is 'first and foremost a system for the protection of human rights'.[102] Exceptions to human rights must therefore, according to the Court, be interpreted restrictively.[103] Protection of human rights is the rule, justified restrictions are the exception.[104] The ECtHR has stated that, when human rights are opposed by a public interest, the Court 'is faced not with a choice between two conflicting principles but with a principle of freedom of expression [or another human right] that is subject to a number of exceptions which must be narrowly interpreted'.[105]

The same goes for situations in which human rights clash with hierarchically 'lower' rights: 'where restrictions are imposed on a right or freedom guaranteed by the Convention in order to protect "rights and freedoms" not, as such, enunciated therein … only indisputable imperatives can justify interference with enjoyment of a Convention right'.[106]

This is a far cry from Beatty's and Möller's 'strict optimization model' of proportionality. Proportionality analysis under the ECHR instead follows what Luc Tremblay terms the 'priority of rights model' of proportionality.[107] Indeed, as Steven Greer and Sébastien Van Drooghenbroeck have convincingly argued, the ECtHR relies on a priority-to-rights principle,[108] under which it grants human rights principled, but defeasible, priority over non-rights considerations.[109]

101 Eva Brems and Laurens Lavrysen, '"Don't Use a Sledgehammer to Crack a Nut": Less Restrictive Means in the Case Law of the European Court of Human Rights', 15 *Human Rights Law Review* (2015), 139–168.

102 *Chapman v the United Kingdom* [2001] ECHR 43, para 70; *Konstantin Markin v Russia* [2010] ECHR 1435, para 126; *Kurić and Others v Slovenia* [2012] ECHR 1083, para 387.

103 *Perez v France* [2004] ECHR 72, para 73; *Demir and Baykara v Turkey* [2008] ECHR 1345, para 146; *Stoll v Switzerland* [2007] ECHR 1060, para 61; *Klass and Others v Germany* [1978] ECHR 4, para 42; *Gorzelik and Others v Poland* [2004] ECHR 73, para 95; *Kudrevičius, supra* note 17 at para 142.

104 Van Drooghenbroeck, *supra* note 97 at 50–51.

105 *Sunday Times v the United Kingdom (No. 1)* [1979] ECHR 1, para 65.

106 *Chassagnou, supra* note 18 at para 113 (emphasis added).

107 Tremblay, *supra* note 77 at 864.

108 Steven Greer, *The European Convention on Human Rights – Achievements, Problems and Prospects* (Cambridge University Press, 2006), 196 and 208–210; Van Drooghenbroeck, *supra* note 97 at 242. Note that Van Drooghenbroeck, writing in French, uses the equivalent term 'préférence abstraite'.

109 *Case "relating to certain aspects of the laws on the use of languages in education in Belgium" v Belgium* (9 February 1967), 28 ('[t]he Convention therefore implies a just balance between the protection of the general interest of the Community and the respect due to fundamental human rights *while attaching particular importance to the latter*'; emphasis

Human rights adjudication by the ECtHR aligns not with Beatty's and Möller's 'strict optimization model' of proportionality, but with Schauer's 'rule of weight' conception of proportionality, which 'recognizes that rights are worth more than non-rights protected interests'.[110]

Although the ECtHR thus favours a 'priority-to-rights' conception of proportionality, it does not grant *absolute* priority to human rights over non-rights considerations. Under the ECHR, most human rights can be – and frequently are – overridden by public or private interests.[111] The Convention's human rights are therefore not 'trumps',[112] at least not in the strong sense intended by Ronald Dworkin.[113] Instead, they are arguably closer to Schauer's 'shields against government actions',[114] offering right holders presumptive, but defeasible protection against the public interest.[115]

The need for a distinct framework for conflicts between human rights

Thus far, I have explained that, under the ECHR, human rights hold special – presumptive, but defeasible – normative force over non-rights considerations. And, as Schauer would argue, that is as it should be, since this special normative force

added); *Brand v the Netherlands* [2004] ECHR 196, para 65 ('a reasonable balance must be struck between the competing interests involved. On this point, reiterating the importance of Article 5 in the Convention system, the Court is of the opinion that in striking this balance particular weight should be given to the applicant's right to liberty').

110 Schauer, *supra* note 66 at 177.

111 This is true for all relative human rights. Only the absolute human rights of Articles 3, 4, 7 and 9 (1) ECHR could be said to function as genuine 'trumps'.

112 For an alternative view, see Letsas, *supra* note 46 (attempting to reconstruct the ECtHR's proportionality test in terms of a reason-blocking conception of human rights). On the reason-blocking conception of (human) rights, see Ronald Dworkin, *Taking Rights Seriously* (Harvard University Press, 1977); Richard Pildes, 'Why Rights Are Not Trumps: Social Meanings, Expressive Harms, and Constitutionalism', 27 *Journal of Legal Studies* (1998), 725–763; Richard Pildes, 'Dworkin's Two Conceptions of Rights', 29 *Journal of Legal Studies* (2000), 309–315.

113 Dworkin, *supra* note 112 at xi and xv. On different possible conceptions of the 'trump model of rights', see Klatt and Meister, *supra* note 65 at 17–44 (distinguishing between a strong trump model, a medium trump model and a weak trump model; and favouring the last).

114 Schauer, *supra* note 37 at 429 ('[w]earing a suit of armor would protect me against arrows, knives, blackjacks, fists and small bullets, and thus it is plain that wearing a suit of armor provides me with a degree of protection I would otherwise not have had. But that suit of armor does not protect me against large bore ammunitions, bombs, or artillery fire and is as a result less than totally protective. Just like rights ... what rights *do* is to protect against certain low justification (small bore) efforts to restrict the activities that the rights are rights to, but do not protect against high justification (large bore) efforts to restrict those activities' (emphasis in original)).

115 Note that George Letsas has argued that two dominant conceptions of rights – what Jeremy Waldron terms 'the immunities theories' and 'the reason-blocking theories of rights' – can both accommodate limitation clauses to human rights, such as those of the ECHR. See Letsas, *supra* note 84 at 101–105.

is inherent in the very idea of human rights. Taking the special normative force of human rights seriously, I posit, requires the development of a distinct framework for the resolution of conflicts between them.[116] Since the priority-to-rights principle is deeply engrained in the very structure of the ECtHR's proportionality test, that test must be reserved for 'traditional' human rights cases in which human rights are opposed by a public interest (or other non-human-rights considerations).[117] When human rights conflict, conversely, there are no (weak) trumps to be played or shields to be wielded. Conflicting human rights should instead enter an *alternative* framework on *equal* footing, as norms that merit principled equal respect.[118]

Treating (conflicts between) human rights as special is not only mandated by the normative-theoretical arguments I have advanced thus far. A failure to do so also has detrimental consequences in and for human rights practice. On a 'priority-to-rights' conception of proportionality, such as employed by the ECtHR, treating human rights conflicts identical to 'traditional' human rights cases causes what I term 'preferential framing'.[119]

The idea that the Court's case law on conflicting human rights is subject to 'framing effects' was first hypothesised by Olivier De Schutter and (then ECtHR Judge) Françoise Tulkens.[120] De Schutter and Tulkens recognised that the Court's version of the proportionality test entails 'an implicit priority of the right which is invoked by the applicant over the interest put forward by the defending state in order to justify the restriction'.[121] Application of that test to conflicts between human rights would, according to De Schutter and Tulkens, result 'in one right being recognized a priority over another, simply because it has been invoked by the applicant'.[122]

116 *Contra* Van Drooghenbroeck, *supra* note 97 at 312–313 ('en termes de *méthode de résolution*, le conflit de droits et libertés n'appelle pas d'autres instruments que ceux utilisés dans le cadre du conflit «classique»: de part et d'autre, la proportionnalité est conviée à effectuer l'arbitrage'; emphasis in original).

117 See also Olivier De Schutter and Françoise Tulkens, 'Rights in Conflict: The European Court of Human Rights as a Pragmatic Institution', in Eva Brems (ed.), *Conflicts between Fundamental Rights* (Intersentia, 2008), 188–190; Leto Cariolou, 'The Search for an Equilibrium by the European Court of Human Rights', in Eva Brems (ed.), *Conflicts between Fundamental Rights* (Intersentia, 2008), 261 and 266; Frédéric Sudre, 'Les conflits de droits. Cadre général d'approche dans la jurisprudence de la Cour européenne des droits de l'homme', in Laurence Potvin-Solis (ed.), *La conciliation des droits et libertés dans les ordres juridiques européens* (Bruylant, 2012), 251–252.

118 Once more, this applies primarily to conflicts between relative human rights. Conflicts involving absolute rights on one or both sides of the equation are not tackled in detail in this book.

119 See also Chapter 5, where I test the hypothesis that the Court's case law on human rights conflicts is subject to 'preferential framing' effects, through a statistical and substantive analysis of its defamation case law.

120 De Schutter and Tulkens, *supra* note 117.

121 Ibid. at 170.

122 Ibid. at 190.

Indeed, conflicting human rights do not arrive in Strasbourg on an equal footing.[123] Due to the structure of human rights, *i.e.* as rights held against the state, ECtHR cases invariably posit right holders against states. Thus, a case that involves a horizontal clash of rights at the domestic level is transformed, as it were, in a vertical conflict between one of the right holders and the state in front of the ECtHR. The state will usually attempt to justify the rights infringement as necessary to protect the human rights of others, but those 'others' are not directly involved in the proceedings.[124]

The procedural logics of the ECHR system are partially responsible for 'preferential framing' effects, leading the Court to frame the case around the directly invoked human right, while disregarding (to a greater or lesser extent) the importance of the other human right at stake. The other – conflicting – human right threatens to fade into the background as a result of the vertical nature of the Court's proceedings between a right holder and a state.[125] This 'preferential framing' process, which I evaluate in detail in Chapter 5, is further compounded when the Court applies its 'priority-to-rights' model of the proportionality test to conflicts between human rights.

Under the 'priority-to-rights' model, the invoked human right is granted principled (but defeasible) priority over the considerations invoked to justify its infringement. Protection of the invoked human rights is the rule; justified restrictions are the exception. The Court's proportionality test is thus loaded in favour of the invoked human right. This is mandated by the special normative force of human rights and makes perfect sense when a human right is opposed by a public interest. But if the same logic is applied to conflicts between human rights, 'preferential framing' effects unjustifiably skew the Court's reasoning in favour of the directly invoked human right, and against the other human right at stake. This, in turn, threatens to render the outcome of Strasbourg judgments dependent on an arbitrary factor: the result of the domestic proceedings. Let me elaborate this point a bit.

If a conflict between human right A of person X and human right B of person Y is decided in favour of Y's human right B by the domestic courts, X can claim a violation of human right A at the ECtHR in Strasbourg. If the Court applies its 'priority-to-rights' conception of proportionality, according to which exceptions to human rights should be interpreted restrictively, its reasoning would be skewed in favour of human right A. Yet, if the *exact same case* would be decided differently at the domestic level, Y could claim a violation of human right B in Strasbourg. The Court's reasoning would, then, be skewed in favour of human right B,

123 Eva Brems, 'Conflicting Human Rights: An Exploration in the Context of the Right to a Fair Trial in the European Convention for the Protection of Human Rights and Fundamental Freedoms', 27 *Human Rights Quarterly* (2005), 305.

124 Although they could present arguments by way of third party interventions. For examples of cases in which this actually occurred, see *Ahrens v Germany* [2012] ECHR 515; *Lombardi Vallauri v Italy* [2011] ECHR 1636; *Obst v Germany* (23 September 2010).

125 De Schutter and Tulkens, *supra* note 117.

although the conflict remains identical. This, clearly, is an undesirable state of affairs, which should be avoided.

The need to avoid 'preferential framing' effects lends further support to the central argument of this book: taking the special normative force of human rights seriously requires the development of a distinct framework for the resolution of conflicts between them. The ECtHR, however, is not convinced. As demonstrated by Peggy Ducoulombier,[126] although the Court has recognised the existence of conflicts between human rights in (part of) its case law,[127] it by and large tackles these conflicts in the same manner as it does 'traditional' human rights cases: through proportionality analysis.[128] Nevertheless, in one particular area of its case law, the Court has gone through an evolution that arguably marks sensitivity to the 'preferential framing' argument: its defamation case law.

The text of the ECHR itself does not include a human right to reputation. For a long time, the Court therefore refused to treat a person's reputation as a matter of human rights.[129] Instead, it subsumed reputation as a 'mere' interest in proportionality analysis under Article 10 (2) ECHR.[130] As a result, protection of the ***human right*** to freedom of expression was the rule, protection of the ***interest*** in reputation the exception. This famously led Judge Loucaides to complain about historic under-protection of (the right to) reputation under the ECHR:

> [f]or many years the jurisprudence of the Court has developed on the premise that, while freedom of speech is a right expressly guaranteed by the Convention, the protection of reputation is simply a ground of

126 Ducoulombier, *supra* note 6 at 350 and 370. See also De Schutter and Tulkens, *supra* note 117 at 188–189.

127 See, most notably, *Chassagnou*, *supra* note 18.

128 For a recent example, see *Couderc and Hachette Filipacchi Associés v France* [2014] ECHR 604, paras 91–96 (in which the Court recognises that it faces a conflict between freedom of expression and the right to private life, but nevertheless states that, as a matter of principle, (a) 'the test of "necessity in a democratic society" requires the Court to determine whether the interference complained of corresponded to a "pressing social need", whether it was proportionate to the legitimate aim pursued and whether the reasons given by the national authorities to justify it are relevant and sufficient'; (b) 'The Court has already had occasion to lay down the relevant principles which must guide its assessment in this area … [identifying] a number of criteria in the context of ***balancing*** the competing rights' (emphasis added); and (c) 'there is little scope under Article 10 § 2 of the Convention for restrictions on freedom of expression when a matter of public interest is at stake'). See also *Fernández Martínez*, *supra* note 20 at paras 123–124; *Perinçek v Switzerland* [2015] ECHR 907, para 228.

129 *Lingens v Austria* [1986] ECHR 7.

130 *Cf.* Schauer, *supra* note 66 at 175 ('suppose … that there is a *right* to drive at sixty miles per hour … the strength of the evidence or arguments necessary for override [of this right] would have to be stronger than the evidence or arguments sufficient to outweigh the *interest* in driving at sixty miles per hour were that interest not understood as, or protected by, a right').

> permissible restriction on the right in question ... as a restriction on a right under the Convention it has to be (like any other restriction on such rights) strictly and narrowly interpreted... As a consequence of this approach, the case-law on the subject of freedom of speech has on occasion shown excessive sensitivity and granted over-protection in respect of interference with freedom of expression, as compared with interference with the right to reputation.[131]

Swayed by the arguments of Judge Loucaides and others, the Court eventually included the right to protection of reputation under Article 8 ECHR.[132] Subject to a threshold requirement,[133] the Court started treating reputation as a matter of human rights under the ECHR, *i.e.* as meriting a higher level of protection than a 'mere' interest in reputation.[134] As a result, defamation cases now entail a conflict between human rights. Yet, if the Court had continued to apply the proportionality test as described by Judge Loucaides, its reasoning would have been 'contaminated' by arbitrary elements, chief among which the result of the domestic proceedings. 'Preferential framing' effects would have taken hold and the Court would have failed to treat both human rights on an equal footing. Initially, this is exactly what happened. The Court continued to apply the proportionality test in most defamation cases.[135] As I show in Chapter 5, there are strong indications that the outcome in such cases was, as a result, skewed by 'preferential framing' effects.[136]

Yet, as Judge Schäffer has lucidly pointed out,

131 Dissenting opinion of Judge Loucaides in *Lindon, Otchakovsky-Laurens and July v France* [2007] ECHR 836.

132 *Pfeifer v Austria* [2007] ECHR 935, para 35.

133 See *supra* note 91 and accompanying text.

134 *Cf. Karacsony v Hungary* [2014] ECHR 939, para 51 ('the notion of "the authority and dignity of Parliament" ... cannot be equated to that of human beings ... [it] is a mere institutional interest of Parliament, that is, a consideration not necessarily of the same strength as "the protection of the reputation or rights of others"').

135 See, for instance, *Frankowicz v Poland* [2008] ECHR 1712; *Csánics v Hungary* [2009] ECHR 90; *Kuliś v Poland* [2008] ECHR 210; *Dyundin v Russia* [2008] ECHR 1076. Note that this applies only to Article 10 ECHR cases, which concern negative interferences (*i.e.* the state's failure to respect freedom of expression), whereas the Court has always applied a 'fair balance' test in positive obligations cases (*i.e.* cases in which the state has failed to protect human rights), including defamation cases brought under Article 8 ECHR. The fact that 'preferential framing' effects can also be seen at work in Article 8 cases (see Chapter 5) shows that the 'priority-to-rights' – or rather 'priority-to-the-invoked-right' – principle is deeply engrained in the Court's case law, not only in negative obligations cases, but also in positive obligations cases.

136 See *contra* Spielmann and Cariolou, *supra* note 24 at 584 (arguing that the 'assumption [of "preferential framing"] is debatable', since there is 'no reason in principle why the outcome of the Court's analysis would depend on how an application is framed, particularly given the nature of the Court's examination that involves precisely the application of the same principles concerning freedom of speech').

> where both values [freedom of expression and the right to private life] are at stake, the result of the Court's balancing exercise ought not to depend on which particular Article of the Convention has been relied on in the case before it.[137]

Indeed, both conflicting human rights should be treated with equal respect. The Grand Chamber finally acknowledged as much in *Axel Springer v Germany*:

> [i]n cases such as the present one [*i.e.* cases of conflict between freedom of expression and the right to reputation] ... the outcome of the application should not, in principle, vary according to whether it has been lodged with the Court under Article 10 of the Convention by the publisher who has published the offending article or under Article 8 of the Convention by the person who was the subject of that article. Indeed, as a matter of principle these rights deserve equal respect.[138]

In *Axel Springer*, the Court further developed a new balancing test which would, although imperfectly applied in the aftermath of the judgment,[139] henceforth structure the Court's reasoning in defamation cases.[140] My primary aim in this book is to go one step further than the ECtHR has gone so far, by proposing a *general* framework for the resolution of conflicts between human rights, *i.e.* a framework that is not narrowly tailored to one specific conflict, but applicable to a wide range of human rights conflicts.[141]

137 Dissenting opinion of Judge Schäffer in *Pfeifer*, *supra* note 132 at para 5.

138 *Axel Springer*, *supra* note 26 at para 87. See also, in the context of other conflicts, *Von Hannover (No. 2)*, *supra* note 26 at para 106; *Sindicatul "Păstorul cel Bun" v Romania* [2013] ECHR 646, para 160.

139 See, for instance, *Mladina d.d. Ljubljana v Slovenia* [2014] ECHR 425; *Brosa v Germany* [2014] ECHR 432 (in both defamation cases, the Court does not cite, nor apply the balancing test of *Axel Springer*, instead it harkens back to the proportionality test; a potential explanation for this apparent deviation from *Axel Springer* is that both cases concerned speech against politicians; neither judgment mentions the right to reputation, nor the notion of conflict; the Court may thus have been of the opinion that these politicians, as government representatives, did not qualify for a right to reputation and that the cases therefore did not involve a conflict between human rights; if accurate, this actually supports my claim that the proportionality test should be reserved for 'traditional' human rights cases, while an alternative test is to be applied to conflicts between human rights).

140 *Axel Springer*, *supra* note 26. The balancing test is composed of the following criteria: contribution to a debate of general interest; how well known is the person concerned and what is the subject of the report; prior conduct of the person concerned; method of obtaining the information and its veracity; content, form and consequences of the publication; severity of the sanction imposed. See also *Von Hannover (No. 2)*, *supra* note 26 (decided on the same day as *Axel Springer* and providing a similar list of criteria to balance freedom of expression and the right to private life).

141 As indicated before, the framework deals primarily with conflicts between relative human rights, although its first two steps can also be applied to conflicts that involve absolute human rights on one or both sides of the equation.

A general framework for the resolution of human rights conflicts

The framework for the resolution of conflicts between human rights I propose in this book – and develop in Chapters 3 and 6, in particular – is composed of three consecutive steps. The three steps range from the most optimal to the least optimal approach to human rights conflicts: (1) defusing conflicts as fake; (2) reaching a compromise between the human rights in conflict; and (3) balancing the human rights against each other.

The first step of the framework – defusing conflicts as fake – examines two particular questions: (1) are the human rights genuinely in conflict with each other, in the sense of being mutually incompatible; and (2) is the state really under conflicting duties, *i.e.* duties that it cannot simultaneously fulfil? The second step of the framework – reaching a compromise – investigates whether it would be feasible and appropriate to have conflicting human rights make mutual, but minimal sacrifices, so that both (or all) rights may 'survive' the conflict as intact as possible. The third step of the framework – balancing – consists in a structured balancing as reasoning test, aimed at determining which of the conflicting human rights should prevail under the circumstances.

The first and second steps of the framework target the conflict. In aiming to either defuse or minimise it, their objective is to keep the human rights at stake either entirely intact (defusing conflicts as fake) or to the maximum extent possible (reaching a compromise). The third step, by contrast, deals with conflicts that cannot be defused or minimised. It thus turns its gaze from the conflict towards the human rights in the conflict, aiming to determine which right should prevail over the other (and, concomitantly, which right should be 'sacrificed').

At face value, the three steps of my framework bear some resemblance to the three stages of 'classic' proportionality analysis (suitability, necessity, balancing). This is true to some extent, but there are also important differences, which are worth highlighting before we proceed.

Of all three steps, the final step of my framework is perhaps most in line with the 'classic' proportionality test. It even shares its name with the last stage of proportionality analysis: balancing. Yet, as I will argue in Chapters 4–7, the structured balancing as reasoning test I propose deviates significantly from proportionality's rather mechanical balancing of interests test. Most importantly, it aims to do better than Alexy's Weight Formula balancing test, which I critique in Chapter 7.

The differences between my framework and 'classic' proportionality analysis are more pronounced in relation to the first and second steps of the framework, when contrasted with the suitability and necessity stages of proportionality analysis. Those suitability and necessity stages – which aim at 'optimization relative to the factual possibilities'[142] – are usefully summarised by Kai Möller:

142 Alexy, *supra* note 48 at 28.

> The principle [of proportionality] is best understood as providing guidance in the structured resolution of a *conflict* between a (prima facie) right and another right or a public interest … The suitability stage determines the extent to which there is a genuine conflict between the two in the sense that one can only be realized at the cost of the other: when a policy which interferes with a right does not contribute to the achievement of the legitimate goal, then there is no conflict between the right and the goal. The necessity stage requires that the conflict be resolved in a way that is as respectful of the right as possible; thus, the less restrictive but equally effective alternative must be chosen.[143]

The first step of my framework (defusing conflicts as fake) is in line with proportionality analysis insofar as it – like proportionality's suitability stage – investigates whether both human rights are genuinely incompatible with each other. Additionally, however, it also asks whether the state is under conflicting duties. Implicit within that question is not only a factual determination, but also an element of legal creativity: could the state have adopted a different approach or taken measures that would have *rendered* its human rights duties compatible (thereby removing the conflict)? This question is generally not asked under the suitability (nor necessity) stage of the 'classic' proportionality test, which investigates 'optimization relative to the *factual* possibilities'.[144] The exact nature of the difference will, I trust, become clear when I detail the first step of my framework in Chapter 3.

The second step of my framework – reaching a compromise – is fundamentally distinct from the necessity stage of proportionality, although the devil is in the detail. The necessity stage of proportionality asks whether measures less detrimental to the invoked right, but equally effective for the legitimate aim pursued, are or were available. Under the necessity stage, the *differentiated* impact on the invoked right is thus assessed against the backdrop of an *unaltered* level of protection of the legitimate aim. The second step of my framework, conversely, examines whether *both* conflicting human rights could and should make minor sacrifices to minimise the conflict.[145] By taking the equal respect due to conflicting human rights seriously, the second step of my framework thus declines to restrict itself to examining factual alternatives that would be less detrimental to the invoked human right, while keeping the level of protection of the countervailing human right intact (as the 'classic' proportionality test does). Instead, finding a

143 Möller, *supra* note 45 at 156 (emphasis in original).
144 Alexy, *supra* note 48 at 28 (emphasis added).
145 In the rudimentary description of the framework offered in the text, I refer to 'both' human rights in conflict. I do so to not render the description of the framework overly complex. As I explain later (see Chapters 6 and 7, in particular), conflicts between human rights need not be strictly binary (*i.e.* between two human rights) but may very well be multipolar (*i.e.* involving multiple human rights). The use of 'both' in the text should thus be read to also include, where appropriate, 'all'.

compromise entails, once more, an exercise in legal creativity, whereby attempts are made at accommodating both conflicting human rights. I offer concrete examples in Chapter 3, where it will become clear that the second step of my framework investigates crucially distinct avenues from those examined under proportionality's necessity stage.

In an important sense, the central difference between my framework and the 'classic' proportionality test rests in how conflicts are perceived and tackled. The 'classic' proportionality test asks questions aimed at determining whether or not the infringement of a human right was justified. The issue is thus examined – at least under the suitability and necessity stages – from the viewpoint of the invoked human right. As Frederick Schauer lucidly points out 'courts [applying proportionality] do not typically say that the loss in public order can be no more than necessary in light of the goal of pursuing freedom of expression'.[146] Instead, they 'say that the restriction on freedom of expression can be no more than necessary in light of the goal of pursuing public order'.[147] Indeed, only the last, balancing stage of the 'classic' proportionality test examines 'traditional' human rights cases from both angles, *i.e.* from the viewpoint of both the human right and the legitimate aim invoked to justify its restriction. My framework, conversely, deliberately and consistently examines conflicts between human rights from both angles throughout all three of its steps. This, I posit, is mandated by the equal respect due to human rights, when they (appear to) conflict. But much, I trust, will become clear when I develop the framework in detail throughout this book.

Conclusion

The normative backbone of this book, set out in this opening chapter, is a dual proposition: (1) human rights carry special normative force; and (2) taking that special normative force seriously requires the development of a distinct framework to tackle conflicts between human rights. The 'priority-to-rights' model of proportionality, such as employed by the ECtHR, should therefore be reserved for 'traditional' human rights cases, in which human rights are opposed by non-human-rights considerations.[148] Lest judicial reasoning be skewed by 'preferential

146 Schauer, *supra* note 66 at 180. See also Stephen Gardbaum, 'Positive and Horizontal Rights: Proportionality's Next Frontier or a Bridge Too Far?', available at http://papers.ssrn.com/sol3/papers.cfm?abstract_id=2726794 (last accessed 4 March 2016) ('where in a given context a state has conflicting constitutional duties to grant a criminal defendant a fair trial and not to interfere with the media's freedom of expression and elects to give priority to the latter, it cannot really be said that it limits the defendant's right in order – or as a means – to promote free expression. It is not acting with this latter as its goal but rather to resolve a constitutional conflict by balancing the two duties/rights to determine which is weightier in the circumstances').

147 Schauer, *supra* note 66 at 180.

148 Throughout this book, I remain agnostic – at the level of normative theory – about how 'traditional' human rights cases *should* be tackled (as opposed to how they currently are tackled by the ECtHR). Whether the special normative force of human rights is best

framing' effects, conflicts between human rights should, conversely, be tackled through a distinct resolution framework.

In this chapter, I have sketched the outline of such a distinct framework, consisting of three steps: (1) defusing conflicts between human rights; (2) reaching a compromise between human rights in conflict; and (3) balancing human rights. I have further outlined the major differences between my framework and the 'classic' proportionality test. Ultimately, however, I am agnostic about whether my framework is considered truly distinct or rather an alternative conception of proportionality. What matters is that, in distinguishing itself from the 'classic' proportionality test, the framework takes the special nature of (conflicts between) human rights seriously. What remains to be determined is whether it works, both in theory and in practice. Before the framework can be tested, however, its object – conflicts between human rights – must be clearly defined. That is the task of the next chapter.

protected through a reason-blocking model of adjudication (Letsas), a 'priority-to-rights' model of proportionality (Schauer), an 'optimization' model of proportionality that accommodates the priority of rights (Klatt) or yet another model is an important and interesting question. In this book, however, I do not aim to answer it.

2 Defining conflicts between human rights

Taking the special normative force of human rights seriously requires the development of a distinct framework to tackle conflicts between them. Or so I have argued in the previous chapter. But when do human rights genuinely conflict with one another? The question and its answer are crucial, since the framework I develop throughout this book is specifically designed to only tackle genuine conflicts between human rights. 'Traditional' human rights cases, conversely, should be resolved through the 'priority-to-rights' model of the proportionality test; or another test that takes the special normative force of human rights seriously.[1] That is, at least, one of the core arguments of this book.

Much thus turns on the definition of conflicts between human rights I adopt in this chapter. In proposing that definition, I pursue a dual objective. First, I aim to exclude cases that might *appear* to involve human rights on both sides of the equation, but are in reality more akin to 'traditional' human rights cases, in which a human right is opposed by a public interest. Second, I aim to exclude cases that *do* involve human rights on both sides, but in which the conflict is apparent, rather than real. Throughout this chapter, I explain how arguments based on insincere human rights rhetoric, aggregation and speculation mandate exclusion of the first set of cases. I moreover offer a set of criteria to guide exclusion of the second set of cases. I further propose a single definition of genuine conflicts between human rights, which provides the foundation for the remainder of the book's argument. I conclude the chapter by proposing a double test – composed of a 'converse situation' test and a 'conflicting duties' test – to identify genuine human rights conflicts in judicial practice.

Human right or public interest? On human rights rhetoric, aggregation and speculation

Common sense seems to demand that situations in which human rights are restricted in pursuit of a public interest are categorically excluded from any

1 As noted before, throughout this book I remain agnostic about the best way to ensure that the special normative force of human rights is taken seriously in human rights adjudication. See Chapter 1, note 148.

definition of conflicts between human rights. Otherwise – if they are not excluded – we risk bringing the public interest back in through the backdoor. As a result, the efforts of the previous chapter to take the special normative force of human rights seriously, by erecting a barrier between human rights conflicts and 'traditional' human rights cases, will have been for nought.

The need for such a strict barrier is, however, contested. Peggy Ducoulombier, among others, argues that cases in which human rights restrictions pursue public interests such as 'public order' or 'protection of health' should not *a priori* be excluded from the category of human rights conflicts, since those public interests reflect individuals' human rights.[2] Angelika Nussberger, judge at the ECtHR, concurs in her extra-judicial writings:

> the difference between multipolar human rights conflicts and 'normal human rights conflicts' is only a gradual, not a substantial one. Even in a classical conflict opposing an individual and the State the infringement of the relevant human right has to be justified on the basis of the 'rights and freedoms of others', even if they may be hidden behind an abstract concept such as 'public safety' or 'prevention of disorder and crime', or 'health and morals'. Every human rights conflict can thus be construed as 'multipolar'.[3]

Nussberger and Ducoulombier thus insist on a broad definition of human rights conflicts. I disagree. To counter arguments based on aggregation and speculation, I submit, conflicts between human rights should be interpreted narrowly. Their definition should, as a matter of principle, exclude situations in which human rights are opposed by a public interest. In substantiating that argument, I will first explain how broad interpretations of human rights conflicts invite insincere human rights rhetoric by governments.

Public interests masquerading as human rights

To some, it is certainly appealing to interpret 'public order', 'the prevention of crime' and other public interests as encapsulating the human rights of all individual

2 Peggy Ducoulombier, 'Conflicts between Fundamental Rights and the European Court of Human Rights: An Overview', in Eva Brems, (ed.), *Conflicts between Fundamental Rights* (Intersentia, 2008), 223. See also Janneke Gerards, 'Fundamental Rights and Other Interests: Should it Really Make a Difference?', in Eva Brems (ed), *Conflicts between Fundamental Rights* (Intersentia, 2008), 655–690; Xiaobing Xu and George D. *Wilson*, 'On Conflict of Human Rights', 5 *Pierce Law Review* (2006), 37 ('the reason why utilitarian values such as national security, public safety, public order, public health, and public morality may outweigh human rights is that they contain human rights elements'); Kai Möller, *The Global Model of Constitutional Rights* (Oxford University Press, 2012), 136 ('We often speak of something being in the *public* or *general* interest. This is really only a short form of saying that it serves everyone's autonomy interests' (emphases in original)).

3 Angelika Nussberger, 'Subsidiarity in the Control of Decisions Based on Proportionality: An Analysis on the Basis of the Implementation of ECtHR Judgments into German Law', in Anja Seibert-Forh and Mark E. Villiger (eds), *Judgments of the European Court of Human Rights – Effects and Implementation* (Nomos Verlagsgesellschaft, 2014), 173.

members of society (or a particular segment thereof). Governments, in particular, are prone to deploy argumentative strategies that equate public interests with human rights in a bid to avoid liability for human rights violations. As Jacco Bomhoff argues, 'if the elaboration of the "public"-side to conflicts between *individual* and *public* interests runs into difficulty, the conceptual move of understanding this "public"-side as an aggregation of individual rights becomes highly attractive'.[4] In making this 'conceptual move', governments deliberately justify human rights restrictions in the name of the human rights of others, instead of the public interest. In doing so, they hope to come across as (more) 'human rights-friendly' and stand a better chance of avoiding liability for human rights violations. Indeed, Emmanuelle Bribosia and Isabelle Rorive indicate that governments are starting to realise that:

> [o]nce there is no longer wide acceptance of traditional values (such as general interest, public order and public security), which had been used as the basis for restricting rights and freedoms, it may be worth, in order to persuade judges or public opinion, classifying these values within the discursive register of fundamental rights.[5]

Analysis of the case law of the ECtHR confirms that governments sometimes employ 'human rights rhetoric' to avoid liability under the ECHR.[6] Upon closer examination, however, the relevant cases turn out not to involve a genuine conflict between human rights.

A prominent example,[7] in which the ECtHR ignored the government's human rights rhetoric, is *Saadi v Italy*.[8] *Saadi* concerned the deportation of an alleged

4 Jacco Bomhoff, '"The Rights and Freedoms of Others": The ECHR and Its Peculiar Category of Conflicts between Individual Fundamental Rights', in Eva Brems (ed.), *Conflicts between Fundamental Rights* (Intersentia, 2008), 638 (emphasis in original).

5 Emannuelle Bribosia and Isabelle Rorive, 'In Search of a Balance between the Right to Equality and Other Fundamental Rights', European Commission (2010), 14, available at http://ec.europa.eu/social/main.jsp?catId=738&langId=en&pubId=548&type=2&furtherPubs=no (last accessed 11 March 2016).

6 Sébastien Van Drooghenbroeck, 'Conflits entre droits fondamentaux, pondération des intérêts: fausses pistes(?) et vrais problèmes', in Jean-Louis Renchon (ed.), *Les droits de la personnalité* (Bruylant, 2009), 307 (referring to governments as employing 'un registre «rhétorique»').

7 For another example, see *Yordanova and Others v Bulgaria* [2012] ECHR 758. *Yordanova* concerned the removal of a Roma community from an illegally constructed settlement on government property. In Strasbourg, the Bulgarian government argued that 'had the Bulgarian authorities remained inactive in the face of the safety and sanitary risks that the applicants' settlement represented, they would have risked liability under the Convention for failure to discharge their positive obligation to protect life and health' (para 94). The Court, however, remained unconvinced by this human rights rhetoric. It concluded that the removal order had not been motivated by concerns for the lives and safety of the Roma applicants, but by a desire to sell the land to a private investor and a concern for complaints by neighbours about hygiene risks and disturbances of public order (paras 114 and 124). See further *Folgerø and Others v Norway* [2007] ECHR 546, paras 72–73, 78 and 88–89; *Ciorap v Moldova* [2007] ECHR 502, paras 73 and 83.

8 *Saadi v Italy* [2008] ECHR 179.

terrorist from Italy to Tunisia, where he would face a real risk of being tortured. The United Kingdom, intervening in the case, portrayed *Saadi* as a conflict between the alleged terrorist's freedom from torture and the right to life of Italy's entire population:

> Terrorism seriously [endangers] the right to life … [Therefore,] the threat presented by the person to be deported must be a factor to be assessed in relation to the possibility and the nature of the potential ill-treatment. That would make it possible to … weigh the rights secured to the applicant by Article 3 of the Convention against those secured to all other members of the community by Article 2.[9]

The Court, however, rejected this 'human rights' argument as 'misconceived':[10]

> [t]he concepts of 'risk' and 'dangerousness' … do not lend themselves to a balancing test … Either the evidence adduced before the Court reveals that there is a substantial risk if the person is sent back or it does not. The prospect that he may pose a serious threat to the community if not returned does not reduce in any way the degree of risk of ill treatment that the person may be subject to on return.[11]

In *Saadi*, the ECtHR thus declined to follow the United Kingdom's lead in characterising the case as a human rights conflict. But in other cases the Court has failed to expose the government's human rights rhetoric. Instead, it has gone along with it, thereby misconstruing cases in terms of a human rights conflict.

The domestic violence case of *Opuz v Turkey* marks a clear – and particularly troublesome – example. In *Opuz*, the Turkish government argued that it had to discontinue criminal proceedings against the suspect in a grave domestic violence case after the victims had withdrawn their criminal complaint, because 'further interference by the authorities would have amounted to a breach of the victims' Article 8 rights'.[12] Yet, the victims had withdrawn their criminal complaint due to death threats and pressure exerted by the suspect, not in a bid to secure their own right to private and family life under Article 8 ECHR.[13] The Turkish government's 'human rights' argument, intended to justify the state's failure to act in the face of grave domestic violence, was clearly insincere. Rather than rejecting the government's insincere argument, however, the ECtHR went along with it. The Court held that its role in *Opuz* was to 'examine whether the local authorities struck a proper balance between the victim's Article 2 and Article 8 rights'.[14]

9 Ibid. at paras 119 and 122.
10 Ibid. at para 139
11 Ibid.
12 *Opuz v Turkey* [2009] ECHR 870, para 137.
13 Ibid.
14 Ibid. at para 140 (the Court utilises the term 'victim' (singular), since the other victim – the applicant's mother – was killed and was thus not an applicant in Strasbourg).

This catastrophically misconstrues *Opuz* in terms of a conflict between human rights, pitting the victims' right to life (Article 2 ECHR) against their *own* right to private and family life (Article 8 ECHR).[15] Adding insult to injury, the Court dramatically missed the salient point: the victims had withdrawn their criminal complaint because they feared retaliation, *not* because they wished to have their private and family life respected.[16] Sadly, the suspect ended up killing one of the victims.

Cases like *Saadi* and *Opuz* illustrate why it is imperative to prevent human rights rhetoric by governments from 'infecting' human rights adjudication. Both cases, however, point towards distinct risks. *Saadi* exemplifies the threat of aggregation: once the human rights of the many find their way into judicial reasoning, it may be difficult for courts – like the ECtHR – to rule that they are outweighed by the human rights of the few. *Opuz*, conversely, epitomises the peril of speculation: once courts – like the ECtHR – accept that human rights are in play on both sides of a case, this might influence the outcome, even if one set of human rights was not really at stake. To counter the threat of aggregation and elude the peril of speculation, I posit, conflicts between human rights should be defined restrictively.

Countering aggregation and eluding speculation: the need for restrictive interpretation of human rights conflicts

'Public order', 'public safety', 'the prevention of crime' and other public interests are vague terms whose common meaning is more closely connected to the general interest than it is to individual human rights.[17] There should thus be a strong presumption against classifying *prima facie* 'traditional' human rights cases, in

15 For other cases in which the Court unjustly relied on the government's characterisation of cases as entailing a conflict between human rights, see *Refah Partisi (The Welfare Party) and Others v Turkey* [2003] ECHR 87; *TV Vest As and Rogaland Pensjonistparti v Norway* [2011] ECHR 2151.

16 The Court eventually found a violation of Article 2 in *Opuz*, *supra* note 12. It thus reached the correct outcome. But in order to do so it had to overcome the balancing problem it had itself created. In the process, the Court was forced to recognise that 'in some instances, the national authorities' interference with the private or family life of the individuals might be necessary in order to protect the health and rights of others or to prevent commission of criminal acts' (para 144). It found that, under the particular circumstances, '[t]he seriousness of the risk to the applicant's mother rendered such intervention by the authorities necessary in the present case' (para 144). But the seriousness of the risk to the applicant's mother should not have been balanced against the government's obligation to not interfere with her private and family life in the first place. Rather, there was no human rights obligation to be overridden. In misconstruing *Opuz* as a human rights conflict, the Court invited the unacceptable possibility that, had the risk to the mother's life been less serious, the Turkish government might have gotten away with a failure to prosecute domestic violence by insincerely relying on its obligation to protect the private and family life of the victims.

17 John Rawls, *A Theory of Justice* (Harvard University Press, 1999), 83; Michel Hottelier, 'Les conflits de droits de l'homme et la sécurité juridique', in X. (ed.), *Annuaire international des*

which public interests are invoked to justify rights infringements, in terms of conflicts between human rights. Such principled exclusion is needed to safeguard courts like the ECtHR from being lured in by *speculation* and trapped by *aggregation*.[18]

When governments invoke public interests such as 'public order' to justify human rights restrictions, the question whether the human rights of others are actually at stake *within* these public interests is necessarily a matter of speculation.[19] Governments do not generally know whether the rights-restrictive measures they are taking in the name of 'public order' will contribute to the actual protection of the human rights of concrete individuals.[20] Instead, they rely on the *probability* of a risk to those other human rights. The rights-restrictive measures at issue are usually not aimed at protecting identified individuals. Instead, they aim to protect the *entire population* against the *possibility* of rights infringements. In the absence of concrete evidence that the human rights of identified – or identifiable – individuals are actually at stake, such situations do not entail genuine human rights conflicts.[21] As the above analysis of *Saadi* shows, the opposite conclusion invites a threat under which aggregation of the 'human rights' of the many determines the outcome of cases that should not be ruled by utilitarian considerations.

Reflections on speculation and aggregation, much like the ones I have just described, lay at the heart of disagreement within the ECtHR's Grand Chamber in *Austin and Others v the United Kingdom*.[22] *Austin* concerned the containment of a large number of protestors in a full police cordon, for seven hours, during a demonstration in central London. In Strasbourg, the UK government argued that the full cordon had been absolutely necessary 'to prevent serious public disorder involving a substantial risk of death or serious injury'.[23] The government thus combined a public order defence with a need to protect the human rights of others. In its judgment, the majority of the Grand Chamber accepted the government's characterisation of the case: 'in certain well-defined circumstances, Articles 2 and 3 may imply positive obligations on the authorities to take preventive operational measures to protect individuals at risk of serious harm from the criminal acts of other individuals'.[24] But because Article 5 ECHR does not provide

droits de l'homme (Bruylant, 2009), 133; Ronald Dworkin, *Taking Rights Seriously* (Harvard University Press, 1977), 194.

18 Dworkin, *supra* note 17 at 202–204.

19 Ibid.

20 Note that what I have in mind here is judicial review of state action in concrete cases, not the process the legislator goes through when promulgating laws. In that respect, as intimated in the Introduction, a distinction should be made between how conflicts between human rights arise at the legislative level, where they are *necessarily abstract*, and how they play out in front of courts, where judges should first determine whether the *concrete* circumstances entail a *genuine* conflict between human rights.

21 Dworkin, *supra* note 17 at 203–204.

22 *Austin and Others v the United Kingdom* [2012] ECHR 459.

23 Ibid. at para 42.

24 Ibid. at para 55.

for an explicit 'public order' exception to the human right of personal liberty, the majority subsequently found itself in a predicament. Its way out was an ***implicit*** balancing exercise – disguised as contextualisation – between the protestors' human rights and the 'public order interest in averting a real risk of serious injury or damage'.[25]

Austin is relevant for our current concerns to the extent that it demonstrates how the (implicit) characterisation of a case as a human rights conflict may steer its outcome. The majority in *Austin* arguably viewed the case as follows: a number of persons were restricted in their freedom of movement to protect both themselves ***and*** those outside the cordon against breaches of their right to life and freedom from ill-treatment. Aggregating the latter rights in an implicit balancing exercise, the majority concluded – not unsurprisingly – that the protestors had to endure the temporary restriction of their freedom of movement: the speculative 'human rights' of the many outweighed the concrete human rights of the few.[26]

The dissenting judges in *Austin*, however, critiqued the majority's very characterisation of the case. They claimed that it had 'not been established … that there was a clear and present danger to life or limb'.[27] The dissenters thus argued that the facts of the case were insufficiently connected to the United Kingdom's positive obligations under the rights to life and physical integrity. In the terms I have been utilising, the dissenting judges – unlike the majority – refused to be lured in by speculation and trapped by aggregation.

Analysis of *Austin* directs us to a key question in defining human rights conflict: when – if ever – do public interests *sufficiently* represent individuals' human rights to warrant inclusion of relevant cases in the category of genuine conflicts between human rights? In order to answer that question, we require tools to determine when the protection of 'public order', 'the prevention of crime' and other public interests actually contribute to the protection of individuals' concrete human rights. To that end, I propose we borrow – and adapt – a tool from moral philosophy: Judith Jarvis Thomson's 'High-Threshold Thesis'. Thomson argues that the increment of good achieved by infringing a person's claim, for instance the claim that she not be kicked, is a relevant consideration in assessing the legitimacy of the infringement.[28] Thomson insists that, when the distribution of good takes the form of tiny increments to a large amount of people, the claim cannot justifiably be overridden: 'surely it is on *no* view permissible to kill a person to save billions from a minor headache'.[29] Applying a similar idea to human rights law, George Letsas argues that certain human rights, such as freedom of speech, are so central to the values of democracy and social justice that

25 Ibid. at paras 59–67.

26 Note that the few were, moreover, counted *among* the many, given that the measures – allegedly – aimed to protect them as well.

27 Dissenting opinion of Judges Tulkens, Spielmann and Garlicki in *Austin*, *supra* note 22 at para 8.

28 Judith Jarvis Thomson, *The Realm of Rights* (Harvard University Press, 1990), 166.

29 Ibid. at 169 (emphasis in original).

it is 'important to ensure that these liberties are not limited for *speculative* or *marginal* benefits to the interests of others'.[30]

Thomson's 'High-Threshold Thesis', combined with Letsas' argument on the speculative nature of a benefit, has an intuitive appeal to it. I propose, however, to not use them in quite the sense intended by Thomson and Letsas: as a normative argument to protect (human) rights claims against infringements for particular kinds of reasons. Rather, I suggest we adapt the 'High-Threshold Thesis', transforming it from a normative tool into an analytical one that may be utilised to determine when cases featuring a public interest defence should be excluded from the category of conflicts between human rights. Under the modified 'High-Threshold Thesis', such exclusion is particularly called for when cases involve a large degree of speculation *and* the distribution of good is far removed from the protection of the concrete human rights of identified or identifiable individuals.

To make things more tangible, imagine the following situation: a suspect of a violent robbery is placed in pre-trial detention in pursuit of 'the prevention of crime'. In this situation, the good that is being distributed by the suspect's detention consists of tiny increments to a large number of persons (potentially the entire population of a country). The immediate benefit each individual receives is moreover not greater protection of their human rights, but an increased feeling of security. Any impact of the suspect's detention on individuals' concrete human rights is necessarily speculative. Given that (A) the suspect's detention only leads, in terms of distribution of good, to tiny increments to a large amount of people, and (B) the impact on individualised human rights remains (highly) speculative, the detention should be characterised as pursuing a general interest, *not* the protection of concrete human rights.[31]

The above brings to mind Dworkin's argument – reflected in the ECtHR's case law[32] – that states are under a more stringent obligation to protect the lives of concrete individuals in *actual* danger than to *prevent* endangerment of statistical and anonymous persons.[33] While the former situation may lead to a conflict between human rights (if a suspect is detained or monitored during his

30 George Letsas, *A Theory of Interpretation of the European Convention on Human Rights* (Oxford University Press, 2007), 118 (emphasis in original). Letsas offers the example of a demonstration: '[i]t causes great inconvenience to allow demonstrations on a regular basis in a city centre. But unless they pose a clear and present danger to the lives of others then they should not be banned …' (ibid.).

31 See also Bomhoff, *supra* note 4 at 647–648 (insisting, in his assessment of 'the rights of others', on a need to 'single out those cases where the interests of those seen as "others" are not distinguishable to a sufficient degree from the general interests shared by all members of society').

32 See, for instance, *Choreftakis and Choreftaki v Greece* (17 January 2012), para 59 ('l'absence de lien de causalité direct et solide entre les modalités d'application du système grec et la mort du fils des requérants, *exigerait une défaillance évidente* de la loi appliquée en l'espèce *pour engager la responsabilité* de l'Etat défendeur sur le champ de l'article 2 de la Convention' (emphases added)).

33 Ronald Dworkin, *Justice for Hedgehogs* (Harvard University Press, 2011), 279.

private life), the latter is a paradigmatic 'traditional' human rights case, in which a human right is opposed by a public (or general) interest.

Despite the salience of these arguments, the ECtHR has repeatedly ruled that a conflict between human rights was at issue in cases that, when examined through the lens of the modified 'High-Threshold Thesis', turn out to be 'traditional' human rights cases.[34] Take *Colon v the Netherlands*, for example. *Colon* revolved around an order by Amsterdam's mayor, designating the old centre of the city as a security risk zone. As a result of the order, public prosecutors were granted the power to issue preventive search orders under which – during a randomly selected period of 12 hours – any person in the old centre of Amsterdam could be subjected to a search for the presence of weapons. In ruling on *Colon*, the ECtHR considered that it was:

> faced, not for the first time, with the need to balance two interests protected by Article 8 against each other. The first is the protection of the individual against arbitrary interference by public authority, which the Court has consistently held to be the essential object of Article 8. The second is constituted by the protection of … the physical and moral integrity of those within the jurisdiction of the Contracting States, which imposes on the Contracting States not merely the right but the duty to take positive action.[35]

The Court thus characterised *Colon* as a conflict between human rights, pitting the human rights of those subjected to the search order against the human rights of 'those within the jurisdiction of the Contracting [State]', that is everyone in the Netherlands. Yet, *Colon* is a prime example of a case in which the distribution of good achieved by the human rights restrictive measure is far removed from the protection of the concrete human rights of identified individuals. Instead, it consists of tiny increments to a large number of persons: everyone in the Netherlands. Analysis of *Colon* through the modified 'High Threshold Thesis' thus shows that the Court got it wrong: *Colon* was a 'traditional' human rights case; ***not*** a conflict between human rights.[36]

34 See, apart from the example given in the text, *Colombani and Others v France* [2002] ECHR 521, paras 47, 62 and 68; *Peck v the United Kingdom* [2003] ECHR 44, paras 67 and 79; *Şerife Yiğit* [2010] ECHR 1672, paras 81–82; *Buck v. Germany* [2005] ECHR 267, para 41. For discussion, see Bomhoff, *supra* note 4 at 640 (characterising 'the conflict at the heart of *Colombani*' as 'one between fundamental rights (to expression) and governmental powers (in foreign relation matters), not between the fundamental rights of different individuals').

35 *Colon v the Netherlands* [2012] ECHR 946, para 85.

36 Note that the ECtHR acknowledged this further on in its reasoning in *Colon*, by ruling that '[t]he domestic authorities were entitled to consider that the *public interest* outweighed the subjective disadvantage which the interference with his private life caused to the applicant' (ibid. at para. 95; emphasis added).

Defining genuine human rights conflicts

To preclude the combined threats of aggregation and speculation from eroding the special normative force of human rights, I have argued for the exclusion of 'traditional' human rights cases from the category of conflicts between human rights. In the process, I have indicated a number of elements that are of immediate importance to any definition of human rights conflicts. Such conflicts arise, I have surmised, when (A) the *concrete* human rights of (B) *identified – or identifiable – individuals* are (C) *actually and sufficiently* at stake on both sides. These three elements constitute the pillars (or columns) of my proposed definition of human rights conflicts. They alone, however, do not support a *complete* definition. To finalise the definition, we require an entablature (or frieze) that, as in ancient Roman or Greek temples, brings everything together. The overarching element of the definition – its entablature, if you will – can be found in the correlative of human rights: the duties of the state. Combining all four elements, I propose the following definition of genuine human rights conflicts:

> *A genuine conflict between human rights arises when the state is under incompatible duties to protect/respect the concrete human rights of two or more identified or identifiable individuals and/or entities, provided that these human rights are actually and sufficiently at stake.*[37]

In explicating the definition, I will first unpack its three supporting elements – the pillars – before explaining why incorporation of the duties of the state – the entablature – is needed. Afterwards, I will propose a double test – composed of a 'converse situation' test and a 'conflicting duties' test – to identify genuine human rights conflicts in judicial practice.

37 My proposed definition is broader than the definition of conflicts between fundamental legal rights offered by Lorenzo Zucca. See Lorenzo Zucca, *Constitutional Dilemmas – Conflicts of Fundamental Legal Rights in Europe and the USA* (Oxford University Press, 2007). Zucca, particularly aims to exclude what he terms spurious conflicts, *i.e.* conflicts that can be dispelled by reconciling the claims of both parties or resolved through hierarchical ranking. On his argument, the latter situation covers all cases in which it is possible to determine which claim prevails over the other due to its higher weight: '[i]n the framework of rights conflict, the idea of balance seems more apt to avoid conflicts rather than adjudicate them' (ibid. at 86). Zucca thus only considers conflicts to be genuine if they imply constitutional dilemmas: 'the existence of genuine conflicts of [fundamental legal rights] points to the fact that in certain cases neither a right nor a rational answer are readily available' (ibid. at 25). I consider this definition to be under-inclusive, primarily because it conflates the question of the identification/definition of conflicts with that of their resolution. I favour a broader definition that allows for a clean separation of the questions of identification and resolution, but which is nevertheless sufficiently narrow to exclude 'conflicts' that are merely apparent. For further discussion, see Chapter 7.

Unpacking the three pillars of the definition

The three supporting pillars of the above definition of genuine conflicts between human rights require that, on both sides of the conflict, (A) concrete human rights (rather than abstract considerations), (B) of identified or identifiable individuals (instead of abstract or undetermined persons) are (C) actually and sufficiently at stake (as opposed to merely speculatively).

Incorporation of all three elements in the definition serves to protect the special normative force of human rights. Combined, the three elements – which flow from the modified 'High Threshold Thesis' – avert the threats of aggregation and speculation identified above. They assist in erecting a barrier between 'traditional' human rights cases, subject to the 'priority-to-rights' model of the proportionality test (or an analogous test), and conflicts between human rights, to be tackled through a distinct framework. In fact, the pillars' counterparts are markers of 'traditional' human rights cases: situations in which human rights are restricted in the pursuit of abstract considerations (*e.g.* the public interest in 'prevention of crime') of abstract or undetermined persons (*e.g.* potentially the entire population of a country), which are only speculatively connected to concrete human rights (*i.e.* each individual only receives, in terms of distribution of good, tiny increments that have no concrete impact on their human rights).

A few points are, however, in order. First, the proposed definition is satisfied as soon as the human rights in conflict are actually and *sufficiently* at stake. It does not require that they are *definitively* at stake. This flexibility is intended to cover both situations in which there is no doubt that the human rights were at stake (definitive) and those in which the involvement of the human rights at issue is less than certain, but more than merely speculative (sufficient).[38] Second, the definition not only includes the human rights of *identified* individuals, but also those of *identifiable* individuals. This is meant to capture the idea that the relevant right holders must at least be identifiable, before a genuine conflict between human rights can arise. Third, the definition not only mentions the human rights of *individuals*, but also those of *entities*. This last point is fairly obvious: since human rights can be enjoyed by entities, including newspapers (freedom of expression), trade unions (freedom of assembly), churches (freedom of religion) and companies (right to property), any definition of conflicts between human rights should make room for the possibility of conflicts that not only involve individuals, but also entities. The two other points, however, require more extensive clarification.

First, we need to revisit the question whether a purported conflict between human rights can be genuine, despite the fact that it involves a level of *speculation*

38 The latter point, in particular, was explicitly recognised by the Grand Chamber of the Court, in *Sindicatul "Păstorul cel Bun" v Romania* [2013] ECHR 646, para 159 ('a mere allegation by a religious community that there is an actual or potential threat to its autonomy is not sufficient to render any interference with its members' trade-union rights compatible with the requirements of Article 11 of the Convention. It must also show, in the light of the circumstances of the individual case, that the risk alleged is real and substantial').

as to whether both human rights were actually at stake. Earlier, I rejected speculative arguments insofar as they take the form of human rights rhetoric, in which public interests masquerade as human rights. In other contexts, however, elements of speculation and indeterminacy arise in what seem to be real human rights conflicts.

Osman v the United Kingdom is a case in point. In *Osman*, a teacher who had become obsessed by one of his pupils attacked the pupil and his father. He failed to kill the pupil, but succeeded in murdering the father. In its judgment, the ECtHR indicated that *Osman*-like cases may involve a conflict between human rights:

> bearing in mind the difficulties involved in policing modern societies, the unpredictability of human conduct and the operational choices which must be made in terms of priorities and resources ... not every claimed risk to life can entail for the authorities a Convention requirement to take operational measures to prevent that risk from materialising. Another relevant consideration is the need to ensure that the police exercise their powers to control and prevent crime in a manner which fully respects the ... guarantees contained in Articles 5 and 8 of the Convention.[39]

The Court thus construed *Osman*-like cases as entailing a *potential* conflict between the human rights to personal liberty and private life of the (future) assailant, on the one hand, and the human right to life of his (future) victims, on the other hand. Whether the conflict *actually* arises, however, depends on the extent of the risk to life involved. As the Court indicated, 'not every claimed risk to life' counts.

Indeed, *Osman*-like cases revolve around *future* risks, which are necessarily speculative. A genuine conflict between human rights arguably only materialises when the risk is more than merely speculative. Only when there are sufficient indications that the right to life of identified individuals is actually in danger does the question arise whether measures should be taken that interfere with the (future) assailant's personal liberty and/or private life (*e.g.* detaining him and/or searching his home).[40] Only when the circumstances involve more than mere speculation do both sets of human rights genuinely conflict.

Second, we need to draw a line between *identified*, *identifiable* and *undetermined* individuals, capable of explaining why genuine conflicts between human rights only arise where the human rights of the former two categories are at stake, and not where the putative human rights of the latter are concerned. Part of the explanation has been offered above: situations in which the alleged human rights

39 *Osman v the United Kingdom* [1998] ECHR 101, para 116.

40 In *Osman*, the ECtHR ruled that, *in casu*, the police authorities could not be criticised for having held the reasonable view that the risk to the life of the pupil and his father was insufficiently substantiated to warrant interference with the teacher's Article 5 and 8 rights.

of undetermined individuals are at stake, should principally be classified as 'traditional' human rights cases, rather than genuine human rights conflicts. Indeed, relevant cases will often be *Austin*-like, in the sense that the human rights restrictions they entail are more accurately described in terms of protection of the public or general interest than of concrete human rights.

Analysis of the ECtHR's case law on insult to religious feelings further elucidates the point. In *Otto-Preminger-Institut v Austria* and other relevant cases,[41] the Court has held that when speech insults religious feelings, a human rights conflict arises between freedom of expression and freedom of religion.[42] Certain scholars have, however, criticised the Court's interpretation of insult to religious feelings as a human right, thereby denying that the relevant cases involve a real conflict.[43] Here, I will not enter the normative debate on whether freedom of religion should – or should not – entail a right to be free from insult of one's religious feelings. Instead, I will assume that it does and examine whether the concrete case of *Otto-Preminger-Institut* truly entailed a human rights conflict.

In *Otto-Preminger-Institut*, the Austrian authorities banned the showing of a film about Oskar Panizza's play *Das Liebeskonzil* in select cinemas in Tirol, because the film allegedly insulted the religious feelings of Roman Catholics, which constituted 87 per cent of the population of Tirol at the time. The reason for the restriction immediately raises a red flag, since it signals majoritarian bias. More importantly, however, characterisation of the case as a human rights conflict rested on unsubstantiated speculation that the human rights of undetermined individuals were at stake. Indeed, the film was banned before it had been screened and without the Austrian authorities having received any actual complaints. The ban was thus based on mere speculation on the part of the Austrian authorities about the film's supposed impact on the religious feelings of 'others'.[44] The alleged

41 *Wingrove v the United Kingdom* [1996] ECHR 60; *Murphy v. Ireland* [2003] ECHR 352.

42 *Otto-Preminger-Institut v Austria* [1994] ECHR 26, para 55. For analysis of the case in terms of proportionality, see Matthias Klatt and Moritz Meister, *The Constitutional Structure of Proportionality* (Oxford University Press, 2012), 153–164 (arguing that the case should have been decided in favour of the applicant's freedom of expression).

43 See, for instance, George Letsas, 'Is There a Right Not to be Offended in One's Religious Beliefs?', in Lorenzo Zucca and Camil Ungureanu (eds), *Law, State and Religion in the New Europe: Debates and Dilemmas* (Cambridge University Press, 2012), 239–260; Stavros Tsakyrakis, 'Proportionality: An Assault on Human Rights?', 7 *International Journal of Constitutional Law* (2009), 481; Hottelier, *supra* note 17 at 135; Bomhoff, *supra* note 4 at 648–649. See also the dissenting opinion of Judges Palm, Pekkanen and Makarczyk in *Otto-Preminger-Institut*, *supra* note 42 (arguing that '[t]he Convention does not, in terms, guarantee a right to protection of religious feelings. More particularly, such a right cannot be derived from the right to freedom of religion, which in effect includes a right to express views critical of the religious opinions of others'). For discussion, see Ian Leigh, 'Damned if They Do, Damned if They Don't: The European Court of Human Rights and the Protection of Religion from Attack', 17 *Res Publica* (2011), 55–73.

44 *Cf.* the dissenting opinion of Judge Lohmus in *Wingrove*, *supra* note 41 at para 3 ('[i]n cases of prior restraint (censorship) there is interference by the authorities with freedom of expression even though the members of the society whose feelings they seek to protect have

'victims' moreover remained undetermined, potentially comprising anywhere between zero persons to 87 per cent of the population of Tirol. The combination of mere speculation and absence of identified – or identifiable – right holders mandates, I posit, that cases like *Otto-Preminger-Institut* be excluded from the category of genuine conflicts between human rights.

Constructing the entablature of the definition[45]

Having elucidated the three pillars of the definition of conflicts between human rights, I will now explain why that definition requires an overarching entablature, comprised of the correlative of human rights: the – incompatible – duties of the state.[46]

A useful starting point for the discussion is Wesley Newcomb Hohfeld's seminal article on fundamental legal conceptions.[47] In his article, Hohfeld argues that the generic term 'right' has historically been misused to describe what are, in reality, different entitlements: claims (rights), privileges (liberties), powers and immunities.[48] These four legal conceptions, Hohfeld continues, each have a correlative: duties, no-rights, liabilities and disabilities.[49] For our current concerns with the definition of genuine conflicts between human rights, four of Hohfeld's fundamental legal conceptions are of immediate relevance: claims[50] and liberties,[51] on the one hand, and their correlatives duties and no-rights, on the other.

Hohfeld defines claims (rights) through a concrete example: 'if X has a right against Y that he shall stay off the former's land, the correlative (and equivalent) is that Y is under a duty toward X to stay off the place'.[52] He then defines liberties

not called for such interference. The interference is based on the opinion of the authorities that they understand correctly the feelings they claim to protect. The actual opinion of believers remains unknown').

45 The analysis that follows is based on Stijn Smet, 'On the Existence and Nature of Conflicts between Human Rights at the European Court of Human Rights, *Human Rights Law Review* (forthcoming).

46 Jeremy Waldron, 'Rights in Conflict', 99 *Ethics* (1989), 503–519.

47 Wesley N. Hohfeld, 'Some Fundamental Legal Conceptions as Applied in Judicial Reasoning', 23 *Yale Law Journal* (1913), 16–59. See further, on the use of Hohfeldian analysis, John Finnis, 'Some Professorial Fallacies about Rights', 4 *Adelaide Law Review* (1972), 377–388.

48 Hohfeld, *supra* note 47 at 30.

49 Ibid.

50 To avoid the confusion against which Hohfeld aimed to warn in his seminal article, I will use the term 'claim' throughout, instead of the term 'right'. See ibid. at 32: '[i]f, as seems desirable, we should seek a synonym for the term "right" in this limited and proper meaning, perhaps the word "claim" would prove the best'.

51 Since it is the more established term in contemporary Hohfeldian analysis, I will use 'liberty' throughout, instead of 'privilege', although the latter is the term actually utilised by Hohfeld.

52 Hohfeld, *supra* note 47 at 32.

(privileges) as 'the opposite of a duty and the correlative of a "no-right"'.[53] He goes on to clarify that

> [i]n the example last put, whereas X has a *right* or *claim* that Y, the other man, should stay off the land, he himself has the *privilege* of entering on the land; or, in equivalent words, X does not have a duty to stay off. The privilege of entering is the negation of a duty to stay off.[54]

Hohfeld finally summarises the difference between claims (rights) and liberties (privileges) as follows: 'the correlative of X's right that Y shall not enter on the land is Y's duty not to enter; but the correlative of X's privilege of entering himself is manifestly Y's 'no-right' that X shall not enter'.[55]

Now, it is imperative to note that on a strict Hohfeldian framework – as just described – conflicts can only arise between claims. Conflicts between Hohfeldian claims are possible, because two individuals who hold claims against each other are under a duty to refrain from interfering with the claim of the other.[56] Whenever those duties cannot simultaneously be fulfilled, a conflict between the correlative claims arises. But conflicts between a claim and a liberty, and conflicts between liberties, are not possible on a strict Hohfeldian framework. Indeed, Hohfeld himself argues that a 'claim and privilege ... could not be in conflict with each other'.[57]

The inability of a claim and a liberty to conflict, on a strict Hohfeldian framework, can be illustrated by way of a hypothetical example. Imagine that A wishes to play the saxophone (liberty) on the property of her neighbour B (claim). B may, in exercising his claim over his property, demand that A leave. A must comply, since she is under a duty to not interfere with B's claim. But B cannot use his property claim to prevent A from going back to her own home to play the saxophone there, because – outside the area of protection of his claim – B has no-right that A not exercise her liberty. Thus, A's liberty and B's claim exist in

53 Ibid.

54 Ibid. (emphases in original).

55 Ibid. at 33.

56 See also Waldron, *supra* note 46 at 506; George C. Christie, *Philosopher Kings? The Adjudication of Conflicting Human Rights and Social Values* (Oxford University Press, 2011), 14.

57 Hohfeld, *supra* note 47 at 37. Hohfeld came to this conclusion via a similar route. Applying his framework to what had been described by the courts as 'an apparent conflict or antinomy between ... the right of the plaintiffs to be protected in the legitimate exercise of their trade, and the right of the defendants to carry on their business as seems best to them', Hohfeld first clarified that the characterisation of the latter legal entitlement as a 'right' is erroneous: 'by "the right of the defendants" in relation to the plaintiffs a legal privilege must be intended'. Hohfeld then went on to explain why the right and the privilege cannot be in conflict with each other: '[t]o the extent that the defendants have privileges the plaintiffs have no rights; and conversely, to the extent that the plaintiffs have rights the defendants have no privileges'.

two completely secluded areas of protection, which cannot intersect. As a result, no conflict between A's liberty and B's claim arises, at least not on a strict Hohfeldian framework.[58]

The same applies to situations in which two persons want to exercise a liberty. In such situations, neither person is under a duty to respect the other's liberty.[59] Instead, they each have a no-right that the other person not exercise his liberty. They can thus not prevent each other from using their respective liberties. For instance, both A and B can freely play the saxophone on their own property. Similarly, when meeting in the street both A and B can exercise their freedom of expression simultaneously. They may not be able to hear each other over their own shouting, but neither is under a duty to remain silent and listen.

This brief discussion of conflicts on a strict Hohfdeldian framework might tempt us to conclude that there is little room for genuine conflicts between human rights after all. Yet, and here we come to the crux of the problem, Hohfeld's scheme was designed for relationships between individuals only.[60] It was never intended to be applied to human rights as rights held against the state. Before we can apply Hohfeldian analysis to human rights, we therefore need to make important adjustments. Once those adjustments are made, it will become clear that conflicts between human rights are not limited to claims. They can also arise between a claim and a liberty, and between liberties.

Let us start by considering some concrete examples in the realm of human rights. An example of a conflict between claims could, in a human rights context, be a conflict between the freedom from torture of a suspect who allegedly kidnapped a child and the right to life of the child, whose location – the police assumes – can only be found by torturing the suspect.[61] Applied to such a human rights case, the premise of the strict Hohfeldian framework – individual claim holders are under a duty to refrain from interfering with each other's claims – proves unworkable. In the human rights context, we need to adjust the Hohfeldian framework to incorporate the (duties of the) state. Indeed, under human rights systems, claims of individuals are correlative to duties of the state, not of other individuals. In our example, it is the *state* that is under a duty not to torture the first person, while at the same time being under a duty to *protect* the right to life of the child. Whenever both duties are incompatible – as is the case in our example – it remains fair to speak of a conflict between human rights. Having established as much, let us move on to more complex situations: conflicts between a claim and a liberty and conflicts between liberties.

An example of a conflict between a claim and a liberty could, under a human rights system, be a case in which the right to property of one person (John) over a piece of land clashes with the freedom of expression of another person (Jane)

58 See also Phillip Montague, 'When Rights Conflict', 7 *Legal Theory* (2001), 271–272.

59 Hohfeld, *supra* note 47 at 36–37.

60 Zucca, *supra* note 37 at 32.

61 The example is inspired by *Gäfgen v Germany* [2010] ECHR 759.

who wishes to distribute leaflets on that land.[62] Here, employing a strict Hohfeldian framework creates problems, because only Jane would be under a duty not to interfere with the right to property (claim) of John. John, conversely, would not be under a duty to allow Jane to exercise her freedom of expression (liberty) on his land. On a strict Hohfeldian framework, the solution would thus be simple: Jane cannot exercise her freedom of expression, because she is under a duty to not interfere with John's right to property. Yet, this conclusion is troubling when transposed to the human rights context, because it would imply that a human right formulated as a liberty can under no circumstances 'trump' a human right formulated as a claim. This conclusion is drastically out of line with human rights theory – according to which all human rights are principally worthy of equal respect – and actual human rights practice.[63] What has gone wrong, here, is a double failure to recognise that (A) human rights are held against states and (B) they may take the form of complex rights, *i.e.* rights that are made up of several Hohfeldian entitlements.[64]

Once we take into account that all human rights are held against the state, it becomes clear that, insofar as they are phrased as liberties, they must be what Jeremy Bentham has termed 'vested liberties'.[65] Crucially, Bentham's 'vested liberties' are surrounded by a 'protective perimeter', composed of additional Hohfeldian entitlements.[66] In the case of human rights, H. L. A. Hart has argued, this protective perimeter includes a claim of non-interference.[67] Human rights phrased as liberties, freedom of expression for instance, exhibit precisely this structure. They consist of a liberty to act, for example a liberty to express one's opinion, combined with a claim to non-interference, as well as a claim to protection.[68] These latter claims are held by the individual against the state. They thus impose correlative duties on the state.

Applied to the earlier example of John and Jane, human rights thus impose two concurrent duties on the state: a duty to respect Jane's freedom of expression and a duty to protect John's right to property. The true nature of the conflict between John's right to property and Jane's right to freedom of expression thus comes to

62 The example is inspired by *Appleby and Others v the United Kingdom* [2003] ECHR 222.

63 See, for instance, the many cases in which the ECtHR has held that freedom of expression (liberty) prevailed over the right to reputation (claim). For an example, see *Romanenko and Others v Russia* [2009] ECHR 1476.

64 See also Zucca, *supra* note 37 at 53. On the notion of complex rights, see Carl Wellman, *The Moral Dimensions of Human Rights* (Oxford University Press, 2011), 18–19; Jeremy Waldron, 'Introduction', in Jeremy Waldron (ed.), *Theories of Rights* (Oxford University Press, 1984), 10.

65 Herbert L. A. Hart, *Essays on Bentham – Studies in Jurisprudence and Political Theory* (Clarendon Press, 1982), 172.

66 Ibid. at 171–173.

67 Ibid. at 172.

68 See, *mutatis mutandis*, Mathew H. Kramer, 'Rights Without Trimmings', in Matthew H. Kramer *et al.*, *A Debate over Rights – Philosophical Enquiries* (Oxford University Press, 1998), 111; Wellman, *supra* note 64 at 24.

light when we examine the duties of the state. When Jane enters John's land to distribute leaflets, the state is simultaneously under a duty to protect John's right to property and under a duty to respect Jane's freedom of expression.[69] Since the state cannot simultaneously fulfil both duties, we again face a genuine conflict between human rights.

Finally, a similar argument to the above applies when we adjust the Hohfeldian framework to accommodate conflicts between liberties in the realm of human rights. A conflict between liberties may, in human rights terms, arise when protestors outside a mosque shout anti-Islam slogans, thereby utilising their freedom of expression to disturb the freedom of religion of Muslims attending the prayer inside and outside the mosque.[70] In such a case, the state again finds itself under incompatible duties: a duty to respect the freedom of expression of the protestors, on the one hand, and a duty to protect the religious freedom of the Muslims, on the other. Since both duties are incompatible, we once more face a genuine conflict between human rights.

Conclusion: a double test for the identification of genuine human rights conflicts

In this chapter, I have proposed the following definition of conflicts between human rights:

> A genuine conflict between human rights arises when the state is under incompatible duties to protect/respect the concrete human rights of two or more identified or identifiable individuals and/or entities, provided that these human rights are actually and sufficiently at stake.

I have explained why the definition's base is composed of three pillars: genuine human rights conflicts involve (1) the concrete human rights of (2) identified or identifiable individuals or entities that (3) are actually and sufficiently at stake. These three elements, combined, prevent threats of aggregation and speculation from eroding the special normative force of human rights. The definition is completed by its overarching entablature: genuine human rights conflicts

69 The situation is phrased in terms of the state's 'duty to respect Jane's freedom of expression', because, if the state chooses to protect John's right to property, it will do so by interfering with Jane's freedom of expression (either by preventive means or by imposing a sanction afterwards). This representation of the conflict is compatible with the test Dworkin developed in *Taking Rights Seriously* to determine when one is faced with competing rights: 'The test we must use is this. Someone has a competing right to protection, which must be weighed against an individual right to act, if that person would be entitled to demand that protection from his government on his own title, as an individual...'. See Dworkin, *supra* note 17 at 194.

70 The example is inspired by *Karaahmed v Bulgaria* [2015] ECHR 217.

only arise when the state is under incompatible duties to protect/respect both (or all) human rights at stake. Here, by way of conclusion, I will propose a double test to identify genuine conflicts between human rights – as defined above – in judicial practice.

The double test is composed of a 'converse situation' test,[71] linked to the definition's pillars, and a 'conflicting duties' test, connected to the definition's entablature. Both tests are relatively straightforward and, thus, easy to apply. The 'converse situation' test invites human rights courts, like the ECtHR, to assess the opposite scenario from the one they are actually confronted with. If that 'converse situation' does not meet the three pillar elements of the definition, the alleged conflict between human rights is apparent, rather than real. The 'converse situation' test is thus designed to avoid, *inter alia*, overzealous confidence by human rights courts in 'human rights rhetoric' by governments. Indeed, courts like the ECtHR are used to carefully scrutinising whether the human right invoked by an applicant is actually at stake. But when the government justifies infringement of that right in the name of the human rights of others, those others – and their human rights – are not necessarily visible to courts. In assessing whether they face a genuine human rights conflict, courts should therefore determine who those others are and whether their human rights were actually and sufficiently at stake. That is the aim of the 'converse situation' test. The 'conflicting duties' test, conversely, compels courts, like the ECtHR, to examine whether the state was really under incompatible duties to respect/protect the human rights at stake. The precise implications of both tests will be fully explored in the next chapter (Chapter 3). Here, I will offer two examples to elucidate how they (should) function.

The first example, *Evans v the United Kingdom*, is of a genuine conflict between human rights, *i.e.* a case in which both the 'converse situation' test and the 'conflicting duties' test are met.[72] In *Evans*, the applicant – Ms Evans – was diagnosed with serious pre-cancerous tumours in both ovaries. At the time of her diagnosis, she was still in a relationship with her partner (J.). Because the tumours were growing slowly, it was possible to extract a number of eggs for *in vitro* fertilisation (IVF). Six eggs were extracted, successfully fertilised with J.'s sperm and frozen. During the process, both Ms Evans and J. signed a consent form. They were informed that either party could withdraw his/her consent for

71 See also Ian Leigh and Andrew Hambler, 'Religious Symbols, Conscience, and the Rights of Others', 3 *Oxford Journal of Law and Religion* (2014), 2–24 (defending a similar test, which they label the 'reversibility test').

72 The double test is able to identify a wide range of conflicts in, among others, defamation cases, cases involving the publication of photographs in the press, paternity cases, child custody cases and cases involving the dismissal of employees by a religious organisation for reasons to do with actions taken in their private lives. See, among many other possible examples, *Axel Springer AG v Germany* [2012] ECHR 227; *MGN Limited v the United Kingdom* [2008] ECHR 1255; *Von Hannover v Germany (No. 2)* [2012] ECHR 228; *Mikulić v Croatia* [2002] ECHR 27; *Larissis and Others v Greece* [1998] ECHR 13; *Hokkanen v Finland* [1994] ECHR 32; *Fernández Martínez v Spain* [2014] ECHR 615; *Gäfgen*, *supra* note 61.

the use of the embryos at any stage, as long as they were not implanted in Ms Evans' uterus. Several months later, Ms Evans and J. ended their relationship. J. subsequently withdrew his consent for further use of the embryos. As a result, the clinic was under a legal obligation to destroy them. Ms Evans objected and instituted legal proceedings, seeking an injunction order requiring J. to restore his consent. But the domestic courts refused to grant the order. Ms Evans' case eventually reached the ECtHR, which held that the right to respect for private life 'incorporates the right to respect for both the decisions to become and not to become a parent', but ultimately ruled against Ms Evans.[73]

Evans involves a genuine conflict between human rights, because it meets both the 'converse situation' test and the 'conflicting duties'; and thus all elements of the definition of genuine human rights conflicts. In applying the 'converse situation' test, we are invited to imagine the converse situation from the one that reached the Court. On such a hypothetical scenario, in which Ms Evans is successful in the domestic proceedings, J. would certainly have a case in Strasbourg. He could argue that the court order restoring his consent violates his right to respect for private life. In the converse situation, the *concrete* human rights of the *identified* J. would thus *actually and sufficiently* be at stake. Therefore, no matter the outcome of the domestic proceedings in *Evans*, one of the parties could claim a *prima facie* violation of his/her right to private life in front of the ECtHR. Thus, the 'converse situation' test is met. And the same goes for the 'conflicting duties' test. Indeed, in *Evans* the United Kingdom was under *incompatible* duties to respect J.'s decision not to become a parent and protect Ms Evans' right to respect for the decision to become a (genetic) parent. For the state, complying with one duty automatically meant breaching the other.[74] Thus, identification of the conflicting duties of the state in *Evans* confirms that the case entailed a genuine conflict between human rights.

Evans can be usefully contrasted with another case, *Dahlab v Switzerland*, in which the double test was not met, and in which there was thus no genuine conflict between human rights.[75] *Dahlab* concerned the dismissal of a primary school teacher in a public school in Switzerland for refusing to remove her Islamic headscarf in class. In ruling on *Dahlab*, the Court relied on a proselytism argument that suggests the case involved, at least in part, a conflict between the teacher's freedom to manifest her religion and her pupils' freedom *from* religion:

73 *Evans v the United Kingdom* [2006] ECHR 265, para 71.

74 Frédéric Sudre, 'Les conflits de droits. Cadre général d'approche dans la jurisprudence de la Cour européenne des droits de l'homme', in Laurence Potvin-Solis (ed.), *La conciliation des droits et libertés dans les ordres juridiques européens* (Bruylant, 2012), 235 ('Il nous semble alors possible de définir les «conflits de droits de l'homme» comme la contradiction entre deux droits individuels [telle que] la garantie de l'un des droits ne peut être assurée qu'en portant atteinte à l'autre droit').

75 Compare *Larissis, supra* note 72. For other examples of cases in which the double test is not met – and there is thus no genuine conflict – see *Leyla Şahin v Turkey* [2004] ECHR 299; *Association Rhino and Others v Switzerland* [2011] ECHR 2426.

> [t]he Court accepts that it is very difficult to assess the impact that a powerful external symbol such as the wearing of a headscarf may have on the freedom of conscience and religion of very young children. The applicant's pupils were aged between four and eight, an age at which children wonder about many things and are also more easily influenced than older pupils. In those circumstances, it cannot be denied outright that the wearing of a headscarf might have some kind of proselytising effect.[76]

Yet, the teacher had never been accused of 'indoctrinating' behaviour. Instead, her dismissal was motivated by the supposed proselytising effect of her headscarf on the young children in her class. Constructing the case in terms of proselytism makes it seem as though a conflict between human rights was involved. The Swiss authorities certainly considered themselves to be under a duty to protect the pupils' freedom from religion, a duty that – along with other reasons[77] – outweighed their duty to respect the teacher's freedom of religion. *Dahlab* thus *prima facie* meets the 'conflicting duties' test. Yet, that is mere appearance.

The true nature of *Dahlab* – as a fake conflict, rather than a real one – comes to light when we apply the 'converse situation' test. The purported conflict in *Dahlab* arose because the concrete human rights (freedom from religion) of identifiable individuals (the pupils in the teacher's class) were allegedly at stake. But – and this is crucial – the case for a conflict rested *entirely* on speculation. At this point, the strength of the 'converse situation' test shows itself. It urges human rights courts like the ECtHR to look beyond the *appearance* of a threat to the human rights of others and evaluate whether those rights were actually and sufficiently at stake. In *Dahlab*, there was no concrete evidence that the children's freedom from religion was in peril. There was no sign – or even claim – of indoctrination on the part of the teacher, nor was there proof that being confronted with her Islamic headscarf had any influence on the pupils' freedom to form their own religious beliefs. To fully appreciate the salience of the latter point, we may compare *Dahlab* to *Lautsi v Italy*, an ECtHR case on the display of crucifixes on the wall of public school classrooms. In *Lautsi*, the Court – diverging from its reliance on speculation in *Dahlab* – held that:

> [t]here is no evidence … that the display of a religious symbol on classroom walls may have an influence on pupils and so it cannot reasonably be asserted that it does or does not have an effect on young persons whose convictions are still in the process of being formed.[78]

76 *Dahlab v Switzerland* [2001] ECHR 899, 13.

77 Another prominent reason, not touched upon here, was gender equality. For discussion, see Stijn Smet, 'Freedom of Religion v. Freedom from Religion: Putting Religious Dictates of Conscience (Back) on the Map', in Jeroen Temperman (ed.), *The Lautsi Papers: Multidisciplinary Reflections on Religious Symbols in the Public School Classroom* (Martinus Nijhoff Publishers, 2012), 113–142.

78 *Lautsi and Others v Italy* [2011] ECHR 2412, para 66.

Crucially, the same applies to the Islamic headscarf worn by the teacher in *Dahlab*. In *Dahlab*, the Court arguably acted too swiftly in accepting the government's argument on the need to protect the pupils' freedom from religion. Indeed, the 'converse situation' to *Dahlab* – in which the teacher would have been allowed to wear her headscarf – would not have entailed a *prima facie* violation of the pupils' freedom from religion, since 'there is no evidence ... that the [wearing] of a religious symbol may have an influence on pupils ... whose convictions are still in the process of being formed'. Because the 'converse situation' test was not met, *Dahlab* did not – upon closer inspection – entail a genuine conflict between human rights. Instead, it was a fake conflict.

Importantly, defusing conflicts as fake constitutes the first step of the framework I develop throughout this book to tackle conflicts between human rights. The arguments of the current chapter – especially the double test – will thus prove relevant to the next chapter as well. In that next chapter, I propose that the optimal approach to conflicts between human rights entails defusing them, closely followed by minimising their impact through compromise.

3 Defusing and minimising conflicts between human rights

When a human rights conflict comes before a human rights (or constitutional) court, judges on the bench face a dilemma. They are forced to make difficult choices between superior norms that deserve equal respect. The dilemma is particularly acute at courts that employ a 'priority-to-rights' model of proportionality (or an equivalent test that takes the special normative force of human rights seriously). Such courts, like the ECtHR, are habituated to treating human rights protection as the rule and their restriction as the exception. They thus grant human rights principled, but defeasible priority over non-rights considerations. Under the ECHR, in particular, human rights arguably function as 'shields' that protect individuals from some, but not all non-rights considerations.[1] When human rights conflict, however, there are no priorities to be enjoyed or shields to be wielded. Instead, judges have to make difficult choices between superior norms. They thereby face a dilemma: it seems as if, no matter which choice they make, one human right needs to be sacrificed to protect the other.

When courts fixate on assessing the strength of the human rights in conflict, for instance by balancing them against each other, this is precisely what happens. In balancing human rights against each other, judges determine which right should be granted priority over the other. They thereby inevitably end up sacrificing one human right to safeguard the other. Yet this is arguably the least desirable outcome of a human rights conflict. If judges were to direct their

1 Unless the ECtHR is driven to defer to states by legitimacy concerns, it will generally demand strong reasons before allowing human rights to be overridden by non-rights considerations. The ECtHR tends to defer to states, *inter alia*, when human rights cases are closely connected to socio-economic policy (*e.g.* in social security matters) or when there is no European consensus on how to deal with sensitive issues (*e.g.* euthanasia). In such cases, the Court will often employ its margin of appreciation doctrine to defer to the state. As noted in the Introduction, I will not engage with the margin of appreciation doctrine in this book. For discussion in the context of human rights conflicts, see Stijn Smet, 'When Human Rights Clash in "The Age of Subsidiarity": What Role for the Margin of Appreciation?', in Petr Agha (ed.), *Human Rights between Law and Politics: The Margin of Appreciation in Post-National Contexts* (Hart Publishing, forthcoming 2017).

immediate attention not to the human rights at stake, but rather to the conflict itself, more optimal avenues would become available. First, judges could defuse the conflict itself, while keeping the human rights involved entirely intact. Defusing conflicts is the optimal outcome to a purported human rights conflict: the conflict itself disappears, the rights survive. But even when conflicts cannot be defused, it may well prove possible to minimise the *impact* of the conflict on the human rights involved, by reaching a compromise between them. As long as human rights in conflict make mutual, but *minimal* sacrifices, a compromise solution is superior to balancing, which inevitably sacrifices one human right entirely to safeguard the other.

In order to grant human rights in conflict the equal respect they deserve – *qua* human rights – courts like the ECtHR should thus aim to defuse or minimise conflicts, before balancing the human rights implied within them. Therefore, the framework I develop throughout this book aims to: (1) defuse conflicts and (2) minimise conflicts by reaching a compromise, before (3) balancing the human rights involved. In this chapter, I will elucidate the first and second steps of the framework. In the remainder of the book – Parts II and III – I will turn to balancing.

Defusing conflicts

The optimal approach to purported conflicts between human rights is to remove the conflict itself, while keeping the human rights involved entirely intact.[2] This approach is optimal, because it avoids any sacrifice on the part of the human rights at stake. It thus takes the equal respect due to human rights seriously. When courts, like the ECtHR, are confronted with a purported human rights conflict, they should thus first aim to defuse the conflict itself as fake. As the term indicates, fake conflicts do not meet the definition of genuine human rights conflicts provided in Chapter 2.

One way to establish that purported conflicts are fake is to apply the 'converse situation' and 'conflicting duties' tests of Chapter 2. Whenever these tests are – *as a matter of fact* – not met in the concrete circumstances, the alleged conflict is not genuine, but fake. Here, however, I am not concerned with such factual determinations, which have been sufficiently explored in Chapter 2. I am, rather, concerned with *active strategies* that courts may pursue to defuse conflicts, *beyond* mere factual determinations. Actively defusing conflicts requires substantive and creative reasoning on the part of courts to conclude that either (A) the concrete human rights of identified – or identifiable – individuals are not actually and sufficiently at stake, or (B) the state is not under incompatible duties towards those human rights.

2 Eva Brems, 'Conflicting Human Rights: An Exploration in the Context of the Right to a Fair Trial in the European Convention for the Protection of Human Rights and Fundamental Freedoms', 27 *Human Rights Quarterly* (2005), 302–303.

Two strategies are thus, *prima facie*, available to courts that aim to defuse conflicts. Courts may focus on (A) and *remove* one of the human rights involved from the equation, through a definitional approach along the lines of the specificationist strategy I critiqued in Chapter 1. This defuses the purported conflict, since one of the human rights is held, by definition, to be inapplicable to the situation at hand. But even when courts decline to pursue (A), they may still defuse purported conflicts by focusing on (B) instead. Courts may indeed find that the human rights involved in a purported conflict are actually and sufficiently at stake, while employing creative reasoning to conclude that the state is not under incompatible duties towards those human rights. If alternative solutions can be found, under which the state's duties towards all relevant human rights holders are rendered compatible, the seeming conflict is – once more – defused.

Although both approaches succeed in defusing conflicts, one is clearly superior to the other. The salient difference between both approaches is the drastically divergent impact they have on the human rights involved in a purported conflict. The first approach – in focusing on (A) – deliberately sacrifices one of the human rights (allegedly) at stake. The second approach – by focusing on (B) – is determined to keep the human rights involved entirely intact. The first approach can thus be labelled 'negative', whereas the second can be termed 'positive'. Crucially, only the 'positive' approach provides an optimal solution to purported human rights conflicts: it removes the conflict, while keeping the human rights involved intact. Unlike the 'negative' approach, the 'positive' takes the equal respect due to conflicting human rights seriously. The latter is thus superior to the former. To establish as much, I will first examine – and discard – the 'negative' approach.

The 'negative' approach to defusing conflicts

The 'negative' approach to defusing conflicts entails an argumentative strategy under which judges remove one of the human rights in seeming conflict from the equation. Judges thus escape the purported conflict through a definitional process, echoing the specificationist argument I critiqued in Chapter 1.

The ECtHR, for instance, has pursued this strategy in a number of situations. It has, for example, done so in application of the abuse of rights clause of Article 17 ECHR, which states that '[n]othing in this Convention may be interpreted as implying … any right to engage in any activity or perform any act aimed at the destruction of any of the rights and freedoms set forth therein'.[3] The Court has *inter alia* relied on Article 17 to categorically deny certain forms of speech the protection normally granted by Article 10 ECHR,[4] especially in relation to

3 Sébastien Van Drooghenbroeck, *La proportionnalité dans le droit de la convention européenne des droits de l'homme: prendre l'idée simple au sérieux* (Bruylant, 2001), 111.

4 For an example in which the Court has applied Article 17 ECHR to a case involving a different human right – the freedom of assembly normally protected by Article 11 ECHR – see *Hizb Ut-Tahrir v Germany* [2012] ECHR 1045, para 74.

Holocaust denial,[5] but also in a number of hate speech cases.[6] The latter cases, in particular, involve an apparent conflict between freedom of expression and the prohibition of discrimination. Yet, by applying Article 17, the Court removes freedom of expression from the equation, thereby defusing the conflict.[7]

Another prime example of such 'defusing-through-definition' can be found in *Gillberg v Sweden*, a case we discussed in Chapter 1. In *Gillberg*, the Court escaped a potential conflict between a professor's freedom of expression, on the one hand, and his university's right to property and other researchers' right to access information, on the other hand, by removing the former from the equation. The Court held that the professor did not have a

> negative right within the meaning of Article 10 of the Convention not to make ... research material available [because] finding that [he] had such a right ... would run counter to the property rights of [his university] ... [and] would impinge on [other researchers'] rights under Article 10 ... to receive information in the form of access to the public documents concerned.[8]

In Chapter 1, I argued that *Gillberg* illustrates the Court's inability to come to grips with the intricacies of human rights conflicts. Rather than confronting the conflict inherent in *Gillberg*, the Court escaped it by 'negatively' defusing it. In holding that the professor's freedom of expression did not apply by definition, the Court resorted to the specificationist strategy to deny human rights conflicts. Yet, as I argued in Chapter 1, the specificationist strategy fails to convince, normatively, and is out of line with how human rights function under the ECHR, analytically. Given the failure of the specificationist strategy, human rights conflicts cannot – and should not – be defined away. They should not be defused through 'negative' approaches. But they can be defused in 'positive' terms.

The 'positive' approach to defusing conflicts

'Negative' approaches to defusing human rights conflicts focus on removing one of the human rights from the equation. They thereby fail to take the equal respect due to conflicting human rights seriously. Yet, another avenue is available to defuse conflicts. Instead of focusing their creative attention on the human rights

5 See, among many examples, *Garaudy v France* (24 June 2003).

6 See, for instance, *Norwood v the United Kingdom* [2004] ECHR 730; *Pavel Ivanov v Russia* (18 December 1996).

7 For a critique, see Hannes Cannie and Dirk Voorhoof, 'The Abuse Clause and Freedom of Expression under the European Human Rights Convention: An Added Value for Democracy and Human Rights Protection?', 27 *Netherlands Quarterly for Human Rights* (2011), 54–83. For an example of a case in which the Court did not apply Article 17 to the hate speech in question – thus letting the conflict play out – see *Vejdeland and Others v Sweden* [2012] ECHR 242.

8 *Gillberg v Sweden* [2012] ECHR 569, paras 92–94.

that are seemingly in conflict, judges may direct it to the correlative of those rights: the duties of the state. Only when the state is under incompatible duties towards the human rights at stake – *i.e.* duties it cannot simultaneously fulfil – does a genuine human rights conflict arise. Thus, if alternative solutions can be found under which the state's human rights duties are rendered compatible, the purported conflict disappears. Courts would do well to explore such 'positive' approaches to defusing conflicts. The ECtHR has, in fact, already done so, albeit possibly unreflectively.[9]

Eva Brems, who coined the term 'fake conflict',[10] suggests that interventions by the state can 'resolve' certain apparent human rights conflicts in a manner that keeps both rights entirely intact.[11] By way of example, Brems discusses cases in which procedural limits are imposed on the accused during a criminal trial, but not on the prosecutor, in order to guarantee the delivery of a judgment within a reasonable time.[12] Here, an apparent conflict arises between the right to equality of arms and the right to a trial within a reasonable time, both aspects of the human right to a fair trial (Article 6 ECHR). As Brems points out,[13] however, the ECtHR held in *Wynen v Belgium* that states are under a duty to realise the reasonable time objective *without* impinging on the equality of arms.[14] Hence, the Court's case law imposes a duty on states to organise their judicial system in such a manner as to safeguard *both* human rights at stake. As a result, purported conflicts between the right to equality of arms and the right to a trial within a reasonable time are defused. This is made possible due to the triadic relationship, in the human rights context, between two human right holders and the state. Indeed, when human rights conflict, the duties correlative to those rights are held by the state. Faced with purported conflicts between human rights, courts like the ECtHR may thus resort to creative substantive reasoning to impose *compatible* duties on states.

9 For an example, apart from the ones discussed in the text, see *Fransesco Sessa v Italy* (3 April 2012). *Sessa* concerned the authorities' refusal – for reasons to do with their duty to deal with cases within a reasonable time – of a lawyer's request to reschedule a court hearing so that he would be able to adhere to Jewish religious holidays. As indicated by the dissenting judges, the applicant's freedom of religion could have easily been reconciled with the right of others to a hearing within a reasonable time. Thus, both human rights could have been kept entirely intact, thereby defusing any potential conflict between them. For an example outside the ECtHR's case law, see André Van der Walt, 'The State's Duty to Protect Property Owners v The State's Duty to Provide Housing: Thoughts on the *Modderklip* Case', 21 *South African Journal on Human Rights* (2005), 155 (explaining how the Supreme Court of Appeal of South Africa, in its judgment in the *Modderklip* case, focused on the state's duty to protect rights in order to defuse an apparent conflict between the right to property and the right to housing).

10 Eva Brems, 'Introduction', in Eva Brems (ed.), *Conflicts between Fundamental Rights* (Intersentia, 2008), 4.

11 Brems, *supra* note 2 at 301–302 and 305–306.

12 Ibid. at 305–306.

13 Ibid. at 305.

14 *Wynen and Centre hospitalier interrégional Edith-Cavell v Belgium* [2002] ECHR 715, para 32.

In doing so, courts may defuse conflicts that *appear* real when considered between the respective human right holders alone.

Conscientious objection to abortion may serve to illustrate the point. In abortion cases, an apparent conflict may arise between the right to decisional privacy of a woman who wishes to have an abortion and the religious freedom of a doctor who conscientiously objects to performing the abortion. When considered strictly between the human rights holders (the woman and the doctor), the conflict appears intractable. The doctor cannot perform the abortion without violating his own deeply held convictions. Yet, if he refuses to perform it the woman suffers a grave breach of her right to private life. This, however, only describes the conflict as it exists between the right holders. In the human rights context, we must also consider the role of the state. When called upon to intervene, the state has different avenues available. It may respond by forcing the doctor to perform the abortion (thereby interfering with his rights) or by denying the woman access to abortion (thereby failing to protect her rights). But the state may also adopt a third approach. It may, in particular, organise its health system in such a way as to *simultaneously* guarantee doctors a right to conscientious objection and ensure that women have effective access to abortion. This entails, *inter alia*, providing a steady roster of doctors who *are* willing to perform abortions and ensuring that women do not have to travel excessive distances to obtain an abortion. When the right conditions are put in place by the state, the purported conflict between human rights can thus be defused. This is precisely how the ECtHR tackled the conflict in *R.R. v Poland* and *P. and S. v Poland*:

> States are obliged to organise their health service system in such a way as to ensure that the effective exercise of freedom of conscience by health professionals in a professional context does not prevent patients from obtaining access to services to which they are entitled under the applicable legislation.[15]

According to the Court, states should thus find ways to accommodate both sets of rights. By rendering states' duties towards both human rights holders – doctors and women – compatible, the Court defused what appeared to be an intractable conflict.[16]

Yet, there are limits to this 'positive' approach to defusing conflicts. We may encounter those limits when we move from the abortion case to a *prima facie*

15 *P. and S. v. Poland* [2012] ECHR 185, para 106; *R.R. v. Poland* [2011] ECHR 828, para 206.

16 This, of course, is subject to the guarantee that the woman's right to decisional privacy is not rendered illusory or does not face serious obstacles. If her right is *not* kept entirely intact, the conflict cannot be defused. See, for instance, *P. and S.*, *supra* note 15, in which the procedural guarantees put in place under national law were not complied with, forcing the applicant to travel 500 km to obtain an abortion, although she had received, as required under national law, the necessary permission to have an abortion (ibid., paras 105 and 107).

analogous issue: conscientious objection by civil servants to same-sex marriages. When civil servants refuse to register same-sex marriages for religious reasons, an apparent conflict arises between their religious freedom and the right to non-discrimination of same-sex couples. At first glance, a similar solution to that in the abortion case is available to defuse the conflict: the state could organise its registration system to accommodate both sets of rights. It could, for instance, ensure a steady roster of non-objecting civil servants to register same-sex marriages.

Yet, in ruling on the issue in *Ladele v the United Kingdom*, the ECtHR rejected this accommodation solution. Instead, it accepted the UK courts' rulings, which had granted categorical priority to non-discrimination. Elsewhere, I argue that, although *Ladele* may *appear* to involve a human rights conflict that can be defused, the UK courts' rulings to the contrary can be explained in terms of expressive harm.[17] Even if the state were to reorganise its registration system, it could arguably not avoid same-sex couples suffering expressive harm, *i.e.* the harm caused to a person 'when she is treated [by the state] according to principles that express negative or inappropriate attitudes toward her'.[18] Therefore, the state's duties in the same-sex marriage case cannot be rendered entirely compatible: accommodating the civil servant would still damage same-sex couples' human rights. Thus, no solution is available to keep both human rights entirely intact. The conflict between them cannot be defused. When conflicts cannot be defused, they can nevertheless – under certain circumstances – be minimised by reaching a compromise. It is to such human rights compromises that I will now turn.

Minimising conflicts through compromise

In discussing the defusing of conflicts, I focused on the conflict itself, aiming to remove it while keeping the human rights within entirely intact. Once we move to balancing, we will turn our gaze to the human rights in conflict, aiming to determine which should prevail over the other (and, concomitantly, which should be sacrificed to safeguard the other). Minimising conflicts through compromise targets the 'middle ground': compromises aim to reduce, as far as possible, the impact the conflict has on the human rights involved.

Since we are now dealing with genuine conflicts – *i.e.* conflicts that cannot be defused – there will always be *some* impact. When a conflict is genuine, the human rights involved cannot escape the conflict intact. Attempt can, however, be made to minimise the impact of the conflict by having the human rights involved make *mutual*, but *minimal* sacrifices. In other words, we can aim for a compromise between human rights in conflict. Since compromises take the equal respect due to conflicting human rights seriously, they provide a more optimal solution

17 Stijn Smet, 'Conscientious Objection to Same-sex Marriages: Beyond the Limits of Toleration', 11 *Religion & Human Rights* (2016), 114–139.

18 Elizabeth Anderson and Richard Pildes, 'Expressive Theories of Law: A General Restatement', 148 *University of Pennsylvania Law Review* (2000), 1527.

to human rights conflicts than balancing, which inevitably entails sacrificing one human right entirely to the benefit of the other.[19] Hence, courts like the ECtHR should first attempt to reach a compromise between conflicting human rights, before balancing them against each other.

Yet, for compromises to provide an optimal solution to genuine human rights conflicts, the human rights involved must make *mutual*, but *minimal* sacrifices. Indeed, the very notion of compromise implies that those involved – in our case not persons, but human rights – give way to each other. They abandon the quest for the optimal solution for themselves, in order to reach a solution that is optimal for all involved. In terms of human rights conflicts, we thus refuse to pick a 'winner' – and 'loser' – through balancing, but aim for a solution that keeps *both* human rights as intact as possible. For such a compromise solution to work, the sacrifices it entails must be minimal. If the impact on one of the human rights in conflict would be so extensive as to effectively hollow out its protection, there can be no question of compromise.

Let me explain the latter point through a concrete example. In certain defamation cases, a compromise could be reached between a newspaper's freedom of expression and an individual's right to reputation. Judges could, for instance, rule that a newspaper should add a disclaimer to an article in its online archive, referring to pending defamation proceedings in front of the courts, brought by the subject of the article.[20] This solution could, under certain circumstances, achieve a viable compromise between the human rights in conflict. By adding the disclaimer to the article in its online archive, the newspaper accepts a small sacrifice on the part of its freedom of expression. The subject of the article, conversely, sacrifices a small part of his right to reputation by allowing the article's continued existence in the newspaper's archive, but with a disclaimer that clearly indicates its allegedly defamatory nature. Freedom of expression and the right to reputation thus make mutual, but *minimal* sacrifices, thereby achieving a compromise solution to the conflict between them.

But this does not mean that newspapers can simply add a disclaimer whenever they publish an article they know to be defamatory, nor that the subject of

19 Brems, *supra* note 10 at 5; Brems, *supra* note 2 at 303; Olivier De Schutter and Françoise Tulkens, 'Rights in Conflict: The European Court of Human Rights as a Pragmatic Institution', in Eva Brems (ed.), *Conflicts between Fundamental Rights* (Intersentia, 2008), 203; David Kosař, 'Conflicts between Fundamental Rights in the Jurisprudence of the Constitutional Court of the Czech Republic', in Eva Brems (ed.), *Conflicts between Fundamental Rights* (Intersentia, 2008), 372; Van Drooghenbroeck, *supra* note 3 at 383 (all writing in terms of *praktische Konkordanz* or 'practical concordance'). Since there is disagreement on the precise content of this German doctrine, however, I speak of 'compromise' instead. For discussion, see Thilo Marauhn and Nadine Ruppel, 'Balancing Conflicting Human Rights: Konrad Hesse's Notion of "*praktische Konkordanz*" and the German Federal Constitutional Court', in Eva Brems (ed.), *Conflicts between Fundamental Rights* (Intersentia, 2008) 273–296.

20 *Węgrzynowski and Smolczewski v Poland* [2013] ECHR 690, para 66; ECtHR, *Times Newspapers Ltd v the United Kingdom (Nos. 1 and 2)* [2009] ECHR 451, para 46.

newspaper articles can always demand the publication of such a disclaimer. Indeed, under changing circumstances the sacrifices made by (one of) the human rights may no longer be minimal. If the article is written in good faith on an issue of great public interest, for instance. Or, conversely, if it is deliberately written to insult the individual in the absence of any public interest. In those circumstances, the publication of a disclaimer cannot achieve a compromise between the human rights in conflict, since one of the rights involved is forced to make great – and therefore unacceptable – sacrifices. Hence, balancing becomes inevitable. When no viable compromise can be reached, courts need to determine which of the conflicting human rights should prevail over the other.

But before I turn to balancing, I will examine some concrete examples of compromise in the case law of the ECtHR.[21] These examples serve both to illustrate how compromises function in the ECHR context and to demonstrate how reaching a compromise requires creativity on the part of judges. The examples that follow further reveal the central role of the state in achieving compromises between human rights. As is the case in defusing conflicts, creative approaches to the state's human rights duties may render it possible to achieve a compromise, rather than sacrificing one human right to safeguard the other.[22]

A first set of ECtHR cases that is ideally suited to be resolved through compromise involves counter-demonstrations.[23] Several scholars have pointed towards one particular case on counter-demonstrations, *Öllinger v Austria*, as a prime example of compromise in the case law of the Court.[24] *Öllinger* concerned a counter-demonstration against the gathering of Comradeship IV, an association

21 For further examples, apart from those discussed in the text, see *Dupuis and Others v France* [2007] ECHR 5563 (in which the Court indicated a compromise between freedom of expression and the presumption of innocence in the context of media reports about ongoing criminal trials); *Sporer v Austria* [2011] ECHR 180 (in which the Court found a violation due to the inability under Austrian law to grant a father joint custody over a child born out of wedlock, which categorically precludes any sort of compromise solution from being reached).

22 De Schutter and Tulkens, *supra* note 19 at 206.

23 See, apart from the case discussed in the text, *Plattform "Ärzte für das Leben" v Austria* [1988] ECHR 15; *Fáber v Hungary* [2012] ECHR 2026. Unlike *Öllinger v Austria*, discussed in the text, *Fáber* concerned a direct conflict between the right to peaceful protest of two opposing groups. In *Fáber*, the Court ruled that 'the State has to fulfil its positive obligations to protect the right of assembly of both demonstrating groups, and should find the least restrictive means that would, in principle, enable both demonstrations to take place [including by taking] preventive measures, such as police presence keeping the two assemblies apart and offering a sufficient degree of protection' (paras 43–44). The Hungarian authorities in *Fáber* had taken measures to ensure optimal protection of the human rights of both demonstrating groups. By ensuring police presence and imposing certain limiting factors on both demonstrating groups, including forcing them to keep at a certain distance from each other, the Austrian authorities had imposed mutual, but minimal sacrifices on the right to peaceful protest of both demonstrating groups. As a result, a compromise was reached that allowed both groups to exercise their human rights to the fullest extent possible, under the circumstances.

24 See, for instance, De Schutter and Tulkens, *supra* note 19 at 204–205.

consisting mainly of former members of the SS. Comradeship IV had been granted permission to hold a commemoration service at a cemetery to remember SS members who had died during World War II. A number of individuals wished to organise a counter-demonstration to remind the public of the crimes committed by the SS and to commemorate the Jews murdered by them. The concurrence in time and venue with the commemoration ceremony of Comradeship IV was an essential part of the intended counter-demonstration. Yet, the Austrian authorities refused to authorise the counter-demonstration. Their refusal not only aimed at protecting the rights of Comradeship IV to a peaceful assembly, but also the 'normal' cemetery-goers' right to freedom of religion. The Austrian authorities feared that any counter-demonstration would lead to disturbances on the cemetery grounds.

At the national level, the Austrian Constitutional Court had already ruled that protection of the gathering of Comradeship IV could not justify the prohibition of the counter-demonstration. The ECtHR therefore focused its attention on examining whether the need to protect the cemetery-goers' freedom of religion could offer sufficient justification for the ban. In its judgment, the Court held that it did not. The Court first pointed out that the counter-demonstration would have had a tiny number of participants (six) who moreover envisaged a peaceful and silent protest (they intended to carry commemorative messages and had explicitly ruled out the use of chanting or banners).[25] The Court subsequently ruled that

> [i]n these circumstances, the Court is not convinced by the Government's argument that allowing both meetings while taking preventive measures, such as ensuring police presence in order to keep the two assemblies apart, was not a viable alternative which would have preserved the applicant's right to freedom of assembly while at the same time offering a sufficient degree of protection as regards the rights of the cemetery's visitors.[26]

The Court concluded that the Austrian authorities had given

> too little weight to the applicant's interest in holding the intended assembly and expressing his protest against the meeting of Comradeship IV, while giving too much weight to the interest of cemetery-goers in being protected against *some rather limited disturbances.*[27]

In *Öllinger*, the Court thus ruled that the domestic authorities should have allowed the counter-demonstration to take place. The Court also indicated that the Austrian authorities could have taken measures to ensure that the effects of

25 *Öllinger v Austria* [2006] ECHR 665, para 47.
26 Ibid. at para 48.
27 Ibid. at para 49 (emphasis added).

the counter-demonstration on the cemetery-goers' freedom of religion would have been minimal. The Court thereby expressed, without using the term, its preference for a compromise solution to the conflict in *Öllinger*. This compromise solution would have entailed mutual, but minimal sacrifices on the part of the counter-demonstrators' freedom of assembly and the cemetery-goers' freedom of religion. The counter-demonstrators had already indicated their willingness to make minimal concessions in exercising their freedom of assembly by not chanting or holding banners. The Austrian authorities, conversely, could have taken further protective measures – such as ensuring police presence – to guarantee that the cemetery-goers would only suffer 'some rather limited disturbances' in their religious freedom.

A second set of human rights conflicts that is particularly apt at being resolved through compromise involves the protection of witnesses at criminal trials. When states take measures to protect the rights to life and physical integrity of witnesses, for instance by excusing them from testifying in open court, this has an impact on the right to a fair trial of criminal defendants. In this context, several scholars have cited *Van Mechelen v the Netherlands* as a prime example of compromise.[28] In its relevant case law, the ECtHR has indeed ruled that 'States should organise their criminal proceedings in such a way that [the] interests [of witnesses] are not unjustifiably imperilled'.[29] Thus, the Court has held,

> [w]hen a witness's fear is attributable to the defendant or those acting on his behalf, it is appropriate to allow the evidence of that witness to be introduced at trial without the need for the witness to give live evidence or be examined by the defendant or his representatives – even if such evidence was the sole or decisive evidence against the defendant.[30]

But the Court has also looked at the other side of the conflict. It has held that the right to a fair trial of a criminal defendant should be respected to the fullest extent possible. The Court has clarified that 'given the extent to which the absence of a witness adversely affects the rights of the defence … allowing the admission of a witness statement in lieu of live evidence at trial' will only be allowed if 'all available alternatives, such as witness anonymity and other special measures, would be inappropriate or impracticable'.[31] The Court has moreover held that

> where a hearsay statement is the sole or decisive evidence against a defendant … sufficient counterbalancing factors, including the existence of strong

28 *Van Mechelen and Others v the Netherlands* [1997] ECHR 22. See, for instance, Van Drooghenbroeck, *supra* note 3 at 385.

29 *Doorson v the Netherlands* [1996] ECHR 14, para 70.

30 *Al-Khawaja and Tahery v the United Kingdom* [2011] ECHR 2127, para 123.

31 Ibid. at para 125.

> procedural safeguards ... that permit a fair and proper assessment of the reliability of that evidence to take place need to be put in place.[32] [33]

These counterbalancing factors are not set in stone in the Court's case law, but fluctuate on a case by case basis. Counterbalancing factors that have been deemed relevant are: (1) the ability of the judge, jury, prosecutor and counsel for the defence to see and hear the witness give evidence;[34] (2) the ability of counsel for the defence to put questions to the witness;[35] (3) careful and cautious evaluation by the judge or jury of the witness evidence;[36] (4) disclosure of material, based on the witness statements, which allows for cross-examination by defendant's counsel;[37] and (5) the ability of the defence to challenge the reliability of the evidence given by the witness.[38]

Crucially, the Court imposes the duty to provide these counterbalancing factors on the state to minimise the damage to the defendant's right to a fair trial caused by the measures taken to protect the witness's right to life and physical integrity. But also the witness suffers minimal damage to her human rights. She has to testify in some form or other and consequently exposes herself to some extent. Even if measures are put in place to protect her identity, in offering testimony she puts her human rights more – even if marginally – at risk than by outright declining to testify. As in the counter-demonstration cases, the human rights involved in the witness case thus make *mutual* sacrifices, while the state takes measures to *minimise*, to the fullest extent possible, the impact of the conflict on both human rights. Hence, a compromise is reached between defendants' right to a fair trial and witnesses' right to life and physical integrity.

A third set of compromises I will discuss here, by way of a final example, relates to the liability of intermediaries for speech in the online context. Think, for instance, of a music company, such as Sony Music Entertainment, which claims damages from an internet service provider (ISP) to compensate it for illegal downloads of Shakira's latest album by the ISP's users. Or think of a politician who institutes defamation proceedings against an online news platform, claiming that it is liable for insulting remarks made by its users in the comments section

32 Ibid. at para 147. See also *Doorson*, *supra* note 29 at para 72.

33 Note that the Court has developed similar principles in cases involving allegations of sexual abuse of minors. Also in those cases, the Court has held that 'certain measures may be taken for the purpose of protecting the [right to private life of the] victim, provided that such measures can be reconciled with an adequate and effective exercise of the rights of the defence'. See *A.S. v Finland* [2010] ECHR 1362, para 47; *S.N. v Sweden* [2002] ECHR 551, para 55.

34 *Ellis and Simms and Martin v the United Kingdom* [2012] ECHR 813, para 82; *Pesukic v Switzerland* [2012] ECHR 2031, para 50; *Doorson*, *supra* note 29 at para 73.

35 *Doorson*, *supra* note 29 at para 73; *S.N.*, *supra* note 33 at para 50; *A.S.*, *supra* note 33 at para 56.

36 *Ellis and Simms and Martin*, *supra* note 34 at paras 83–84.

37 Ibid. at para 86.

38 Ibid. at para 87; *S.N.*, *supra* note 33 at para 52; *Pesukic*, *supra* note 34 at para 50.

hosted by the news platform. In these and similar cases, three sets of human rights collide: (1) the freedom of expression and right to privacy of internet users; (2) the human rights to intellectual property, reputation, etc. of the alleged victims of internet users' speech; and (3) the freedom of expression of the intermediary.

Such intermediary liability cases have been prominent in the case law of the Court of Justice of the European Union for well over a decade.[39] In recent years, however, they have started reaching Strasbourg as well. In *Delfi v Estonia* and *Magyar Tartalomszolgáltatók Egyesülete v Hungary*, the ECtHR has indicated that the conflict implied within these cases could be resolved through the imposition, by the state, of a notice-and-takedown system: '[i]f accompanied by effective procedures allowing for rapid response, this system can in the Court's view function in many cases as an appropriate tool for balancing the rights and interests of all those involved'.[40]

Importantly, notice-and-takedown systems rely on burden-sharing between the alleged victim, who claims to have suffered damage caused by – usually anonymous – internet users, and the intermediary through whose services the speech was published online.[41] Under a notice-and-takedown system, the alleged victim is responsible for locating damaging speech and sending the intermediary a notice informing it of the existence of said speech. Only when an intermediary receives a notice is it obliged to take the speech down (or refuse and risk litigation). Variations are, moreover, possible. Under a notice-and-notice system, for instance, the intermediary is not obliged to take the speech down, but merely to forward the notice to the service user.[42] Crucially, however, both notice-and-takedown and notice-and-notice systems refuse to grant one human right – that of the alleged victim or of the intermediary – priority over the other. Instead, the logics behind the system imply a compromise between both human rights: both make concessions in order to survive the conflict as intact as possible.[43]

The three sets of compromises I have just discussed elucidate that conflicts can only be successfully resolved through compromise when two conditions are met: (1) the human rights in conflict must make mutual sacrifices; and (2) those sacrifices must be minimal. When both conditions are not met, which may be the object of reasonable debate, it is not possible – or desirable – to insist on a compromise solution. There are, in other words, clear limits to the potential of

39 See, for instance, *Promusicae* [2007] EUECJ C-275/06; *Netlog* [2012] EUECJ C-360/10; *Scarlet Extended* [2011] EUECJ C-70/10; *UPC Telekabel Wien* [2014] EUECJ C-314/12.

40 *Delfi AS v Estonia* [2015] ECHR 586, para 159; *Magyar Tartalomszolgáltatók Egyesülete and Index.hu Zrt v Hungary* [2016] ECHR 135, para 91.

41 See, for instance, *Digital Millennium Copyright Act* 112 Stat. 2860 (1998) (US).

42 See, for instance, *Copyright Modernization Act* S.C. 2012, c. 20, Section 41.25(1) (Canada).

43 For discussion, see Christina Angelopoulos and Stijn Smet, 'Notice-And-Fair-Balance: How to Reach a Compromise between Fundamental Rights in European Intermediary Liability' (unpublished manuscript, on file with the author).

compromises to provide optimal solutions to human rights conflicts. A few examples may serve to explore these limits.

The limits of compromise solutions relate, first, to the very *possibility* of achieving a compromise. In many situations, it will simply not be possible to reach any sort of compromise between human rights in conflict, because resolution of the conflict *necessarily* entails one human right prevailing entirely over the other.[44] A plethora of examples could be offered here.[45] I will restrict myself, however, to providing a few. Take the conflict between a church's freedom of religion and the right to private life of a church employee who has failed to adhere to religious principles and whom the church consequently wishes to dismiss.[46] Here, it is impossible to strike an effective compromise between the human rights of the church and those of its employee. Either the state allows the church to dismiss the employee, thereby safeguarding the former's religious freedom at the expense of the latter's right to privacy. Or it refuses to allow the dismissal, thereby safeguarding the right to privacy at the expense of religious freedom. No matter how the state acts, it seems, one of the human rights involved will be sacrificed to safeguard the other. No compromise appears available.

The same goes for cases involving establishment of paternity, in which a child requests a DNA test to prove her alleged biological father's paternity.[47] In such cases, the state either orders the DNA test, thereby sacrificing the human rights of the alleged father to safeguard those of the child. Or it does not, thereby sacrificing the human rights of the child to safeguard those of the alleged father. Again, no compromise solution appears available. This is, by way of a final example, also true for a case we discussed at the end of Chapter 2: *Evans v the United Kingdom.*[48] In *Evans*, the state had to choose between ordering a person (J.) to restore his consent to the use of frozen embryos, thereby sacrificing J.'s human rights to safeguard those of his former partner, or decline to grant the order, thereby safeguarding J.'s human rights, but inevitably sacrificing those of his former partner. No compromise solution was available. Instead, difficult choices between the conflicting human rights had to be made.

But even when it is *possible* to achieve a compromise between conflicting human rights, it is not necessarily *desirable* to insist on a compromise, regardless of its costs. Take cases involving a conflict between freedom of expression and the right to private life or the right to reputation, for instance. In such cases, the state

44 Brems, *supra* note 2 at 303.

45 See all cases cited and discussed in Parts II and III of this book.

46 See, for instance, *Fernández Martínez v Spain* [2014] ECHR 615. Note that it may be possible to avoid the conflict by relying on something akin to a 'don't ask, don't tell' policy. Once a church is aware that one of its employees has taken actions in the course of her private life that are out of line with religious rules and principles, however, it appears impossible to reach a compromise.

47 See, for instance, *Mikulić v Croatia* [2002] ECHR 27; ECtHR, *Röman v Finland* [2013] ECHR 90.

48 *Evans v the United Kingdom* [2006] ECHR 265.

could insist that both human rights make mutual sacrifices (*e.g.* by limiting the circulation of a critical publication, through partial censorship of photographs or by having journalists express criticism in modest terms). Yet, I submit, these measures fail to achieve a *viable* compromise, because the sacrifices involved are not minimal. Instead, the damage caused to the human rights in conflict reduces their usefulness beyond what can be expected under a compromise solution. Partial censorship of a photograph, for instance, may leave both the right to private life of the photographed person and the freedom of expression of the magazine or newspaper that publishes it less than satisfactorily protected. Limiting the circulation of a critical publication may similarly leave both the person who is the subject of the publication and the author thereof less than satisfied: the first still suffers the full extent of the damage to his right to reputation *vis-à-vis* the limited number of people who have read the publication, while the latter is prohibited from exercising her freedom of expression towards the entire public.

Whenever it is not possible or desirable to achieve a viable compromise between conflicting human rights, balancing them to determine which should prevail under the circumstances becomes inevitable. Such balancing is the subject of the remainder of this book.

Conclusion

When a purported human rights conflict requires adjudication, judges face a dilemma. They are seemingly forced to make difficult choices between superior norms that deserve equal respect.

Faced with a human rights conflict, judges may – and should – first attempt to remove the conflict itself, before turning their attention to the human rights involved. Defusing human rights conflicts entails, first, factual determinations and, second, legal creativity. When the facts of a concrete case disclose that the 'converse situation test' and the 'conflicting duties test' of Chapter 2 are not met, the conflict is fake, not genuine. Yet, defusing conflicts is not always restricted to a question of fact. It may also be a question of law. Judges should indeed turn to legal creativity in finding ways out of the dilemma caused by apparent human rights conflicts. The implication of the state's human rights duties allows judges to locate alternative ways of approaching a seeming conflict, rendering the state's duties towards the human rights at stake compatible. Hence, the conflict itself disappears, since the state can now fulfil its duties towards both rights.

When conflicts cannot be defused, judges nevertheless do well to *minimise* the impact of genuine human rights conflicts by reaching a compromise between the human rights implicated within. Here, judges should focus their attention on the 'middle ground' between the conflict and the human rights at stake. They should, in particular, locate solutions under which conflicting human rights make *mutual*, but *minimal* sacrifices to have them escape the conflict as intact as possible. Once again, reaching such compromises requires an exercise in legal creativity on the part of judges, whereby they impose duties on the state that aim to keep conflicting human rights as intact as possible, given the factual circumstances.

Often, however, human rights conflicts will be inescapable. Judges will not be able to defuse them, nor will they be able to achieve a viable compromise solution. Instead, they will have to make – often difficult – choices between the human rights at stake. No matter how they choose, judges will end up sacrificing one right to salvage the other. In human rights practice, judges usually make these difficult choices by applying a balancing test. Such balancing is the object of Parts II and III of this book. In Part II, I will tackle the theoretical challenges to balancing (Chapter 4) and identify a number of practical obstacles to balancing (Chapter 5). Afterwards, in Part III, I will propose my own version of a structured balancing test (Chapter 6), which aims to overcome the theoretical challenges and practical obstacles identified in Part II, while outperforming alternative balancing tests (Chapter 7). I will conclude the book by exploring the limits of my structured balancing test in the face of genuine human rights dilemmas (Chapter 8).

Part II

Difficulties in balancing human rights

4 Theoretical challenges to balancing human rights

When a conflict between human rights cannot be defused and no viable compromise between the human rights in conflict can be achieved, a difficult choice between those rights needs to be made. In adjudicating the conflict, judges will have to determine which right should prevail over the other (and, concomitantly, which right should be sacrificed to protect the other). The core argument of Parts II and III of this book is that such difficult choices between human rights in conflict must be made by balancing them against each other. Yet, a number of important theoretical challenges seem to preclude such balancing. In this chapter, I aim to overcome those theoretical challenges, chief among which is the incommensurability challenge to balancing. In the process, I propose to abandon the scales metaphor of balancing, which implies a mechanical 'balancing of interests', and begin to develop a structured 'balancing as reasoning' test instead.

Critiques of balancing

Balancing is unquestionably among the favourite tools in the toolbox of constitutional and human rights courts alike. Yet, despite its ubiquity in human and constitutional rights adjudication, balancing is not without its fair share of critics. On the contrary, a plethora of objections have been raised against balancing as a judicial tool. If successful, these objections would be devastating for the final phase of my project, which aims to 'make balancing work' in the context of human rights conflicts (Part III). Before I am in any position to propose an alternative balancing test, I must therefore evaluate the multiple critiques of balancing.

Many of the core objections against balancing are tied to the imperfections of the balancing metaphor. When taken literally, something one should of course resist doing with metaphors, the balancing metaphor conjures up the image of a pair of scales on which two diametrically opposed items (rights, values, private interests, etc.) are – quite literally – weighed. Each item is placed on one side of the scales and the balancing authority – the ECtHR, for instance – either notes the side to which the scales tip or observes that they stay in equilibrium. Thus presented, the operation of the balancing scales has something profoundly – and confoundingly – mechanical to it: the judge's role appears limited to placing items on the scales and merely observing what happens. As American Circuit Judge Frank Coffin noted decades ago, 'perhaps the biggest problem with the balancing metaphor is that it suggests a mechanistic, quantitative, and utilitarian comparison of the weight or value of two claims according to one scale which is equally appropriate to both'.[1]

This *literal* image of balancing arguably lies at the heart of most of the criticism against balancing in adjudication. Justice Antonin Scalia has famously based his objection to the judicial use of balancing on the idea that 'the scale analogy [of balancing] is not really appropriate, since the interests on both sides are incommensurate. It is more like judging whether a particular line is longer than a particular rock is heavy'.[2] Jürgen Habermas has equally famously criticised balancing: '[b]ecause there are no rational standards [for bringing values into a transitive order with other values], weighing takes place either arbitrarily or unreflectively'.[3] Stavros Tsakyrakis, writing in the ECHR context, has insisted that balancing 'leads to a complete erosion of human rights. It overlooks the idea that human rights are not merely quantities of freedom but protect some basic status of people as human agents'.[4] Alexander Green, also commenting on the ECHR system, has criticised balancing's reliance on 'the obtuse metaphor of "weight"', arguing that 'the balancing test tacitly assumes that there is some common metric by which values … can be measured [while this] idea of "measuring" is … of course nonsense'.[5] Thomas Alexander Aleinikoff, finally, has lamented the obscure nature of balancing methodologies: '[s]ome rough, intuitive scale calibrated in degrees of "importance" appears to be at work. But to a large extent, the balancing takes place inside a black box'.[6]

In short, balancing has been critiqued – among others[7] – for weakening rights,[8]

1 Frank M. Coffin, 'Judicial Balancing: The Protean Scales of Justice', 63 *New York University Law Review* (1988), 19.

2 Concurring opinion of Justice Scalia in United States Supreme Court, *Bendix Autolite Corp. v Midwesco Enterprises, Inc.* [1988] 486 U.S. 888 (108 S.Ct. 2218).

3 Jürgen Habermas, *Between Facts and Norms* (Polity Press, 1996), 259.

4 Stavros Tsakyrakis, 'Proportionality: An Assault on Human Rights?', 7 *International Journal of Constitutional Law* (2009), 490.

5 Alexander Green, 'A Philosophical Taxonomy of European Human Rights Law', *European Human Rights Law Review* (2012), 75.

6 Thomas A. Aleinikoff, 'Constitutional Law in the Age of Balancing', 96 *Yale Law Journal* (1987), 976.

7 Other objections relate, for instance, to the democratic legitimacy argument and the limited role of courts. See ibid. at 984–986; Patrick McFadden, 'The Balancing Test', 29 *Boston College Law Review* (1988), 641–642.

8 Tsakyrakis, *supra* note 4 at 471 and 490–491; Aleinikoff, *supra* note 6 at 991–992; Başak Çali, 'Balancing Human Rights? Methodological Problems with Weights, Scales and Proportions', 29 *Human Rights Quarterly* (2007), 257 and 269.

and for being irrational,[9] arbitrary,[10] subjective or intuitionist[11] and unpredictable.[12] Some of these critiques are, however, not relevant to our current project, since they do not apply to the balancing of human rights (as opposed to balancing rights against the public interest). The argument that balancing weakens rights, in particular, has no real bite in the context of conflicts between human rights.

The objection that balancing weakens the peremptory force of human rights rests on the idea that, on the literal balancing metaphor, the scales start off in a position of equilibrium. The items placed on either end of the scales – human rights *and* public interests – thus enter the balancing test on an equal footing. Yet, according to critics of balancing, this should not be the case. Taking the special normative force of human rights seriously, they posit (and I follow them in this), requires that any test used to determine whether public interests should override human rights, should by definition be loaded in favour of human rights. When human rights conflict, however, there is no need to insist on this otherwise crucial point. Since conflicting human rights are due equal respect, they should enter the test on equal footing. Because the resolution of human rights conflicts does not entail weighing rights against public interests, there is no risk that they will lose their special normative force in a balancing process.[13] Thus, the argument that balancing weakens right does not apply to the balancing of human rights.

The remaining critiques of balancing, however, cannot be so easily dismissed. They require substantive engagement. These critiques – on the irrationality, subjectivity, unpredictability and arbitrariness of balancing – are arguably linked to one core objection to balancing: its alleged impossibility in the face of incommensurability.[14] The notion of incommensurability has its origins in Ancient Greek mathematics.[15] It literally means 'no common measure'.[16] If rights are incommensurable, *i.e.* if no common measure exists to express the relationship

9 Habermas, *supra* note 3 at 259; Green, *supra* note 5 at 75.

10 Habermas, *supra* note 3 at 259; Aleinikoff, *supra* note 6 at 975.

11 Habermas, *supra* note 3 at 259; Aleinikoff, *supra* note 6 at 972–973 and 976; McFadden, *supra* note 7 at 643; Ralf Poscher, 'The Principles Theory: How Many Theories and What is Their Merit?', in Matthias Klatt (ed.), *Institutional Reason: The Jurisprudence of Robert Alexy* (Oxford University Press, 2011), 241.

12 Concurring opinion of Justice Scalia in *Bendix Autolite*, *supra* note 2; Aleinikoff, *supra* note 6 at 975–976; McFadden, *supra* note 7 at 642 and 646.

13 For this reason, I will not engage further with the argument that balancing or proportionality weakens rights. Instead, I refer the reader to the illuminating works of Ronald Dworkin, Stavros Tsakyrakis, Richard Pildes, George Letsas and Mattias Kumm, among others.

14 Aleinikoff, *supra* note 6 at 973 and 975; Habermas, *supra* note 3 at 259; Joseph Raz, *The Morality of Freedom* (Clarendon Press, 1986), 333–334; Matthias Klatt and Moritz Meister, *The Constitutional Structure of Proportionality* (Oxford University Press, 2012), 59; Brett Scharffs, 'Adjudication and the Problems of Incommensurability', 42 *William and Mary Law Review* (2001), 1385 and 1406.

15 Eric Oberheim and Paul Hoyningen-Huene, 'The Incommensurability of Scientific Theories', *Stanford Encyclopedia of Philosophy* (2013), available at http://plato.stanford.edu/entries/incommensurability (last accessed 30 March 2016).

16 Ibid.

between them, it indeed appears impossible to *weigh* rights against each other in the rational and objective manner implied by the scales metaphor. Incommensurability is thus the primary challenge we need to tackle, if we are to make balancing work.[17] Overcoming the incommensurability challenge entails shining some light in the 'black box' of balancing. This, I posit, implies letting go of the scales metaphor of balancing and painting an alternative picture of 'balancing as reasoning' (as opposed to the rather mechanical 'balancing of interests').

Overcoming the incommensurability challenge to balancing

Incommensurability: what are we really talking about?

Incommensurability is a pluriform concept. Although incommensurability is generally tied to Isaiah Berlin's notion of value pluralism,[18] different scholars have put forth distinct conceptions of the concept.[19] Joseph Raz, for instance, equates incommensurability with incomparability: 'A and B are incommensurate if it is neither true that one is better than the other nor true that they are of equal value'.[20] The test of incommensurability is thus, according to Raz, failure of transitivity of options: '[t]wo valuable options are incommensurable (1) if neither is better than the other, and (2) there is (or could be) another option which is better than one but is not better than the others'.[21] Raz illustrates his claim on the equivalence of incommensurability and incomparability by discussing the example of a person faced with a choice between two careers: one in law, the other as a clarinet player.[22] But Raz's test of a failure of transitivity is perhaps easier understood with reference to a simpler example: the choice between two cars.[23]

Assume I am looking to buy a car. Assume further that after laborious research, during which I have filtered numerous options through a number of parameters (fuel consumption, space, price, safety, comfort, etc.), I have narrowed my search down to two cars: a certain Ford and a certain Volvo. I am, however, utterly unable to choose between these two cars. I cannot find any rational criterion that will allow me to choose one over the other. I am left hopelessly undecided. The

17 Scharffs, *supra* note 14 at 1377 ('[t]hese metaphors [of weighing, balancing and measuring] are both powerful and problematic. Their power lies in the promise to provide objective and quantifiable answers to practical choices. The problem is that these very metaphors presuppose the commensurability of the values being weighed, balanced, and measured').

18 Isaiah Berlin, 'Two Concepts of Liberty', in Nigel Warburton (ed.), *Arguments for Freedom* (Open University, 1999), note 10 at 165; Scharffs, *supra* note 14 at 1372.

19 For overviews, see Henry S. Mather, 'Law-making and Incommensurability', 47 *McGill Law Journal* (2002), 345–388; Paul-Erik N. Veel, 'Incommensurability, Proportionality and Rational Legal Decision-making', 4 *Law and Ethics of Human Rights* (2010), 176–228.

20 Raz, *supra* note 14 at 322.

21 Ibid. at 325.

22 Ibid. at 332.

23 The example is taken from Leo Katz, 'Incommensurable Choices and the Problem of Moral Ignorance', 146 *University of Pennsylvania Law Review* (1998), 1465.

failure of transitivity, then, entails that finding a *better* offer on one of these cars will not make my choice between them any easier. For instance, if besides the original Ford I would find *exactly the same* Ford being sold for €500 less, I would certainly choose that Ford over the original one. But that knowledge may not help me dispel my inability to choose between the original Ford and the Volvo. This is due to the failure of transitivity that marks Raz's conception of incommensurability.

So far, so good. But the car example signals that there is something odd about Raz's conception of incommensurability as synonymous with incomparability. It is too narrow. Incommensurability and incomparability should not be equated. Instead, they should remain disentangled. Both concepts are, however, linked in the sense that incomparability can only obtain *after* rational attempts to choose between incommensurable options have failed. While I was shopping for a new car, I engaged in such an attempt. I used a number of parameters that allowed me to choose between multiple incommensurable options: a myriad of cars. Despite the incommensurability between them, I was able to scratch a wide range of cars – BMWs, Toyotas, Renaults, etc. – off my list. I compared them to the Ford and the Volvo and found them to score worse on my predefined parameters. Thus, the incommensurability of the cars did not entail their incomparability. I only faced a problem – an impossibility to choose between the Ford and the Volvo – *afterwards*, when my attempt to compare those specific two cars failed. It is only in the face of such a failure of comparability that rational choice becomes impossible. Incomparability and incommensurability therefore need to be disentangled.

Indeed, unlike Raz, most scholars define incommensurability without reference to comparability, nor to concepts like 'better' or 'worse'. Different conceptions of incommensurability nevertheless remain commonplace. Incommensurability is, in particular, often defined solely with reference to the absence of a common metric along which options, values, goods or rights can be compared. According to Ruth Chang, for instance, two items are incommensurable if they 'cannot be precisely measured by some common scale of units of value'.[24] Chang's definition brings to mind Justice Scalia's objection that balancing 'is more like judging whether a particular line is longer than a particular rock is heavy'.[25] But is Chang's definition really the one we should favour?

I join Brett Scharffs and Cass Sunstein in arguing that we should not. The conception of incommensurability offered by Chang underestimates the incommensurability challenge. Indeed, the absence of a common metric to compare – weigh, if you will – options is only part of the problem. Cass Sunstein points towards the real problem: '[i]ncommensurability occurs when the relevant goods cannot be aligned along a single metric *without doing violence* to our considered judgments about how these goods are best characterised'.[26] The real

24 Ruth Chang, as found in Veel, *supra* note 19 at 182.

25 Concurring opinion of Justice Scalia in *Bendix Autolite*, *supra* note 2.

26 Cass R. Sunstein, 'Incommensurability and Valuation in Law', 92 *Michigan Law Review* (1994), 796 (emphasis added).

problem – or 'the central idea of incommensurability', as Scharffs puts it – is thus *irreducibility*: the impossibility, not only to express the relationship between options along a common metric, but also to *adequately* express what is important about (the relationship between) those options, even when a common metric *is* available.[27] To illustrate the point, Scharffs offers the illuminating example of a man and a book.[28] Although we may express the relationship between a man and a book along the common metric of weight (in kilograms), we learn or gain nothing by doing so. On the contrary, purporting to be comparing a man and a book by stating how much each weighs does violence to our considered judgement about how the relationship between both is best characterised. In tackling the incommensurability challenge, we should thus do more than overcome the absence of a common metric to express the relationship between different options. We should also ensure that we are engaging in *useful* comparisons.

The incommensurability challenge applied to human rights

In terms of the incommensurability challenge, human rights are not all that different from cars. Just as BMWs, Toyotas and Volvos all belong to the larger family of cars, so do freedom of expression, the right to private life and freedom of religion belong to the same larger family: that of human rights. Yet, this simple fact does not render those rights commensurate. Quite the contrary. As with cars, there exists no single common metric to express the relationship between human rights. When human rights conflict, they are, moreover, due principled equal respect. Reducing the relationship between conflicting human rights to a single variable would, in that respect, do violence to our considered judgement of what human rights are. For all intents and purposes, human rights are complex norms that *resist* comparison through a single, common metric. This explains why certain scholars object so strongly to balancing human rights *as if they were commensurable*. James Griffin has aptly summarised this scholarly objection to balancing:

> [m]any who say, "some values are incommensurable" mean something like this ... not all values can be fitted onto a single scale; nor can conflict between them be resolved by measuring them and then, in some arithmetic way, combining the measurements; no such scale exists; no such measurement is possible.[29]

27 Scharffs, *supra* note 14 at 1389–1390. See also Grégoire C. N. Webber, 'Proportionality, Balancing, and the Cult of Constitutional Rights Scholarship', 23 *Canadian Journal of Law and Jurisprudence* (2010), 194 ('two options are incommensurable when it is not appropriate to evaluate both options according to a common measure ... To say that it is "not appropriate" to evaluate both options according to a common measure is to say that applying a common measure to one or both options would distort, transform, or misrepresent the value, importance, or quality of that option').

28 Scharffs, *supra* note 14 at 1391.

29 James Griffin, *On Human Rights* (Oxford University Press, 2008), 47–48.

Griffin speaks of the balancing of values, here. But balancing values is often a shortcut to balancing human rights. The ECtHR, for instance, has held that – when confronted with a human rights conflict – it is tasked to 'verify whether the domestic authorities struck a fair balance when protecting two *values* guaranteed by the Convention which may come into conflict with each other in certain cases'.[30] No matter how one approaches the problem, at its core remains the same objection: since no common metric exists to express the relationship between human rights, values and interests, balancing rights is *by definition* impossible. Stavros Tsakyrakis for instance claims that

> [t]he most effective critique of balancing concerns the assumption of a common metric in the weighing process. The metaphor says nothing about how various interests are to be weighed and this silence tends to conceal the impossibility of measuring incommensurable values.[31]

Or, as Scharffs puts it, '[t]he problem with balancing metaphors is that they slip commensurability in through the back door. If values are incommensurable, they cannot be successfully weighed against each other.'[32]

By combining these critiques with the conception of incommensurability put forth by Scharffs and Sunstein,[33] we are now in a position to formulate the incommensurability challenge as it applies to balancing human rights: given that human rights are incommensurable, *i.e.* since *no common metric* exists to *adequately* capture their relationship, how can we balance them against each other in the rational manner suggested by the balancing metaphor?

A hypothetical example may assist to further illuminate the dual nature of the incommensurability challenge, as it applies to the balancing of human rights: (1) the absence of a *common metric* to (2) *adequately* capture the relationship between human rights.[34] The example draws on the use of money to *create* a common metric – by way of legal fiction – along which otherwise intangible interests can be expressed and compared in law. Take the loss of a family member.[35] Losing a brother as a result of a shooting, for instance, may be compensated in court by, say, €10,000. Although it hereby becomes possible to – at some level – bring the

30 *Axel Springer AG v Germany* [2012] ECHR 227, para 84.
31 Tsakyrakis, *supra* note 4 at 471.
32 Scharffs, *supra* note 14 at 1416.
33 See *supra* notes 26–27 and accompanying text.
34 In the human rights law literature on conflicts of rights, this dual aspect of the incommensurability challenge is often overlooked. Instead, the challenge is often posited only in terms of the absence of a common metric. See, for instance, Lorenzo Zucca, 'Conflicts of Fundamental Rights as Constitutional Dilemmas', in Eva Brems (ed.), *Conflicts between Fundamental Rights* (Intersentia, 2008), 30; Olivier De Schutter and Françoise Tulkens, 'Rights in Conflict: The European Court of Human Rights as a Pragmatic Institution', in Eva Brems (ed.), *Conflicts between Fundamental Rights* (Intersentia, 2008), 191.
35 Frederick Schauer, 'Commensurability and Its Constitutional Consequences', 45 *Hastings Law Journal* (1994), 788; Sunstein, *supra* note 26 at 796.

loss of a brother in relation with other interests, this does not necessarily say anything meaningful about that relationship. Imagine, for instance, that my brother has died of a gunshot wound, inflicted by his neighbour, from whom my brother had just stolen some valuable goods. Through the legal fiction of compensation in monetary terms, a common metric exists to express both my loss (my brother's life) and the potential loss of my brother's neighbour (the goods my brother had just stolen). Yet, whatever one's thoughts may be on the justifiability of the use of lethal force to protect possessions, it surely does violence to our considered judgement to claim that if my brother had stolen goods worth over €10,000, his neighbour was justified in shooting him, while if the stolen goods were worth less than €10,000, my brother was unlawfully killed by his neighbour. Expressing both things – the loss of my brother's life and the theft of goods – in a common metric (money) thus does not render them commensurable. Indeed, the fictional metric created by the law does not *adequately* express the relationship between both things.

The same idea applies to the balancing of human rights, where the crux of the incommensurability challenge is that no common metric is available to adequately express the relationship between conflicting rights. As a result, the core objection to balancing goes, it is not possible to make rational choices between human rights in conflict through balancing.[36] It is this challenge that we must overcome, if we are to make balancing work in the context of human rights conflicts.

Incommensurability and/in human rights practice

Thus far, the incommensurability challenge to balancing human rights has remained rather theoretical. To get a better sense of its impact – if any – on actual human rights practice, we should examine to what extent incommensurability features as a practical obstacle to human rights adjudication. I will, to that end, analyse the case law of the ECtHR in search of traces of the incommensurability challenge. Knowing the potential concerns of the Court will tell us something about the impact of the *theoretical* challenge of incommensurability on the *practical* ability of the Court to resolve cases. Indeed, it is not because scholars insist on theoretical impossibilities that judges necessarily play ball. Judges may not be overly concerned with purported theoretical impossibilities when, in reality, they have no choice but to adjudicate the cases that come before them. In that respect, Brett Scharffs has noted that

> Judges routinely seek to accomplish the impossible – to commensurate incommensurable values. That they attempt to do so with regularity says

36 Grégoire C. N. Webber, *The Negotiable Constitution: On the Limitation of Rights* (Cambridge University Press, 2009), 97; Virgílio Afonso da Silva, 'Comparing the Incommensurable: Constitutional Principles, Balancing and Rational Decision', 31 *Oxford Journal of Legal Studies* (2011), 278 (setting out the objection, before rebutting it).

> something important about the problems of incommensurability, namely that such problems do not foreclose reasoned deliberation and choice.[37]

The ECtHR is no exception. In its case law, the Court continuously balances human rights against each other and against the public interest, *as if* their commensurability obtains. The Court thus does not seem overly preoccupied by the incommensurability challenge. To the best of my knowledge, relevant references to incommensurability only feature twice in the ECtHR's entire case law.[38] This, alone, indicates that the Court is not overly bothered by the alleged impossibility of balancing in the face of incommensurability.[39] Moreover, even in the two judgments that feature relevant references, the Court did not itself invoke incommensurability. In the first judgment, *V. v the United Kingdom*, it was Lord Reed who invoked the concept in his concurring opinion. *V v UK* concerned two young children who had murdered a third young child (James Bulger) and were subsequently tried as adults in criminal court. In his concurring opinion, Lord Reed emphasised that

> it has to be borne in mind that whether a legal system requires a child to be tried in public or in private reflects the way in which a balance is drawn between countervailing, and ***incommensurable***, values. On the one hand, the importance attached to safeguarding the well-being and future of young children who have offended, and promoting their rehabilitation and reintegration into society, point towards holding their trials in private. On the other hand, the public interest (and that of the defendant) in the open administration of justice, and the public interest in freedom of information, point towards holding trials in public.[40]

37 Scharffs, *supra* note 14 at 1374.

38 Note that the terms 'incommensurable', 'incommensurate' and 'incommensurability' feature multiple times in the Court's case law. Yet, in all but two cases, the references are not of immediate relevance to our current concerns. In the majority of cases, the Court uses the terms in an entirely different – often unintelligible – sense to the one we are concerned with here. For a somewhat relevant reference, see the joint dissenting opinion of Judges Ziemele, Sajó, Kalaydjieva, Vučinič and De Gaetano in *Animal Defenders International v the United Kingdom* [2011] ECHR 191, para 7 (noting that the 'present case is not one of balancing between the incommensurable Convention rights of two individuals').

39 See the concurring opinion of Judge Motoc in *Pentikäinen v Finland* [2015] ECHR 926, para 7 (in which she unfortunately obscures the relevance of incommensurability to the case at hand somewhat: 'Although it is broadly considered that the Court uses the triadic structure to assess proportionality, albeit often in a rather obscure manner, other approaches to the proportionality issue have been proposed in terms of moral values, drawing on the stance adopted by Jeremy Waldron, who notes the lack of a common system to "balance" incommensurability but allows the relevant values to be taken into account ... I consider that this judgment implicitly combines both approaches, as do many of the Court's judgments. It analyses the objective, the aims and the question whether the measure helps pursue those aims, and at the same time it highlights the question of the competing moral values').

40 Concurring opinion of Lord Reed in *V. v the United Kingdom* [1999] ECHR 171 (emphasis added).

For all intents and purposes, this remained the opinion of a single judge who moreover did not consider the incommensurability he had himself invoked to preclude rational choice between the 'values' in conflict. On the contrary, Lord Reed went on to endorse the balance struck in the United Kingdom, defending it against other possible balances, as struck in other Member States of the Council of Europe. In doing so, he noted that 'the other important considerations [*i.e.* those of public interest] were considered on balance to require a public trial'.[41] Yet, this is precisely the kind of balanced conclusion that would, on the theoretical argument, be precluded by the incommensurability of values.

If we search for references to incommensurability in the Court's main judgments, the only mention we find is in *Evans v the United Kingdom. Evans*, a case we discussed previously and will return to later,[42] involved a conflict between Ms Evans' right to decisional privacy over becoming a biological parent and the same right of her former partner. The case concerned Ms Evans' last chance to become a biological parent by using frozen embryos, fertilised with the sperm of her former partner. UK legislation included an absolute rule according to which both partners could at all times revoke consent to the use of their sperm or ovum. Since Ms Evans' partner had made use of that rule after the couple's break-up, Ms Evans had lost the ability to have biological children.[43] In its judgment, the ECtHR held that 'the absolute nature of the rule served to promote legal certainty and to avoid the problems of arbitrariness and inconsistency inherent in weighing, on a case-by-case basis, what the Court of Appeal described as "entirely incommensurable" interests'.[44]

The Court, here, did not invoke the notion of incommensurability itself. Instead, it referred to the domestic court's reliance thereon. Throughout its own judicial reasoning, the Court used different terms to describe the conflicting rights in *Evans*, terms such as 'entirely irreconcilable'.[45] It does not seem, therefore, that the Court considered incommensurability to obtain in *Evans*, in the sense that a rational weighing of the interests at stake was impossible.[46] Instead, in describing those interests as 'entirely irreconcilable', the Court emphasised the tragic nature of the case. The Court specifically noted that 'whatever solution the national

41 Ibid.

42 See *supra* Chapter 2 at notes 72–74 and accompanying text; see *infra* Chapter 8.

43 Note that, thanks to advances in medical science in the intervening period, Ms Evans has recently given birth to a biological child. See Lorenzo Zucca, 'The Comedy of Mrs Evans', in Stijn Smet and Eva Brems (eds), *Conflicts of Rights at the European Court of Human Rights* (Oxford University Press, forthcoming 2017; chapter on file with author). At the time of the *Evans* ruling at the ECtHR, however, the available evidence pointed to the absolute impossibility of Ms Evans ever having biological children.

44 *Evans v the United Kingdom* [2006] ECHR 265, para 89.

45 Ibid. at para 73.

46 See *contra* Jacco Bomhoff and Lorenzo Zucca, 'Evans v. UK, European Court of Human Rights – the Tragedy of Ms Evans: Conflicts and Incommensurability of Rights, *Evans* v. *the United Kingdom*, Fourth Section Judgment of 7 March 2006, Application No. 6339/05', 2 *European Constitutional Law Review* (2006), 424–442.

authorities might adopt would result in the interests of one or the other parties to the IVF treatment being wholly frustrated'.[47] This, however, does not imply incommensurability. Instead, it underscores the difficult choices that must often be made in balancing human rights. The Court emphasised this point in its conclusion:

> As regards the balance struck between the conflicting Article 8 rights of the parties to the IVF treatment, the Grand Chamber, in common with every other court which has examined this case, has great sympathy for the applicant ... However ... it does not consider that the applicant's right to respect for the decision to become a parent in the genetic sense should be accorded greater weight than [her partner's] right to respect for his decision not to have a genetically related child with her.[48]

Genuine incommensurability of the interests at stake would, of course, have precluded the Court from reaching this conclusion. It should, however, not come as a surprise that the ECtHR chose to act pragmatically, *as if* commensurability obtained. As Jacco Bomhoff and Lorenzo Zucca have noted in their analysis of the *Evans* case, '[m]uch of fundamental rights law simply is based on the assumption that it must be possible for courts to make rational choices between incommensurable values or interests'.[49] Moreover, on pain of denial of justice, the Court is obliged to adjudicate the cases that come before it.[50] The ECtHR therefore appears to rely on Frederick Schauer's 'instrumental commensurability': a pragmatic attitude that *assumes* or *chooses* commensurability, rather than demonstrating it, and does so for instrumental reasons; simply because the advantages of assuming commensurability are far greater than the disadvantages.[51] Since constitutional and human rights courts like the ECtHR have no choice but to resolve cases, despite the theoretical challenge of incommensurability, they are likely to *assume* – even if unsupported or incorrectly – commensurability at the level of practical adjudication.

Yet, such pragmatic choices and assumptions on the parts of courts will do little – or nothing – to appease critics of balancing. Those critics will point out that herein lies precisely the problem: when judges ignore the incommensurability challenge to balancing, they fail to realise that they cannot – despite their best

47 *Evans*, *supra* note 44 at para 73.

48 Ibid. at para 90.

49 Bomhoff and Zucca, *supra* note 47 at 432.

50 Sébastien Van Drooghenbroeck, *La proportionnalité dans le droit de la convention européenne des droits de l'homme: prendre l'idée simple au sérieux* (Bruylant, 2001), 282; Scharffs, *supra* note 14 at 1410–1411; Janneke Gerards, '"Hard Cases" in Law', in Adriaan in 't Groen *et al.* (eds), *Knowledge in Ferment – Dilemmas in Science, Scholarship and Society* (Leiden University Press, 2007) at 128.

51 Frederick Schauer, 'Instrumental Commensurability', 146 *University of Pennsylvania Law Review* (1998), 1216–1217 and 1225.

intentions – succeed in balancing rights against each other (or against the public interest). Instead, by pressing on in the face of the incommensurability of rights, values and interests, judges engage in arbitrary and subjective reasoning. Or so the critics argue. Taking incommensurability seriously, they insist, entails abandoning all attempts at judicial balancing.[52] The incommensurability challenge can thus not simply be ignored, as courts are wont to do. In this book, at least, it needs to be faced head on.

The incommensurability challenge overcome

The incommensurability challenge to balancing human rights insists that it is not possible to rationally choose between human rights by weighing them against each other, since no common metric exists to adequately express the relationship between them. Here, the shortcomings of the scales metaphor begin to overshadow its benefits. What makes the scales metaphor of balancing particularly attractive is the ease with which it makes balancing accessible. It does so by painting an immediate visual image of what balancing entails. In relation to human or constitutional rights adjudication, the scales metaphor moreover defuses potential charges of judicial law-making by implying that all judges do when they balance rights against each other or against the public interest, is place them on opposite sides of a pair of scales and observe to which side the scales tip. The purported objectivity of the balancing exercise thus obscures (potential) judicial activism.

But the clarity that makes the scales metaphor so attractive also constitutes its major shortcoming: it is hopelessly simplistic. The literal image of the balancing scales invites us to think of balancing rights in the same way as we think of weighing fruit. With two pieces of fruit on either end of the scales, we are at least able to truly say which weighs more. But with rights on each side, we are genuinely comparing apples and oranges. Human rights of course have no physical weight. Yet, on the scales metaphor – even when interpreted symbolically – we are invited to assume that a single common metric is available to weigh rights against each other. This, however, is patently not the case. Even where the law *creates* such a common metric through legal fiction (*e.g.* monetary value), it does not adequately express the relationship between the items in the balance. Conceiving the balancing of human rights in terms of the scales metaphor arguably does violence to our considered judgement of how rights relate to each other. We would therefore do well to abandon the scales metaphor, as well as the notion of weight. Both ultimately do more to confound balancing than to elucidate it.

Yet, it is not because we abandon the scales metaphor of balancing and the search for a common metric to express the relationship between competing human rights that we must necessarily cave in to the incommensurability challenge. On the contrary, we may yet overcome that challenge by designing a balancing test that allows for rational *comparison* – not weighing – of human rights. To fully

52 Tsakyrakis, *supra* note 4; Webber, *supra* note 36.

appreciate the salience of this point, we must delve even deeper into the notion of incommensurability.

When we explore the meaning of incommensurability further than we thus far have, we are bound to discover that a distinction should be made between two modes thereof: weak incommensurability and strong incommensurability.[53] Jeremy Waldron's work is of singular importance here. Waldron describes strong incommensurability as 'genuine incomparability', that is 'the sort of incommensurability that can leave us paralysed, not knowing what to choose'.[54] According to Waldron, strong incommensurability does not necessarily preclude choice, given that an agent will *have* to make a choice if the problem is sufficiently acute.[55] But strong incommensurability does preclude the making of a *rational* choice. Any choice made under strong incommensurability will instead reveal a particular, subjective preference.[56]

Weak incommensurability, conversely, does not preclude rational choice.[57] Under weak incommensurability, items can be brought into objective relation with each other.[58] According to Waldron, weak incommensurability 'is usually expressed in terms of a simple and straightforward rule' that creates an ordering or hierarchy between the items between which we have to choose.[59] In terms of rights, such an ordering is implicit in, for instance, Ronald Dworkin's 'rights as trumps',[60] Robert Nozick's 'rights as side constraints',[61] Frederick Schauer's 'rights as shields'[62] and John Rawls' concept of a 'lexical ordering'.[63]

Waldron sums up his discussion on the difference between strong and weak incommensurability as follows:

> In a case of strong incommensurability, the competing values cannot even be brought into relation with one another: They are genuinely incomparable … In a case of weak incommensurability … the values *can* be brought into relation with one another … Their lack of commensurability refers only to the absence of a common dimension of measurement that would allow trade-offs between them.[64]

53 Jeremy Waldron, 'Fake Incommensurability: A Response to Professor Schauer', 45 *Hastings Law Journal* (1994), 815–817.
54 Ibid. at 815–816.
55 Ibid. at 816.
56 Ibid.
57 Ibid. at 816–817; Scharffs, *supra* note 14 at 1383.
58 Waldron, *supra* note 54 at 817.
59 Ibid. at 816.
60 Ronald Dworkin, *Taking Rights Seriously* (Harvard University Press, 1977).
61 Robert Nozick, *Anarchy, State, and Utopia* (Basic Books, 1974).
62 Frederick Schauer, 'A Comment on the Structure of Rights', 27 *Georgia Law Review* (1993), 415–434.
63 John Rawls, *A Theory of Justice* (Belknap Press, 1971).
64 Waldron, *supra* note 54 at 817 (emphasis in original).

In other words, the absence of a common metric to express the relationship between items, such as conflicting human rights, does not mean they cannot usefully be compared.

It is worth noting that Waldron's conception of weak incommensurability is contested by certain proportionality scholars, insofar as it creates an abstract ordering or hierarchy between rights and the public interest.[65] This corresponds to arguments I made in Chapter 1, where I emphasised the need to safeguard the special normative force of human rights in the face of certain conceptions of proportionality. Here, in attempting to locate a balancing solution to conflicts between human rights, we should have no qualms in accepting Waldron's conception of weak incommensurability. Indeed, Waldron himself has indicated that – under the trumping model, for instance – weighing and balancing may need to take place between the trumps (*i.e.* rights) themselves.[66]

An example may serve to further illustrate the difference between weak and strong incommensurability, easing the transition to the discussion in the context of human rights that follows. The example draws on illustrations that have been offered in the scholarly literature.[67] It involves two artists: a painter and a composer. Both are weakly incommensurable. They cannot be adequately compared with reference to a common metric (such as their weight). This does not necessarily mean, however, that we are not able to choose, with some measure of rational confidence, one over the other. If we take Wolfgang Amadeus Mozart as our composer and compare him to a quite dreadful painter, we should be able to choose – with rational confidence – Mozart over the painter. We are not able to express their relationship with reference to an objectively measurable common metric, but we are able to choose between them on the basis of factors that we deem central to what it means for an artist to be great. These factors include her influence on the development of her field, her uniqueness, her ability to move people, the extent to which she is regarded (by critics and others alike) to be a genius, etc. On the basis of these factors, we should quite easily be able to choose Mozart over the quite dreadful painter, because he 'scores better' on each and every one of the factors mentioned. Crucially, this idea of comparing options according to a set of criteria *is* something we can translate to the realm of human rights, as I explain below and in Chapter 6.[68]

If we replace our quite dreadful painter with Pablo Picasso, however, we may suddenly find it much more difficult to choose. Not because rational choice between Picasso and Mozart is impossible from the outset – we were, after all, able to choose between Mozart and the quite dreadful painter – but because our attempts at rational choice will fail. We might ultimately be able to say 'I prefer Picasso over Mozart' (or the other way around), but that choice will merely

65 See, for instance, Afonso da Silva, *supra* note 37 at 280–282.
66 Waldron, *supra* note 54 at 816–817.
67 See, for instance, Afonso da Silva, *supra* note 37 at 283 (comparing Bach and Madonna).
68 See *infra* notes 76–77 and accompanying text.

express a subjective preference that is not supported by reason. It would, thus, be a sign of the strong incommensurability between Picasso and Mozart.

Translated to the realm of human rights in conflict, weak incommensurability implies that it is not possible to measure human rights with reference to a single metric. We may nevertheless overcome such weak incommensurability, provided that we are able to choose between human rights in conflict, with some measure of rational confidence. This implies being able to rationally *compare* human rights. I submit that, for such comparison to work, we need to focus our efforts on developing a 'balancing as reasoning' test,[69] as opposed to the mechanical 'balancing of interests' test implied by the scales metaphor of balancing.[70] Only when such a 'balancing as reasoning' test fails to provide a solution, will we be confronted with strong incommensurability in the sense of genuine incomparability. Yet, such strong incommensurability will only rarely obtain.[71] It is particularly likely to arise, not in the average hard case, but in the context of genuine dilemmas. Indeed, as Waldron emphasises, strong incommensurability 'is the stuff of tragic choices'.[72] Further on, I dedicate a separate chapter to such strong incommensurability and the genuine dilemmas it causes (Chapter 8).

Until then, I focus on developing a structured 'balancing as reasoning' test, aimed at making balancing work in the face of weak incommensurability between human rights (Chapter 6). I will moreover defend that structured balancing test against possible alternative approaches to balancing (Chapter 7). By advocating for balancing, I engage in *rapprochement* with (certain) proportionality scholars, from whom I took principled distance earlier in this book (particularly in Chapter 1). In proposing a 'balancing as reasoning' test, I most notably align myself with Kai Möller (Chapter 7).[73] Yet, I will also critique the specific balancing test defended by (most) proportionality scholars: Robert Alexy's Weight Formula

69 I reject other attempts at overcoming the incommensurability challenge, including the insistence that a common metric does exist (*e.g.* utilitarianism's 'greatest happiness for the greatest number'), the creation of such a common metric within a balancing test (*e.g.* Aharon Barak's 'marginal social importance') and value monism (*e.g.* Ronald Dworkin's right to equal concern and respect). On these other strategies, see Dworkin, *supra* note 61; Aharon Barak, *Proportionality: Constitutional Rights and Their Limitations* (Cambridge University Press, 2012); Griffin, *supra* note 29 at 48; Afonso da Silva, *supra* note 37 at 284 and 301.

70 See, in support, Matthias Jestaedt, 'The Doctrine of Balancing – Its Strengths and Weaknesses', in Matthias Klatt (ed.), *Institutional Reason: The Jurisprudence of Robert Alexy* (Oxford University Press, 2011), 172 (generally critical of balancing, but accepting that, if the 'claim of the doctrine of balancing is reduced to the status of a subject-specific analytical theory directed to the structure of competing fundamental rights ... then there is no reason why it should not have a prominent place in fundamental rights doctrine, and plenty of reasons why it should').

71 Scharffs, *supra* note 14 at 1375; Sunstein, *supra* note 26 at 810.

72 Waldron, *supra* note 54 at 816.

73 Kai Möller, 'Proportionality: Challenging the Critics', 10 *International Journal of Constitutional Law* (2012), 715 and 721–722; Kai Möller, *The Global Model of Constitutional Rights* (Oxford University Press, 2012), 25 and 137–139. But see *infra* notes 79–80 and accompanying text, for an important point of departure from Möller's views.

test (Chapter 7). In this chapter, I will restrict myself to sketching the outline of my structured balancing test, with a view to explaining how it overcomes the challenge from weak incommensurability. I develop the test in full in Chapter 6.

The outline of a structured balancing test

In addressing the incommensurability challenge to balancing, I do not intend to provide a magical 'balancing of interests' test that would somehow *convert* the value of human rights into a common metric so that they may be weighed, quite literally, against each other. Balancing is not – or should not be – that simplistic. Instead, to make balancing work I will propose a structured test that relies on 'balancing as reasoning' – *i.e.* a form of practical reasoning – to determine which right should prevail under the specific circumstances of a given conflict. Balancing thus understood implies *comparing* the strength of *reasons* – not the *measuring* of *weights* – in favour of, and against, human rights in conflict.[74]

To enable such comparison of reasons, we require criteria to guide the balancing exercise. To that end, I propose a limited set of seven criteria that make up a structured balancing test: a value criterion, impact criterion, core/periphery criterion, additional rights criterion, general interest criterion, purpose criterion and responsibility criterion. I explain each criterion in detail in Chapter 6. In order to engage in the kind of useful comparison of reasons that will overcome the challenge from weak incommensurability, the seven criteria of the balancing test need to be combined so as to allow us to adequately express the relationship between human rights in conflict. In Chapter 6, I explain that this aim is best achieved by constructing 'nets of arguments', as opposed to 'chains of arguments'.[75] I propose to discard the deductive reasoning of 'chains of arguments' – if P1 is valid, then P2 is valid and therefore P3 follows – because it implies an intuitive or subjective moment at the start of the chain and since it entails that a reasoned argument is only as strong as its weakest link. In 'nets of arguments', conversely, the elements of a reasoned argument *mutually reinforce* each other (P1, P2 and P3 support each other).

In more practical terms, the idea is the following. In balancing human rights, judges first construct two (or more) nets of arguments, one for each of the human rights in conflict. In constructing those nets of arguments, judges turn to the seven criteria of the structured balancing test to determine whether they provide

74 See also Griffin, *supra* note 29 at 69 and 131 (arguing that '[f]or a pair of values to be commensurable … there must be a bridging notion in terms of which the comparison can be made' and offering, as an example of such a bridging notion, 'the notion of a "reason": "this reason is stronger than that"').

75 Aleksander Peczenik, *On Law and Reason* (Kluwer Academic Publishers, 1989), 137; Leonor Moral Soriano, 'A Modest Notion of Coherence in Legal Reasoning. A Model for the European Court of Justice', 16 *Ratio Juris* (2003), 319 (introducing the idea of constructing 'nets of arguments', rather than chains). See also Scharffs, *supra* note 14 at 1423 (using the metaphor of reasons being woven into a cable of cumulative strength, rather than a net).

reasons in favour of – or against – the human rights in conflict. Once constructed, each net of arguments expresses the strength of the reasons in favour of – and against – each of the human rights in conflict. By comparing the strength of the reasons woven into each net of arguments, judges should be able to determine which human right is supported by stronger reasons and should therefore prevail over the other human right(s), with which it conflicts. But much, I trust, will become clear when I develop the structured balancing test in detail in Chapter 6.

Balancing: contextual or categorical?

The 'balancing as reasoning' test I have just outlined could be labelled as a structured *ad hoc* balancing test. The test relies on *ad hoc* balancing, rather than the definitional or categorical variety, in that it requires a balance to be struck between human rights *in the specific circumstances* of a given conflict.[76] The test thus rejects, in principle, predefined solutions provided by categorical or definitional balancing, under which one human right by definition 'trumps' the other (in all situations; or at least given a particular set of circumstances).[77] Instead, human rights enter the test on equal footing, as rights that principally deserve equal respect. Taking this equal respect seriously, I posit, requires *contextual* balancing, not *predefined* outcomes. Nevertheless, three crucial points must be made.

First, abstract differences in value between human rights in conflict *can* be expressed within the workings of the test (as I explain in Chapter 6). But – and this is crucial – such differences in value are incorporated in the *ad hoc* balancing exercise. They do not foreclose the argument, as definitional/categorical balancing is wont to do. Second, over time – once the contextual balancing test has been repeatedly applied to adjudicate a specific conflict – patterns may start to emerge. Analysis of those patterns may allow us to predict future outcomes in that, given similar sets of circumstances, certain human rights are likely to prevail over others. In that respect, categorical balancing rules might result from repeated application of the contextual balancing test. But – and this, again, is crucial – such rules will merely be the result of repeated contextual balancing and are therefore not set in stone. Indeed, new circumstances and/or new normative evaluation of those

76 On the difference between *ad hoc* and definitional (or categorical) balancing, see Melville B. Nimmer, 'The Right Time to Speak from *Times* to *Time*: First Amendment Theory Applied to Libel and Misapplied to Privacy', 56 *California Law Review* (1968), 939–945. For discussion, see Aleinikoff, *supra* note 6 at 948 and 979–980; Mark Tushnet, 'An Essay on Rights', 62 *Texas Law Review* (1984), 1371–1372; Aharon Barak, 'Proportionality and Principled Balancing', 4 *Law & Ethics of Human Rights* (2010), 2–18.

77 Note, however, that we are dealing with conflicts between *relative* human rights here. The resolution of conflicts involving absolute rights may very well involve resolution techniques analogous to definitional balancing, in the sense that absolute rights – by their very nature – 'trump' relative rights. I would, however, be loath to label this balancing of any sort.

circumstances may cause deviation from 'established' categorical balancing rules.[78] Contextual balancing will – or should – thus remain at the heart of adjudication of human rights conflicts.

Third, the above does not mean, however, that balancing need be arbitrary and unpredictable. Although the test I propose relies on *ad hoc* balancing, it is – and this, once more, is crucial – not an open ended test. I critique such *open ended* balancing tests, including the one currently employed by the ECtHR, in Chapter 5. On this particular point, I also deviate from Kai Möller, who equates 'balancing as reasoning' to the idea that 'we have to make a moral argument as to which of the competing interests takes priority in the case at hand'.[79] Franscisco Urbina has critiqued Möller's argument as implying directionless 'open-ended moral reasoning'.[80] To avoid the shortcomings of open ended balancing or moral reasoning (see Chapter 5 for details), I propose a *structured* test that *limits* the kinds of considerations that may enter the balancing exercise and *predefines* the appropriate relation between those considerations within the balancing exercise (see Chapter 6). The desired structure comes from the seven criteria that make up the structured 'balancing as reasoning' test, and from bringing those criteria into relation through the construction of nets of arguments. The test I propose thus combines features of *ad hoc* balancing and of what Aharon Barak has termed 'principled balancing'.[81] Ultimately, however, it remains a test that relies on contextual balancing, under which the outcome depends on the specific circumstances of a case, instead of categorical balancing, under which the outcome is predefined.

Conclusion

To overcome the incommensurability challenge to balancing human rights, we should abandon the scales metaphor of 'balancing of interests' and develop a structured 'balancing as reasoning' test. In this chapter, I have sketched the outline of such a structured balancing test, composed of seven criteria, that should allow judges to determine the strength of reasons in favour of – and against – human rights in conflict. By comparing the strength of those reasons, woven together in 'nets of arguments', judges will often be able to choose between human rights in conflict (Chapter 6). Judges may thereby overcome the challenge from weak incommensurability. When their attempts at comparison fail, however, judges will be confronted with genuine dilemmas, which entail strong incommensurability and cannot, therefore, be resolved rationally (Chapter 8).

78 Aleinikoff, *supra* note 6 at 979–980.

79 Möller, 'Proportionality…', *supra* note 74 at 715.

80 Francisco Urbina, '"Balancing as Reasoning" and the Problems of Legally Unaided Adjudication: A Reply to Kai Möller', 12 *International Journal of Constitutional Law* (2014), 214–215 and 220.

81 Barak, *supra* note 77 at 12.

The balancing test I have outlined in this chapter moreover relies on contextual balancing, as opposed to categorical balancing. Yet, because it is a *structured* test, it avoids the pitfalls of the open ended balancing tests courts, including the ECtHR, currently often employ in resolving human rights conflicts. The structured balancing test I propose thereby also aims to address important practical obstacles to balancing in human rights adjudication. These practical obstacles are the subject of the next chapter.

5 Practical obstacles to balancing human rights

The previous chapter addressed the alleged irrationality of balancing in the face of the theoretical challenge of incommensurability. But critics of balancing do more than point out theoretical impossibilities. They also critique how balancing functions in judicial practice. In this chapter, I will deal with the most salient *practical* obstacles to balancing human rights: alleged subjectivity in balancing, the impact of intuitive reasoning on balancing, the lack of coherence of balancing decisions and the occurrence of 'preferential framing' effects in the construction of balancing exercises.

In examining these practical obstacles, I will make four key claims. First, I will argue that open ended balancing, generally employed by the ECtHR in resolving human rights conflicts, fails to ward off judges' subjective preferences. Second, I will submit that, in balancing human rights, judges should be nudged towards quasirationality, a mode of cognitive reasoning that lies between pure intuition and pure analysis (or deliberation). Third, I will posit that our primary focus in improving balancing methodologies should be on increasing coherence, both within and across conflicting human rights cases. Fourth, I will show that the adjudication of human rights conflicts may be subject to 'preferential framing' effects, *i.e.* unjustified skewing of judicial reasoning in favour of one of the human rights in conflict.

In evaluating these practical obstacles to balancing human rights, I will explain how the introduction of a structured balancing test may assist judges in overcoming them. Use of a structured balancing test would minimise the influence of subjective preferences, nudge judges towards quasirationality, increase the coherence of judicial reasoning and eliminate preferential framing effects.

Subjectivity in balancing?

Critics of balancing do more than cast doubts on the very possibility of balancing in the face of the theoretical challenge of incommensurability. They also lament the subjectivity of balancing in judicial practice. Lorenzo Zucca, for instance, argues that '[b]alancing often seems arbitrary, and little more than window-dressing for unsophisticated ethical intuitions'.[1] Stavros Tsakyrakis similarly argues that

> the balancing approach fails, spectacularly, to deliver what it promises. At the very least, we would expect that the balancing approach would throw some light on the 'black box' of comparisons of incommensurable values. What we find, instead, is a characteristically impressionistic assessment of the relative weights of the competing considerations, which does not lend itself to a rational reconstruction of the argumentative path that has led to a particular decision.[2]

Interestingly, critiques of judicial balancing are not limited to scholars who principally oppose balancing as such. Scholars who are generally supportive of balancing also criticise the specific balancing methodologies employed by courts like the ECtHR. Matthias Klatt and Moritz Meister, for instance, criticise the Court's failure to develop and apply a 'proper balancing approach' to conflicts between human rights.[3] Sébastien Van Drooghenbroeck similarly points out that any attempt at structuring the Court's balancing test 'is largely deceived by European practice, which seems to prefer "flair" over method'.[4]

Critiques of the subjectivity of judicial balancing are particularly acute – and apt – when judges resort to a particular kind of balancing: open ended *ad hoc* balancing. Much of the subjectivity problem arguably originates in courts, like the ECtHR, utilising open ended balancing to resolve human rights conflicts. In the absence of limiting factors, the ECtHR tends to employ an 'anything goes' strategy. Anything can be brought into balancing exercises, but anything can also be left out. In constructing balancing exercises, the Court's judges do not explain *why* certain factors have been brought in, while others have been left out. They also generally fail to explicate the relationship between invoked factors. Combined, these failures contribute to painting the 'impressionistic' picture of balancing as 'window-dressing' – or as 'flair' being preferred over 'method' – lamented in the literature. As Pieter van Dijk and Fried van Hoof note, judgments of the ECtHR

1 Lorenzo Zucca, '*Evans v United Kingdom*: Frozen Embryos and Conflicting Rights', 11 *Edinburgh Law Review* (2007), 449.

2 Stavros Tsakyrakis, 'Proportionality: An Assault on Human Rights?', 7 *International Journal of Constitutional Law* (2009), 482.

3 Matthias Klatt and Moritz Meister, *The Constitutional Structure of Proportionality* (Oxford University Press, 2012), 157 (criticising the ECtHR's balancing exercise in *Otto-Preminger-Institut v Austria* [1994] ECHR 26: '[a] substantiated balancing test was applied by neither the majority nor the minority of the judges').

4 Sébastien Van Drooghenbroeck, *La proportionnalité dans le droit de la convention européenne des droits de l'homme: prendre l'idée simple au sérieux* (Bruylant, 2001), 306 (author's translation; original: 'est largement déçue par la pratique européenne, qui ... semble préférer 'le flair' ... à la méthode').

> typically contain a (sometimes extensive) listing of the factors to be taken into account, but then somewhat abruptly – without additional arguments as to the weight of the factors concerned – conclude, for instance, that … 'a proper balance was not achieved'.[5]

Indeed, often no insight can be gleaned from the Court's judgments on the comparative strength of human rights in conflict. This, in turn, leaves a stark impression that the Court's balancing exercises are steered by subjective preferences.

A few ECtHR judges have displayed acute awareness of the shortcomings of the Court's open ended balancing test, as applied in concrete cases. A particularly poignant critique can be found in *Fürst-Pfeifer v Austria*, a case concerning the publication of personal health data in the media.[6] In *Fürst-Pfeifer*, a regional newspaper and a regional website had revealed the content of a 15-year-old psychological report in which a psychiatrist, who had acted as a court expert in thousands of child custody cases, was described as suffering from mood swings, panic attacks, suicidal thoughts and hallucinations. In balancing the psychiatrist's right to privacy against the newspaper's and website's freedom of expression, the majority of the ECtHR ruled in favour of the latter. Two dissenting judges expressed their outrage at the 'major flaws' in the majority's balancing exercise.[7] They lamented, in particular, that

> the Court's case-law is applied selectively and offhandedly. Important elements thereof, pertaining to the heart of respect for privacy, are suppressed, whereas those related to the freedom of the media are emphasised … pertinent facts are passed over in silence, and certain important factual questions are not raised at all … these flaws have produced the most regrettable result – a one-sided, unbalanced and, it appears, fundamentally unjust judgment.[8]

The one-sided approach to balancing critiqued by the dissenting judges in *Fürst-Pfeifer* is symptomatic of open ended balancing tests. Such tests invite judges'

5 Pieter van Dijk and Fried van Hoof, as found in Van Drooghenbroeck, *supra* note 4 at 284. See also Frank M. Coffin, 'Judicial Balancing: The Protean Scales of Justice', 63 *New York University Law Review* (1988), 22 ('[a]ll too commonly in judicial opinions, lip service is paid to balancing, a cursory mention of opposing interests is made, and, presto, the "balance" is arrived at through some unrevealed legerdemain'); Javier Martínez-Torrón, 'The (Un) protection of Individual Religious Identity in the Strasbourg Case Law', 1 *Oxford Journal of Law and Religion* (2012), 364 ('the Court often declares formally and solemnly its attachment to certain general principles, deemed immovable, but then it assesses the factual evidence with such concision and lack of detail that sometimes those same principles could have been used to decide the case the opposite way').

6 *Fürst-Pfeifer v Austria* [2016] ECHR 431.

7 Dissenting opinion of Judges Wojtyczek and Kūris in ibid. at para 1.

8 Ibid.

subjective preferences to steer the outcome of concrete cases. Under open ended balancing, judges can construct balancing exercises to fit their subjective preferences on the desired outcome. In the process, they are likely to over-emphasise the human right they favour, while neglecting the competing human right. The end result, as noted by the dissenting judges in *Fürst-Pfeifer*, is a one-sided judgment that fails to convince.

Subjectivity in open ended balancing and 'jumps' in judicial reasoning

Although courts such as the ECtHR do formulate criteria that guide balancing exercises between human rights in conflict (*e.g.* the idea that a political figure should show greater tolerance to criticism in the press than a private individual), they are prone to approach balancing in a casuistic manner that leaves multiple factors implicit or unaddressed. In employing open ended balancing, the ECtHR – in particular – draws on a wide array of factors, at some point or other established as potentially relevant in its vast case law. On the one hand, this allows for great flexibility: the Court is able to truly take the concrete circumstances of each case into account.[9] On the other hand, however, it also invites a risk of subjectivity, as critiqued by the dissenters in *Fürst-Pfeifer*. Because the balancing exercise is open ended, it is entirely up to judges to discretionally decide which factors will be included in a given judgment. Judges may elect to leave certain factors aside entirely, without explaining why they do so. They may also fail to clarify, in their judgments, how invoked factors relate to each other. Combined, both failings preclude the possibility of a *comparative* judgment on the strength of reasons in favour of human rights in conflict.[10]

As a result, the ECtHR's reasoning in conflicting human rights cases tends to entail a 'jump' in legal reasoning, to borrow Aleksander Peczenik's terminology.[11] Peczenik explains that, in legal reasoning, a 'jump from a set of premises S to a conclusion q exists if… q does not follow deductively from S'.[12] In judgments on conflicts between human rights, it is indeed often impossible to directly deduce the Court's conclusion from the premises it offers, because the Court generally (1) does not explain why it has included certain factors in its balancing exercise and left others out, and (2) does not explicate the weight it attaches to invoked factors, nor the relationship between them.[13] This creates an impression of

9 Janneke Gerards, 'Judicial Deliberations in the European Court of Human Rights', in Nick Huls *et al.* (eds), *The Legitimacy of Highest Courts' Rulings – Judicial Deliberations and Beyond* (T.M.C. Asser Press, 2009), 420.

10 On the need for a comparative judgment, see Henry S. Mather, 'Law-making and Incommensurability', 47 *McGill Law Journal* (2002), 366.

11 Aleksander Peczenik, *On Law and Reason* (Kluwer Academic Publishers, 1989), 130.

12 Ibid. at 130–131.

13 Frederick Schauer, 'Balancing, Subsumption, and the Constraining Role of Legal Text', 4 *Law and Ethics of Human Rights* (2010), 39.

subjectivity and arbitrariness. One may even be excused for thinking – in legal realist fashion – that Strasbourg judges decide conflicting human rights cases on the basis of their own unarticulated preferences, to afterwards formulate an (unsatisfactory) balancing exercise in support of these preferences.[14] Marko Novak links such legal realist insights to the particular type of balancing employed by the ECtHR. Novak claims that one of the primary shortcomings of unrestrained balancing is that, under it 'the court does not subject its intuition .... to the rationality (justification) test ... whose categories, if they existed, would offer some possibility of enabling an external review (by the public) of what was going on in the case'.[15]

Open ended balancing: an example

A concrete example from the ECtHR's case law illustrates how open ended balancing between human rights in conflict is prone to suffer from two deficiencies: (1) a failure to explain why certain factors have been included in the balancing exercise, while others have been left out; and (2) a concomitant failure to explicate the weight attached to these factors and the relationship between them.[16]

Palomo Sánchez and Others v Spain illustrates how the ECtHR often leaves certain – *prima facie* relevant – factors unaddressed and/or downplays their relevance, without explaining why it does so.[17] *Palomo Sánchez* involved a conflict between the right to freedom of expression of certain trade union members and the right to reputation of two of their fellow employees and the human resources manager of the company. The facts of the case took place in the context of labour disputes. The applicants were the founders of a trade union set up to defend their interests and those of the other employees of the company. They had already instituted several sets of labour proceedings against their employer. In one of the newsletters of the trade union, the applicants reported on a court ruling that partly upheld their claims.

14 Angelika Nussberger, 'Subsidiarity in the Control of Decisions Based on Proportionality: An Analysis on the Basis of the Implementation of ECtHR Judgments into German Law', in Anja Seibert-Forh and Mark E. Villiger (eds), *Judgments of the European Court of Human Rights – Effects and Implementation* (Nomos Verlagsgesellschaft, 2014), 165–186 ('It might be fair to say that what courts do in the end is not balancing rights, but choosing the right they find more important. Therefore personal preferences will unavoidably be involved in the process'). See also Patrick McFadden, 'The Balancing Test', 29 *Boston College Law Review* (1988), 643.

15 Marko Novak, 'Three Models of Balancing (in Constitutional Review)', 23 *Ratio Juris* (2010), 106.

16 I discuss another example – consisting of a pair of cases – in Stijn Smet, 'Conflicts between Human Rights and the ECtHR: Towards a Structured Balancing Test', in Stijn Smet and Eva Brems (eds), *Conflicts of Rights at the European Court of Human Rights* (Oxford University Press, forthcoming; manuscript on file with the author).

17 *Palomo Sánchez and Others v Spain* [2011] ECHR 1319.

The cover of the newsletter featured a caricature in the form of a cartoon. The cartoon depicted the human resources manager sitting behind a desk, under which the legs of a person sitting on all fours could be seen. It was clear from the context that the person beneath the desk was offering sexual services to the resource manager. Two employees of the company – recognisable from their faces – were standing in front of the desk, waiting for their turn to sexually please the resource manager. The newsletter also featured two articles in which the applicants vehemently denounced the two employees depicted in the cartoon on the cover for having testified in favour of the company in the labour proceedings. The newsletter was distributed among the workers and displayed on the noticeboard of the trade union, located on the company's premises. The company dismissed the trade union members on grounds of serious misconduct.

In its judgment, the ECtHR ruled, in a 12–5 split vote, that there had been no violation of the right to freedom of expression. The majority's reasoning demonstrates how the Court's implementation of open ended balancing invites a subjective selection of the factors employed in the balancing exercise. In *Palomo Sánchez*, the majority ignored and/or downplayed the relevance of two factors that – *prima facie* – are of direct relevance to the balancing exercise: the trade union aspect of the case and the caricatured form of the speech.

The majority first downplayed the importance of the trade union aspect of the case. Instead of strengthening the applicants' position, the fact that the speech was uttered in a labour context rather appears to have weakened their claim. According to the majority, 'certain manifestations of the right to freedom of expression that may be legitimate in other contexts are not legitimate in that of labour relations'.[18] The majority also ignored the form of the speech at issue: a caricature. Despite the availability of case law that specifically deals with caricatures,[19] the majority refused to reference it. It attached no weight to the fact that the accusations were depicted in the form of a cartoon, which by its very nature aims to exaggerate and ridicule.

Both omissions from the majority's reasoning were strongly criticised by the dissenting judges. Regarding the majority's downplaying of the trade union aspect of the case, the dissenting judges lamented that the majority 'brushes aside, somewhat artificially, the trade union dimension of the case'.[20] The dissenters moreover criticised the majority's claim that freedom of expression is more limited in labour contexts: '[w]e are puzzled by such an assertion ... the argument of possible disruption in the workplace is one that has been traditionally used in order to justify *greater* protection of freedom of expression and not *less* protection'.[21] Because the majority ignored the trade union aspect of the case,

18 Ibid. at para 76.

19 *Vereinigung Bildender Künstler v Austria* [2007] ECHR 79.

20 Joint dissenting opinion of Judges Tulkens, David Thór Björgvinsson, Jočienė, Popović and Vučinić in *Palomo Sánchez, supra* note 17 at para 3 (emphasis removed).

21 Ibid. at para 18 (emphases in original).

the dissenting judges finally pointed out, they failed to recognise that the applicants' dismissal constituted a '"chilling effect" on the conduct of trade unionists'.[22]

Regarding the cartoon, the dissenting judges noted that 'it is a caricature, which, whilst being vulgar and tasteless in nature, should be taken for what it is – a satirical representation'.[23] They critiqued the majority's utter failure to attach any weight thereto:

> [i]n other cases the Court has recognised the satirical nature of an expression, publication or caricature. In refusing to take that nature into account in the present case, the judgment gives the curious impression of placing trade union freedom of expression at a lower level than that of artistic freedom and of treating it more restrictively.[24]

Whatever one's opinion on the substantive outcome of *Palomo Sánchez* may be,[25] the majority judgment clearly downplayed the relevance of one factor (the trade union dimension of the case) and outright refused to mention another relevant factor (criticism by way of caricature). The majority judgment moreover failed to explain *why* these factors would be irrelevant to the balancing exercise. Since *prima facie* crucial factors were downplayed within or omitted from the majority's balancing exercise, its judgment should not come as a surprise. One plausible explanation for the majority's failures is that they were needed to secure the outcome the majority wished to obtain: a ruling against the trade union members. Subjective or intuitive preferences on the part of the judges in the majority would explain why crucial factors were downplayed or omitted in the reconstruction of the balancing exercise, which was intended to bolster – rather than inform – the majority's preferred outcome. The open ended balancing methodology employed by the ECtHR allows, if not invites, situations in which such subjective preferences steer the outcome of conflicting human rights cases.

The remedy and a good example

What can be done about this? Subjective or intuitive preferences can be neutralised – or at least minimised – in several ways. First, one may, along with Patrick McFadden and others, insist on (a return to) rule-based syllogism.[26] Second, one may, along with Marko Novak and others, seek refuge in the structured proportionality test.[27] In this book, I will follow neither route. Instead, I aim to

22 Ibid. at para 17.
23 Ibid. at para 11.
24 Ibid.
25 Further on, in Chapter 6, I explain how application of the structured balancing test supports an alternative outcome in *Palomo Sánchez*, against the majority judgment.
26 McFadden, *supra* note 14.
27 Novak, *supra* note 15 at 107–108.

provide a third way. In Chapter 1, I already rejected the relevance of specificationism – which relies on the formulation of exceptions to rights in the form of rules – to conflicts between human rights. In the same chapter, I argued that conflicts between human rights should not be resolved through application of the 'traditional' proportionality test.

Instead, I posit, courts should employ the structured balancing test outlined in Chapter 4 and developed in detail in Chapter 6. Employing that test will go a long way towards addressing the role of subjective preferences in balancing. The structured nature of the test targets the invitation that open ended balancing tests extend to such preferences. Closing the door on subjective preferences entirely may well prove impossible. But narrowing the opening by infusing the balancing test with structure will at least *reduce* the impact of subjective preferences on judicial reasoning. Introducing a structured balancing test composed of a limited number of criteria forces judges to consider all relevant factors, rather than employing a pick-and-choose strategy. By relying on the construction and comparison of nets of reasons, the structured balancing test moreover invites judges to explicate the relationship between invoked factors in balancing. This, finally, nudges judges to render a comparative judgment on the relative strength of reasons in favour of human rights in conflict. Since the outcome of a particular human rights conflict can, if the test is applied correctly, only be determined by running through the steps consecutively, there should be less room for outcomes predetermined by subjective preferences.

Interestingly, the ECtHR has taken important strides in the direction of a more structured balancing test in recent years. The Court's case law thus not only illustrates the bad; it also offers 'best practices'. One key development is the Court's recent elaboration of a limited set of criteria to guide balancing exercises in particular human rights conflicts: between freedom of expression, on the one hand, and the right to private life or the right to reputation, on the other. In *Von Hannover v Germany (No. 2)* and *Axel Springer AG v Germany*, the ECtHR indicated that balancing in these particular conflicts should take place with reference to the following criteria: (1) contribution of the publication to a debate of general interest; (2) how well known the person concerned is and what the subject of the report is; (3) prior conduct of the person concerned; (4) the content, form and consequences of the publication; (5) the circumstances in which the photos were taken/the method of obtaining the information and its veracity; and (6) the severity of the sanction imposed.[28]

By explicitly listing an exhaustive set of criteria to guide the balancing exercise, the Court infused its balancing test with some much needed structure. There remain, however, clear limitations. First, the Court does not apply the *Axel Springer/Von Hannover (No. 2)* criteria consistently. In several subsequent cases, without explaining why, the Court either reverts to criteria established in its

28 *Von Hannover v Germany (No. 2)* [2012] ECHR 228; *Axel Springer AG v Germany* [2012] ECHR 227.

earlier case law or balances without reference to any structuring criteria at all.[29] Second, and more importantly, nearly all the Court's criteria lose their relevance outside the free speech context. They can thus not be applied to resolve other types of conflicts.

Although the exhaustive listing of relevant criteria in *Von Hannover (No. 2)* and *Axel Springer* is certainly an important step forward, it remains an imperfect solution. To arrive at a more comprehensive balancing test for the resolution of conflicts between human rights, I intend to move a few steps further than the Court has gone so far. I will, in particular, propose a structured balancing test that can be applied to a wide range of conflicts. Yet, in the implementation of that test, the *Von Hannover (No. 2)* and *Axel Springer* criteria may well prove relevant, in the sense that they may be utilised to concretise the structured balancing test in applying it to specific types of conflicts.

Intermezzo: a quick quiz

The reader has shown admirable patience thus far. At this stage, I would like to reward her/him with some respite before I continue. A brief intermezzo for your entertainment, if you will. I would kindly invite the reader to take a quick quiz. The results may or may not prove relevant.

1. If it takes 5 machines 5 minutes to make 5 plastic bottles, how long would it take 100 machines to make 100 plastic bottles? ____ minutes.
2. Roberto's father John, who is extremely proud of his heritage and his first name in particular, has three sons. His youngest son is called Jeff. His middle son is called Jack. What is the name of John's oldest and first born son? __ .
3. In a lake, there is a patch of lily pads. Every day, the patch doubles in size. If it takes 48 days for the patch to cover the entire lake, how long would it take for the patch to cover half of the lake? ____ days.
4. Two trains leave different cities at the same time, travelling at different speeds. Train A travels from Paris to Brussels at 80 km/h. Train B travels the opposite trajectory, from Brussels to Paris, at 50 km/h. If the distance between Paris and Brussels is 260 km, how long after their departure will both trains cross each other? After _____ hours and _____ minutes.
5. A baseball bat and a ball cost €1.10 in total. The bat costs €1.00 more than the ball. How much does the ball cost? ____ cents.

Intuitive reasoning and balancing

The quiz does, of course, have a purpose. It is intended to have the reader experience the difference between two modes of reasoning: intuitive and analytical (or deliberative) reasoning. Questions 2 and 4 of the quiz are mere distractions.

29 For an example of the former, see *Brosa v Germany* [2014] ECHR 549. For examples of the latter, see *Armellini and Others v Austria* [2015] ECHR 388; *Fürst-Pfeifer*, *supra* note 6.

The important questions are 1, 3 and 5. If all has gone well, the reader will have given an intuitively attractive, but incorrect answer to at least one of those questions. The intuitive, but incorrect answers to questions 1, 3 and 5 are '100 minutes', '24 days' and '10 cents', respectively. The correct answers are '5 minutes', '47 days' and '5 cents', respectively. Even if the reader has answered all three questions correctly, she/he may have first experienced a 'flash' in which the incorrect answers came to mind. This is no coincidence.

Questions 1, 3 and 5 of the quiz reflect a slightly modified version of Shane Frederick's Cognitive Reflection Test (CRT).[30] The CRT is designed to illustrate and test the difference between intuitive and analytical reasoning. Each question of the test provides an intuitively appealing (*i.e.* easily accessible) answer that appears to be correct, but turns out to be false.[31] Finding the correct answer requires analysis.[32] When unexpectedly confronted with the CRT, most persons – most readers of this book included – fail to provide correct answers to all three questions. When Frederick originally administered the CRT to 3,428 respondents, mostly undergraduates at American universities,[33] the mean CRT score was 1.24 (out of 3).[34] In other words, on average less than half of the questions were answered correctly. Frederick also found that, as hypothesised, the intuitively appealing answers dominated among the wrong answers.[35] He further noted that the respondents who answered correctly had often first considered the intuitively appealing answer.[36]

In a further study, particularly interesting for our concerns with judicial reasoning, Chris Guthrie *et al.* presented Frederick's CRT to 295 unsuspecting circuit court judges in the United States (as part of a longer questionnaire).[37] The 252 judges who answered all three questions scored an average 1.23 out of 3.[38] Guthrie *et al.* further found that judges who had answered incorrectly had often given the intuitively appealing answers (57.4 per cent on the widget (plastic bottles) puzzle, 68 per cent on the lily patch puzzle and 88.4 per cent on the bat-and-ball puzzle).[39] The study by Guthrie *et al.* thus confirms that judges – like the rest of us – may be misled by intuitive reasoning. But does this finding have

30 Shane Frederick, 'Cognitive Reflection and Decision Making', 19 *Journal of Economic Perspectives* (2005), 25–42. The key modifications from the original test are: (1) in relation to question 1, the machines make 'plastic bottles' instead of the original 'widgets'; and (2) in relation to question 5, the word 'baseball' has been added before 'bat' and the amount is expressed in euros instead of US dollars.

31 Ibid.

32 Ibid.

33 Ibid. at 28.

34 Ibid. at 29.

35 Ibid. at 27.

36 Ibid. at 27 (as indicated by introspection, verbal reports and scribbles in the margins).

37 Chris Guthrie *et al.*, 'Blinking on the Bench: How Judges Decide Cases', 93 *Cornell Law Review* (2007), 13.

38 Ibid. at 13–14.

39 Ibid. at 16.

any bearing on the ability of judges to reason well in adjudicating human rights conflicts? I will answer that separate question with a qualified 'yes'.

The role of intuition in judging

The role of intuition in judging is notoriously contested and fiercely debated. Legal formalists insist that judges restrict themselves to applying the law in a rational, logical and deliberative manner.[40] Legal realists, conversely, claim that judges decide cases on the basis of intuitions or hunches,[41] to afterwards rationalise these decisions and present them in the form of deliberative reasoning.[42] I will rely on insights from cognitive psychology to suggest that the truth, as with so many things, probably lies somewhere in the middle: judges arguably often engage in what Kenneth Hammond calls 'quasirationality', a mode of reasoning that lies somewhere in between pure intuition and pure analysis.[43]

Testing this hypothesis is difficult, because – aside from through anecdotal references[44] – we know little about *how* judges actually decide (hard) cases.[45] Most judges are understandably loath to acknowledge reliance, if any, on intuitive reasoning in adjudicating (hard) cases. The results of judicial labour – judgments – cannot assist us either, since they may either offer an accurate reflection of judges' analytical reasoning or merely provide a rationalisation of intuitive thought processes (or something in between). Since the parties and the broader community have to be persuaded of the validity of judgments, they are invariably couched in the language of deliberative reasoning. This does not mean, however, that intuitive

40 See, for instance, David L. Shapiro, 'In Defense of Judicial Candor', 100 *Harvard Law Review* (1987), 731–750.

41 Joseph C. Hutcheson Jr, 'The Judgment Intuitive: The Function of the "Hunch" in Judicial Decision', 14 *Cornell Law Quarterly* (1928), 278 ('when the case is difficult or involved … I, after canvassing all the available material at my command, and duly cogitating upon it, give my imagination play, and brooding over the cause, wait for the feeling, the hunch – that intuitive flash of understanding which makes the connection between question and decision').

42 See, for instance, George Wright, 'The Role of Intuition in Judicial Decisionmaking', 42 *Houston Law Review* (2006), 1381–1424; Hutcheson, *supra* note 41.

43 On the need for legal theory to be responsive to developments in cognitive psychology, see Amelia Amaya, 'Ten Theses on Coherence in Law', in Michał Araszkiewicz and Jaromír Šavelka (eds), *Coherence: Insights from Philosophy, Jurisprudence and Artificial Intelligence* (Springer, 2013), 243–267.

44 See, for instance, Hutcheson, *supra* note 41; Nussberger, *supra* note 14.

45 Seymour Epstein *et al.* have developed a Rational–Experiential Inventory (REI), aimed at measuring the extent to which persons rely on intuitive and analytical reasoning. See Seymour Epstein *et al.*, 'Individual Differences in Intuitive–Experiential and Analytical–Rational Thinking Styles', 71 *Journal of Personality and Social Psychology* (1996), 390–405. To my knowledge, however, the REI – which consists of statements like 'The notion of thinking abstractly is not appealing to me' and 'I believe in trusting my hunches' – has not been tested on judges in ways that are relevant to our current concerns.

thought processes are irrelevant to judging. It just means that these thought processes – if and when they have played a role – are hidden from sight.

Occasionally, however, judges hint at the relevance of intuition – and analysis – to judging.[46] In the ECHR context, in particular, separate opinions shed some light on the role of intuition in judicial reasoning. In their separate opinions, some judges reference the importance of what 'experience and common sense teach[es] us [judges]',[47] while others emphasise the 'self-evident' nature of certain violations.[48] This hints at the potential relevance to adjudication of intuitions or at least quasirationality, which has been equated with 'common sense'.[49] Certain judges also admit, in their separate opinions, that 'on (further) reflection' they have changed their mind about certain cases. This may occur when a judge has heard the same case before the Chamber and the Grand Chamber.[50] On rare occasions, judges in this situation explain that they 'have realised that the third violation of Article [X] ... did not even occur! ... I considered this complaint to be genuine and distinct; on reflection, I consider it artificial and pointless'[51] or that 'the material and arguments before the Grand Chamber did not differ in any significant respect from those before the Chamber. I have, nevertheless concluded, on further reflection, that my previous view on the main issue was wrong'.[52]

Such references to a change of mind (or heart?) 'on reflection' imply that the judges perceive their previous judgment to have been based on insufficient analysis. Presumably, it was thus located more towards the intuitive side of the cognitive spectrum.

We should, however, resist the urge to jump to conclusions here. None of the above examples confirm – or even necessarily imply – that judges rely on intuitive reasoning when adjudicating human rights cases. Yet, they do offer us some insight into the *possibility* thereof. Before we go on to examine whether this is problematic, we need a firmer grasp on the role of intuitive and analytical reasoning in cognition, and in law.

46 Hutcheson, *supra* note 41.

47 Partly dissenting opinion of Judge Palm joined by Judges Jungwiert, Levits, Panţîru, Kovler and Marcus-Helmons to *Cyprus v Turkey* [2001] ECHR 331.

48 Partly dissenting opinion of Judge Costa to *Kyprianou v Cyprus* [2005] ECHR 873, para 6.

49 Kenneth R. Hammond *et al.*, 'Direct Comparison of the Efficacy of Intuitive and Analytical Cognition in Expert Judgment', 17 *IEEE Transactions on Systems, Man, and Cybernetics: Systems* (1987), 755.

50 This is possible because the national judge always sits on both the Chamber and the Grand Chamber in cases against her/his state. The President and Vice-Presidents of the Court, moreover, always sit on the Grand Chamber. If one of them also happened to be part of the Chamber, she/he will thus hear the same case twice.

51 Partly dissenting opinion of Judge Costa to *Kyprianou*, *supra* note 48 at para 7 (emphasis added).

52 Concurring opinion of Judge Bratza to *Dickson v the United Kingdom* [2007] ECHR 1050 (emphasis added).

Intuitive and analytical reasoning in cognition, and in law

In cognitive psychology, widespread agreement exists on the existence of two cognitive processes: intuitive reasoning and analytical (or deliberative) reasoning.[53] As Nobel Prize winner Daniel Kahneman explains,

> [t]here is considerable agreement on the characteristics that distinguish the two types of cognitive processes … labelled System 1 and System 2 … The operations of System 1 [*i.e.* of intuitive reasoning] are fast, automatic, effortless, associative, and difficult to control or modify. The operations of System 2 [*i.e.* of deliberative reasoning] are slower, serial, effortful, and deliberatively controlled.[54]

Both systems thus function differently. Intuitive reasoning functions by way of impressions, which come to mind spontaneously (hence the term intuitive).[55] Intuitive judgments are 'flashes', snapshot considerations of perceptions or problems that 'directly reflect impressions'.[56] This description of intuitive reasoning in cognitive psychology is remarkably similar to (in)famous allusions to intuition in adjudication. Think, for instance, of Judge Hutcheson's description of the 'judicial hunch' as 'that intuitive flash of understanding which makes the connection between question and decision'.[57] Or recall Justice William Brennan's reference to 'passion' in the judicial process as 'the range of emotional and intuitive responses to a given set of facts or arguments, responses which often speed into our consciousness far ahead of the lumbering syllogism of reason'.[58]

The 'lumbering syllogism of reason' that closes Justice Brennan's quote, by contrast, is part of analytical reasoning. Analytical reasoning is more cumbersome

53 Daniel Kahneman, 'Maps of Bounded Rationality: A Perspective on Intuitive Judgment and Choice', Nobel Prize Lecture (8 December 2002), available at http://www.nobelprize.org/nobel_prizes/economic-sciences/laureates/2002/kahnemann-lecture.pdf (last accessed 18 April 2016), 49; Veronika Denes-Raj and Seymour Epstein, 'Conflict between Intuitive and Rational Processing: When People Behave against Their Better Judgment', 66 *Journal of Personality and Social Psychology* (1994), 819–829; Frederick, *supra* note 30 at 26; Guthrie *et al.*, *supra* note 37 at 7. Cass Sunstein has presented his views on the role of intuition and analysis in legal decision-making in several publications. See Daniel Kahneman and Cass Sunstein, 'Indignation: Psychology, Politics, Law', *University of Chicago John M. Olin Law & Economics Working Paper No. 346/Public Law and Legal Theory Working Paper No. 171* (July 2007), available at http://www.law.uchicago.edu/files/files/346.pdf (last accessed 18 April 2016); Cass Sunstein, 'Moral Heuristics and Moral Framing', 88 *Minnesota Law Review* (2004), 1556–1597; Cass Sunstein, 'Some Effects of Moral Indignation on Law', 33 *Vermont Law Review* (2009), 405–433.

54 Kahneman, *supra* note 53 at 450. See also Frederick, *supra* note 30 at 26; Denes-Raj and Epstein, *supra* note 53 at 819.

55 Kahneman, *supra* note 53 at 452.

56 Ibid. at 451.

57 Hutcheson, *supra* note 41 at 278.

58 William J. Brennan Jr, 'Reason, Passion, and "The Progress of the Law"', 10 *Cardozo Law Review* (1988), 9.

than intuitive reasoning. It functions more slowly, is effortful and requires justification through logic and evidence.[59] Question 4 of the quiz I presented earlier typifies what analytical reasoning requires. There is no intuitively appealing answer – no 'flash' response – available for question 4. Most readers will therefore immediately have engaged in analytical reasoning to answer it. This probably took longer and required more effort than answering the other questions, especially if the reader gave the intuitive (but incorrect) answers to questions 1, 3 and 5. The CRT is of course designed to illustrate the drawbacks of excessive confidence in intuitive reasoning. Yet, this does not mean that analytical reasoning necessarily outperforms intuitive reasoning. On the contrary, research shows that intuitive reasoning usually generates correct answers – sometimes even where analytical reasoning offers poorer judgments – and that it does so faster than analytical reasoning.[60] Intuitive reasoning can moreover be trained and improved, particularly in and by experts.[61]

On one key factor, the exact relationship between intuitive and analytical reasoning, cognitive psychology is divided. Traditionally, the relationship has been conceived of in terms of a duality, emphasising the dichotomy between intuitive and analytical reasoning.[62] One of the core functions of analytical reasoning is, then, to control the quality of thought processes by confirming, modifying or overriding intuitive judgments.[63] Yet, more recent research suggests that intuitive and analytical reasoning operate *jointly*, indicating that they are interactive systems.[64] This finding is difficult to square with the dichotomous view of the dual process account. Others have therefore proposed alternative approaches.[65] Kenneth Hammond's 'cognitive continuum' theory is particularly instructive.[66] On the cognitive continuum theory, judgments are placed on a continuum that ranges from fully intuitive to fully analytical. Unlike in the dual process account, there is thus also reasoning 'in between', *i.e.* between both ends of the continuum.[67] Hammond labels such reasoning 'quasirational'.[68] Quasirationality, I posit, is central to understanding judicial reasoning in conflicting human rights cases.

Hammond describes quasirationality 'as "resembling" rationality rather than being identical with it'.[69] He adds that '[i]t is of first importance to recognise that

59 Seymour Epstein *et al.*, *supra* note 45 at 391.
60 Seymour Epstein, 'Cognitive-Experiential Self-Theory', in David F. Barone *et al.* (eds), *Advanced Personality* (Springer, 1998), 234; Hammond *et al.*, *supra* note 49 at 766.
61 For discussion, see James Shanteau, 'Competence in Experts: The Role of Task Characteristics', 53 *Organizational Behavior and Human Decision Processes* (1992), 252–266.
62 Kahneman, *supra* note 53.
63 Ibid. at 481.
64 Denes-Raj and Epstein, *supra* note 53; Seymour Epstein *et al.*, *supra* note 45.
65 See, apart from the alternative discussed in the text, also Epstein, *supra* note 60.
66 Hammond *et al.*, *supra* note 49 at 754.
67 Kenneth R. Hammond, 'Intuition, No! ... Quasirationality, Yes!', 21 *Psychological Inquiry* (2010), 330.
68 Ibid.
69 Ibid.

"quasirationality" is not merely flawed rationality, or rationality poorly carried out'.[70] Instead, it is 'the normal form of cognition—human judgment that is neither purely analytical nor purely intuitive but involves differing proportions of each, depending on which attributes are present in our normal activities'.[71] According to Hammond,

> the modifier 'quasi' is employed because the process fails to achieve logical perfection due to an absence of current knowledge, *or* skill, in organizing the knowledge it is based on, *or* because the person is simply forced to rely on unreliable, partially valid information … as is normally the case.[72]

In other words, because of knowledge, skill or contextual limitations, quasi-rationality is often the best we can aim for. I propose that quasirationality is a prime candidate for describing the kind of reasoning involved in the adjudication of human rights conflicts.[73]

Quasirationality in human rights practice

As noted earlier, we should be careful in drawing conclusions from the study by Guthrie *et al.* on judges' responses to Frederick's Cognitive Reflection Test (CRT). It is not because most judges, like the majority of us, resort to (incorrect) intuitive reasoning to answer the CRT's questions that they necessarily do the same in judging cases that come before them. Indeed, as Guthrie *et al.* note, 'judges undoubtedly exercise greater care when ruling in court than when responding to CRT questions'.[74] There are two reasons to suppose as much. First, there are clear differences between the CRT's questions and the kinds of cases (including human rights conflicts) that judges are routinely asked to adjudicate. Second, judges are generally not experts in resolving the kinds of puzzles included in the CRT, while they *are* (supposed to be) experts in adjudication.

On the second point, the chess master who, unlike the novice, immediately perceives all available options on the board is often invoked to illustrate how intuitive thought processes can be honed through practice and experience.[75] Might the same apply to judges in fulfilling their adjudicatory role?[76] Judge Hutcheson certainly thought that the practical role played by judges requires

70 Ibid.

71 Ibid.

72 Ibid.

73 Ibid. at 333 (referencing the work of Benjamin Cardozo as a prime example of quasirationality in judicial thought processes).

74 Guthrie *et al.*, *supra* note 37 at 18.

75 Kahneman, *supra* note 53 at 453; Guthrie *et al.*, *supra* note 37 at 30; Kahneman and Sunstein, *supra* note 53 at 4–5.

76 See also Brett Scharffs, 'Adjudication and the Problems of Incommensurability', 42 *William and Mary Law Review* (2001), 1420.

reliance on intuitions: '[t]he purely contemplative philosopher may project himself into an abstract field of contemplation where he reasons, but practical men, and in that judges must be included, must have impulses'.[77] Yet, as Richard Posner explains, this must not lead us to 'go to the opposite extreme and suppose intuition a sure guide to sound decision making. An intuitive decision may ignore critical factors that lie outside the range of the person's experience that informs his intuition'.[78] Moreover, as pointed out by Guthrie *et al.*, there are limitations to the ability of judges to hone their intuitive reasoning skills: '[u]nlike chess grandmasters, judges operate in an environment that does not allow them to perfect their intuitive decision-making processes'.[79]

Here, the psychological literature offers crucial insights. James Shanteau explains that judgement and decision research, on the one hand, and cognitive science research, on the other, support opposing views on the ability of experts to avoid the kinds of pitfalls and errors associated with intuitive reasoning.[80] Judgement and decision research, Shanteau states, 'paints a dismal picture of the ability of experts', on which a 'common explanation for [their] low level of performance is that experts often rely on heuristics, which in turn lead to systematic biases'.[81] An example of such a bias, particularly relevant to our concerns with balancing human rights, is 'confirmation bias'.

Confirmation bias occurs when decision makers (say, judges at the ECtHR) test a hypothesis (*e.g.* an intuitive judgment in a conflicting human rights case) by considering more evidence that confirms it than evidence that denies it.[82] Confirmation bias entails the 'overweighting of some aspects of the information and underweighting or neglect of others', which 'usually occurs automatically, without explicit intent to do so'.[83] Applied to judges who balance human rights, confirmation bias may lead them to (unintentionally) mould the balancing exercise to support an outcome they have intuitively 'perceived'. This would explain situations, as described in the discussion on subjectivity in balancing, in which

77 Hutcheson, *supra* note 41 at 286.

78 Richard A. Posner, 'The Role of the Judge in the Twenty-first Century', 86 *Boston University Law Review* (2006), 1064.

79 Guthrie *et al.*, *supra* note 37 at 32.

80 Shanteau, *supra* note 61.

81 Ibid. at 253–254. For an empirical study that tests judges' vulnerability to 'cognitive illusions', which may result from reliance on heuristics, see Chris Guthrie *et al.*, 'Inside the Judicial Mind', 86 *Cornell Law Review* (2001), 777–830 (finding that judges are – to a greater or lesser extent – vulnerable to five 'cognitive illusions': 'anchoring (making estimates based on irrelevant starting points); framing (treating economically equivalent gains and losses differently); hindsight bias (perceiving past events to have been more predictable than they actually were); the representativeness heuristic (ignoring important background statistical information in favor of individuating information); and egocentric biases (overestimating one's own abilities)' (at 784)).

82 Carey K. Morewedge and Daniel Kahneman, 'Associative Processes in Intuitive Judgment', 14 *Trends in Cognitive Science* (2010), 435.

83 Ibid.

judges downplay and/or omit *prima facie* relevant factors in/from open ended balancing exercises.[84] According to judgement and decision research, even expert decision makers – among which we should include judges at the ECtHR – cannot avoid falling prey to these biases.[85]

Yet, this conclusion is disputed by cognitive science research, which has 'shown expert superiority over novices in nearly every aspect of cognitive functioning'.[86] In his research on intuitive reasoning by firemen, Gary Klein, for instance, shows that experienced firemen develop specific expertise that allows them to employ highly adaptive 'recognitional strategies'.[87] Through these recognitional strategies, experienced firemen are – unlike novice firemen – able to make quick and effective decisions in situations that simply do not leave time for the kinds of weighing of options involved in analytical reasoning.[88] Yet, such recognitional strategies – a hallmark of intuitive reasoning – 'are less likely to be used with highly combinatorial problems, in situations where justifications are required, and in cases where the views of different stakeholders have to be taken into account'.[89] Seymour Epstein has also noted that, due to its long evolutionary pedigree, intuitive reasoning 'is often adaptive, but it is ill-suited for solving problems that require logical analysis and an understanding of abstract relations'.[90] In other words, intuitive reasoning skills can be honed by experts in some areas, but not in others.

Shanteau argues that task characteristics are a key factor in explaining why some experts perform well in intuitive decision making, while others do not.[91] Court judges are, studies show, among the experts that perform poorly.[92] Shanteau offers a number of task-related explanations for the poor performance of judges. First, those who perform poorly are generally confronted with 'stimuli [that] are dynamic and generally involve human behavior' (as opposed to 'stimuli that are relatively constant').[93] Second, they perform tasks that are more 'changeable' and in which 'conditions differ frequently' (as opposed to tasks with 'repetitive-similar conditions').[94] Third, they have less 'opportunity to receive and respond to feedback' and thus 'fewer chances to learn'.[95] All three factors apply to judges

84 See *supra* 'Subjectivity in balancing', p. 00.
85 Kahneman, *supra* note 53 at 459; Shanteau, *supra* note 61 at 253–254.
86 Shanteau, *supra* note 61 at 254.
87 Gary A. Klein, 'A Recognition-Primed Decision (RPD) Model of Rapid Decision Making', in Gary A. Klein *et al.* (eds), *Decision Making in Action: Models and Methods (Cognition and Literacy)* (Ablex Publishing, 1993), 138–147.
88 Ibid.
89 Ranaan Lipshitz *et al.*, 'Taking Stock of Naturalistic Decision Making', 14 *Journal of Behavioral Decision Making* (2001), 337 (Gary Klein is one of the co-authors of the Lipshitz *et al.* article).
90 Epstein *et al.*, *supra* note 45 at 391.
91 Shanteau, *supra* note 61.
92 Ibid. at 258.
93 Ibid.
94 Ibid.
95 Ibid. at 259.

at the ECtHR when adjudicating human rights conflicts (and other cases). ECtHR judges are faced with dynamic cases in which human behaviour plays a key role. The conditions of their task are moreover frequently changing, in the sense that the concrete circumstances of any given case may have a profound impact on how judges will go about judging. ECtHR judges, finally, are rarely exposed to feedback, given that most of their judgments – save for those that go to the Grand Chamber – are never appealed.[96] Human rights adjudication, in short, involves the kinds of 'highly combinatorial problems, in situations where justifications are required, and in cases where the views of different stakeholders have to be taken into account'[97] that render intuitive reasoning inapt.

Since overzealous reliance on intuitive reasoning by judges – even as experts – is prone to lead to poor decision making,[98] they should arguably be nudged towards the analytical side of Hammond's cognitive continuum in resolving human rights conflicts.[99] Yet, because of the nature of their adjudicatory task, it is arguably impossible for judges to engage in pure analysis. In adjudicating conflicting human rights cases, judges cannot aim for correspondence with empirical facts. Adjudicating a human rights conflict drastically differs from answering, say, question 3 of the above quiz. There is no predefined true answer against which judges' performance can be measured. The involvement of normative – as opposed to empirical – elements arguably bars access to pure analytical reasoning. Pure analysis may even be an unattractive goal to aim for in the adjudication of human rights conflicts, since adjudication 'closer to the analytic end of the cognitive continuum is a disturbingly dehumanizing experience'.[100] Instead, the most we arguably can – and should – expect from judges is that they engage in quasirationality when balancing human rights.[101]

Under the Court's current open ended balancing test, however, this aim appears to be out of reach. As noted by Olivier de Schutter and Françoise Tulkens, 'the less rigorous the judicial methodology used – the more the judicial decision depends on elements of intuition or "hunch"".'[102] Psychological research, for its

96 See, *mutatis mutandis*, Mandeep K. Dhami *et al.*, 'Quasirational Models of Sentencing', 4 *Journal of Applied Research in Memory and Cognition* (2015), 241 (arguing similarly in the context of their study on sentencing by judges: '[s]entencers receive little or no feedback on the outcomes of their own or others' sentencing decisions … Some form of feedback may be available when a decision is appealed, but this is rare').

97 Lipshitz *et al.*, *supra* note 89 at 337.

98 Guthrie *et al.*, *supra* note 81 (showing that, in experimental settings, 'judges rely on cognitive processes that are likely to induce them to make systematic errors', but noting that their study 'does not conclusively demonstrate that judges actually make such errors in the courtroom' (both at 819)).

99 Ibid. at 245.

100 Ibid.

101 See, *mutatis mutandis*, ibid. (presenting a similar argument in the context of sentencing).

102 Olivier De Schutter and Françoise Tulkens, 'Rights in Conflict: The European Court of Human Rights as a Pragmatic Institution', in Eva Brems (ed.), *Conflicts between Fundamental Rights* (Intersentia, 2008), 202. See further, Wright, *supra* note 42 at 1398 ('[t]hat intuition

part, suggests that the performance of decision makers who are faced with complex task characteristics can be improved through use of decision aids, which are prevalent among experts that do perform well.[103] The structured balancing test I propose in Chapter 6 is the kind of decisional aid that would provide a rigorous judicial methodology for the adjudication of conflicts between human rights. Use of the structured balancing test would nudge judges towards quasirationality, thereby making their judgments more rational than under pure intuitive reasoning.[104] But it would also increase the coherence of judicial reasoning in and across conflicting human rights cases.

Reaching for coherence in judicial reasoning

Because balancing human rights entails answering profoundly normative questions on the strength of reasons in favour of – and against – human rights in conflict, correspondence with empirical facts is an unattainable, and inappropriate, aim to reach for. We are not trying to determine the market value of stolen property here. Instead, we are deeply embroiled in normative questions that are often open to persistent reasonable disagreement. Since no empirically accurate answers are available, achieving full rationality through pure analytical reasoning is arguably too much to ask for. But judges can and should be nudged towards quasirationality, located towards the analytical end of the cognitive continuum. One particularly promising way of getting there is through the use of decisional aids that aim to achieve coherence within and across cases. This should, in turn, go a long way towards minimising subjectivity in the adjudication of human rights conflicts.

Yet, coherence in law is notoriously difficult to define. It certainly requires more than mere consistency, *i.e.* the absence of logical contradictions.[105] Logical consistency is a necessary, but insufficient condition for obtaining coherence in

plays an important role in judicial balancing tests should hardly be a surprise'); Zucca, *supra* note 1 at 449 ('[b]alancing often seems arbitrary, and little more than window-dressing for unsophisticated ethical intuitions'); Paul-Erik N. Veel, 'Incommensurability, Proportionality and Rational Legal Decision-making', 4 *Law and Ethics of Human Rights* (2010), 192 ('intuitive weighing … seems less acceptable as a basis for judicial decisions on the appropriate balancing of parties' rights' than it may be 'as a means of deciding between various dinner options').

103 Shanteau, *supra* note 61 at 260. See also Guthrie *et al.*, *supra* note 81 at 828 ('The legal system might also adopt procedural, evidentiary, and even substantive rules to minimize the deleterious effects of cognitive illusions on judicial decision making').

104 See, *mutatis mutandis*, Dhami *et al.*, *supra* note 96 at 242–245 (arguing, in relation to sentencing, that judges benefit from sentencing guidelines that encourage them to engage in more analytical reasoning, but submitting that quasirationality in sentencing is the most appropriate and practical mode of cognition for the task at hand).

105 Neil MacCormick, 'Coherence in Legal Justification', in Aleksander Peczenik *et al.* (eds), *Theory of Legal Science – Proceedings of the Conference on Legal Theory and Philosophy of Science, Lund, Sweden, December 11–14, 1983* (D. Reidel Publishing Company, 1983), 235; Aldo Schiavello, 'On "Coherence" and "Law": An Analysis of Different Models', 14 *Ratio Juris* (2001), 236.

law.[106] Coherence also requires something that can only be expressed in rather abstract terms. It requires that a legal system 'fits together',[107] 'hangs together'[108] or 'makes sense'.[109] To illustrate the difference between consistency and coherence in law, Neil MacCormick offers his famous example of a statute that imposes different speed limits for different cars, depending on the colour they are painted.[110] MacCormick explains that such a statute is not inconsistent, but *is* incoherent because it fails to make sense.[111] Indeed, no plausible 'rational' justification exists for the difference imposed by the statute. The statute is arbitrary. Some *measure of* rational justification of legal norms and decisions, having them 'make sense', is thus a central element of coherence.

In respect of the adjudication of human rights conflicts, achieving coherence arguably requires two things. First, it requires the absence of logical contradictions within or between cases. Second, it requires that the whole body of case law 'makes sense'. To make the latter requirement more concrete, we could say that it implies that decisions in individual cases should fit together with those in other cases, be maximally rationally justified and give proper guidance for future cases. Coherence thus calls for increased rationality, objectivity and predictability.[112]

With those objectives in mind, let us examine what coherence theories bring to the table. Coherence theories in law aim to present an alternative to both the formal model of rationality of legal positivism and the abandonment of rationality by sceptics. As Amalia Amaya explains: '[f]aced with the failure of attempts to model [legal] rationality after scientific rationality … the only viable response is not skepticism … [instead] [c]oherentism is … proposed as an alternative to scientific models of knowledge'.[113] It is commonplace to note that because legal norms and decisions involve practical and/or moral reasoning, they cannot be 'true' or 'false' in the scientific meaning of the words. Instead, as emphasised by Aleksander Peczenik, they are normative propositions that claim to be *right* or *correct*, rather than true.[114]

The deductive approach of legal positivism, which relies on the truth value of legal norms and decisions, thus knows considerable limitations, not least in the

106 Aleksander Peczenik, 'Law, Morality, Coherence and Truth', 7 *Ratio Juris* (1994), 167.
107 Leonor Moral Soriano, 'A Modest Notion of Coherence in Legal Reasoning. A Model for the European Court of Justice', 16 *Ratio Juris* (2003), 310.
108 MacCormick, *supra* note 105 at 235.
109 Ibid.; Schiavello, *supra* note 105 at 237.
110 MacCormick, *supra* note 105 at 235.
111 Ibid.
112 On the link between coherence and legal certainty, see, for instance, Amaya, *supra* note 43.
113 Amelia Amaya, 'Ten Theses on Coherence and Law' (2012), available at http://papers.ssrn.com/sol3/papers.cfm?abstract_id=2064295 (last accessed 18 April 2016), 25.
114 Peczenik, *supra* note 11 at 45–46, 186–187. See also Scharffs, *supra* note 76 at 1423 ('[w]e routinely speak of judicial conclusions being correct or incorrect. By this we mean that the reasons that were, or that could have been, marshaled on behalf of a particular outcome are or are not more compelling than the reasons that were, or that could have been, marshaled on behalf of the alternatives').

domain of human rights conflicts. In hard cases in law, there exists no one *true* answer that can be logically deduced from a given set of premises, as one may scientifically deduce that, say, the ambient temperature is below 0°C from the fact that water freezes. Instead, lawyers and judges *argue* that one particular answer among several possible ones is the (most) *correct* or *right* one. In hard cases, this is the answer that best responds to the requirements of justice.[115]

In short, formal rationality in law needs to be cast aside in favour of something else.[116] That something else can be scepticism about the ability to rationally justify judicial decisions. But it can also be a positive response, an attempt to put forth a more fitting conception of rationality in the legal context. Coherentism aims to present such a broader conception of rationality.[117] In what follows, I will examine its claims and adapt them to the specific context of the adjudication of human rights conflicts.

Coherence theories in law tend to focus on the meta-level of the legal system.[118] As system theories, they aim to provide the necessary criteria for rendering legal systems coherent. Here, however, we are concerned with the narrower issue of coherence in judicial reasoning. Certain coherence theories also prove valuable in this more specific context. The coherence theory of Aleksander Peczenik, in particular, is of immediate salience to the adjudication of human rights conflicts. Peczenik's theory rests on four central propositions. Peczenik first argues that coherence is the central requirement for legal argumentation's claim to rightness or correctness. He also argues that legal justification, especially in hard cases, is the result of balancing, and that such balancing needs to be underscored by coherent reasons.[119] He further argues that the requisite coherence can be obtained by constructing chains of arguments (P1 supports P2, P2 in turn supports P3, etc.).[120] He finally argues that the last step in balancing is different: it cannot be underscored by further reasons, but necessarily requires a moment of subjectivity or personal intuition.[121]

In light of what preceded, Peczenik's propositions are simultaneously useful and problematic. They are useful to the extent that they provide a clear link between legal justification, balancing in hard cases (which human rights conflicts generally are), and the relevance of coherence to such balancing. Peczenik's

115 This substantive requirement is imperative, because the existence of coherence in law does not say anything about the values pursued by a legal system. As Neil MacCormick explains, the legal system of the NSDAP during the Nazi regime in Germany could have been perfectly coherent, but we would not label it as just. See MacCormick, *supra* note 105 at 243–244.

116 Ronald Dworkin, *Taking Rights Seriously* (Harvard University Press, 1977); Robert Alexy, *A Theory of Constitutional Rights* (Oxford University Press, 2002).

117 Amaya, *supra* note 113 at 26.

118 See, for instance, Peczenik, *supra* note 11; MacCormick, *supra* note 105; Amelia Amaya, 'Legal Justification by Optimal Coherence', 24 *Ratio Juris* (2011), 304–329.

119 Peczenik, *supra* note 106 at 147 and 158; Peczenik, *supra* note 11 at 203.

120 Peczenik, *supra* note 106 at 147; Peczenik, *supra* note 11 at 137.

121 Peczenik, *supra* note 106 at 172; Peczenik, *supra* note 11 at 308.

coherence theory is thus particularly suited to assist in the resolution of human rights conflicts, given that I have insisted that balancing is the proper methodology to resolve such conflicts (when defusing and compromises have failed). As underscored by Amaya, 'coherence methods not only help us realize the different values that the law aims at promoting, but they also crucially help us deliberate about how to weigh and balance these values when they come into conflict'.[122]

But Peczenik's propositions are also problematic, to the extent that they *incorporate* an inevitable element of subjectivity or intuition, rather than aiming to circumvent the need therefor. Peczenik acknowledges that the final step of balancing is necessarily subjective or intuitive. Hence, the entire balancing exercise rests on intuition, while I have proposed to nudge judges towards quasirationality. Peczenik's conclusion, however, is only rendered inevitable by his reliance on *chains* of arguments to achieve coherence. Chains of arguments have two downsides. First, they render reasoning as weak as the weakest link between two arguments in the chain. Second, they are necessarily infinite. Chains of arguments are never fully supportive of a balancing outcome *unless* one argues, as Peczenik is forced to do, that at the end of the chain rests an ultimate argument that is 'taken for granted',[123] *i.e.* assumed to be correct on the basis of subjective or intuitive preferences.[124] Subjectivity and intuition in balancing are thus inevitable. The *inevitability* of this conclusion can, however, be avoided. One way to escape it is to follow Leonor Moral Soriano in search of coherence in judicial reasoning by constructing *nets* of arguments, rather than chains.[125]

Nets of arguments function differently from chains. Netted arguments are *mutually* supportive, whereas chained arguments are *sequentially* supportive. Each argument in a chain of arguments necessarily builds on the previous one (P1 supports P2, P2 in turn supports P3, etc.). This means that, to avoid infinite regress, one *must* accept that the ultimate argument at the outer end of the chain – what Peczenik calls the 'final act of weighing'[126] – cannot be supported by a further argument. Nets of arguments avoid this conclusion. Netted arguments mutually reinforce each other (P1 strengthens P2 and P3, P2 strengthens P1 and P3 and P3 strengthens P1 and P2). By constructing nets of arguments, it thus becomes possible to present a *finite* number of coherent arguments to justify a certain outcome. There is no need for an 'ultimate argument' that relies on subjective or intuitive preferences. This does *not* mean that nets of arguments are immune to subjectivity and intuitive preferences. But reliance thereon is at least no longer inevitable and can therefore – theoretically – be avoided. Because nets

122 Amaya, *supra* note 118 at 322.

123 Peczenik, *supra* note 11 at 308.

124 Ibid.; Peczenik, *supra* note 106 at 172.

125 Moral Soriano, *supra* note 107 at 319. For discussion of coherentism and nets of arguments, see Juan Manuel Pérez Bermejo, 'Coherence: An Outline in Six Metaphors and Four Rules', in Michał Araszkiewicz and Jaromír Šavelka (eds.), *Coherence: Insights from Philosophy, Jurisprudence and Artificial Intelligence* (Springer, 2013), 97–98

126 Peczenik, *supra* note 106 at 172.

of arguments have this clear advantage over chains of argument in achieving coherence in judicial reasoning,[127] I rely on the construction thereof in developing the structured balancing test for the resolution of human rights conflicts (as outlined in Chapter 4 and detailed in Chapter 6).

Preferential framing: a specific problem

In what preceded, I argued that open ended balancing tests, as employed by the ECtHR, allow – or even invite – judges to rely on subjective preferences in adjudicating human rights conflicts. I submitted that the use of a structured balancing test, composed of a limited set of criteria, would go a long way towards curbing such subjective preferences. I further claimed that such a structured balancing test could function as a decision aid to nudge judges towards quasirationality in adjudication, located towards the analytical side of the cognitive continuum. I finally linked quasirationality to the impossibility of correspondence with empirical facts in human rights adjudication. I posited that we should aim for coherence in the adjudication of human rights conflicts instead. This we can achieve by constructing nets of arguments, which – in turn – would avoid the inevitability of subjective and intuitive moments in balancing human rights. And thus, we have come full circle.

Yet, a final practical obstacle to balancing human rights remains. Whereas the previously discussed obstacles are general to human rights adjudication, the final obstacle only arises in particular settings: those in which one of the parties to a human rights conflict is replaced by the state in adjudication. This is what occurs, for instance, when a human rights conflict reaches the ECtHR in Strasbourg. The concomitant obstacle, introduced in Chapter 1, is 'preferential framing' in the construction of the balancing exercise.

Preferential framing in theory

Preferential framing refers to the process by which courts, like the ECtHR, frame conflicting human rights cases around the human right directly invoked in front of them, while neglecting (to a greater or lesser extent) the other human right at stake. In Chapter 1, I explained that the phenomenon of preferential framing is tied to procedural aspects of human rights adjudication, which turn a horizontal human rights conflict into a vertical one. This 'verticalization' process generally occurs in human/fundamental rights adjudication at the constitutional, supranational and international level.

At lower courts, often both parties to a human rights conflict (or their lawyers) appear in court. Think, for instance, of a dispute between a tabloid and a celebrity

127 A further advantage is that, contrary to chains of arguments, the supportive structure of nets of arguments is not as weak as the weakest link between two arguments. Its strength instead depends on the number of arguments and on how well they mutually support each other.

about the unauthorised publication of photographs that depict the latter in a private moment. In such a privacy case, both parties to the dispute will generally argue against each other, claiming priority of their respective rights in front of lower courts. When the human rights conflict reaches the supranational or international level, however, one of the parties will fade into the background. The party who has lost the earlier proceedings will now invoke her human right directly against the state, claiming that state actions in protecting the other party's human right have caused an unjustified human rights breach. The relevant court – the ECtHR, for instance – is thus no longer directly confronted with two right holders. Instead, one of the original parties has been replaced, as it were, by the state. The horizontal conflict between two private parties has transformed into a vertical one between a right holder and the state.

Human rights courts, in particular, are prone to construe such vertical cases in line with their primary task: protecting human rights against unjustified state infringements. They may thereby (unreflectively and unintentionally) focus first and foremost on the directly invoked human right, *i.e.* the right of the party who actually appears in front of them. In the process, the human right of the other party to the original conflict – who is now 'represented' by the state – tends to fade into the background. In other words, the case is framed around the directly invoked right, which thereby gains an edge.

The 'verticalization' of human rights conflicts thus creates a risk of preferential framing. This risk increases when judges on the bench intuitively prefer a finding in favour of the 'victim', *i.e.* the right holder that appears before them. Traditional human rights reasoning at the ECtHR, which operates on the basis of a 'priority-to-rights' principle, bolsters this effect. When judges at the Strasbourg Court frame a conflict around the directly invoked human right, while neglecting (to a greater or lesser extent) the other human right at stake, this may thus have disruptive effects on the outcome. Overemphasis on the directly invoked human right, coupled with a tendency to favour that right, may cause judges to rule in its favour without supporting their ruling with convincing reasons. Judges thereby (unconsciously) fall prey to what Charles Fried warned against more than half a century ago: 'under no circumstances should [a] Court formulate the conflict in a particular case, or identify the elements of the balance to be struck, in such a way that the statement itself prejudices the decision'.[128]

Preferential framing not only threatens to prejudice decisions in conflicting human rights cases. It also introduces an element of arbitrariness in the adjudication of such cases. When skewed by preferential framing effects, adjudication of human rights conflicts depends – at least in part – on the result of earlier proceedings.

When human right A prevails over human right B in earlier proceedings, preferential framing effects will grant the directly invoked right B the edge in front

128 Charles Fried, 'Two Concepts of Interests: Some Reflections on the Supreme Court's Balancing Test', 76 *Harvard Law Review* (1963), 763.

of human rights courts like the ECtHR. But if, in the same case, human right B were to prevail in earlier proceedings, things would be the other way around: preferential framing effects would now give human right A the edge in front of the human rights court. From the viewpoint of human rights theory, however, the outcome of earlier proceedings is an arbitrary factor. As I argue elsewhere,[129] because human rights in conflict deserve principled equal respect, neither should gain a substantive edge in balancing simply due to the outcome of earlier proceedings.[130] The Grand Chamber of the ECtHR recognised as much when it ruled, in setting out its new approach to defamation cases, that

> the outcome of the application should not, in principle, vary according to whether it has been lodged with the Court under Article 10 of the Convention by the publisher who has published the offending article or under Article 8 of the Convention by the person who was the subject of that article. Indeed, as a matter of principle these rights deserve equal respect.[131]

Preferential framing in human rights practice?

Preferential framing, as just described, certainly is a *theoretical* threat to the resolution of human rights conflicts. Yet, it is far from obvious that the problem also obtains in actual human rights practice.[132] For one thing, judges may be aware of the problem and may thus employ counterbalancing strategies. Since such strategies would function at the cognitive level, they may not be explicated in

129 Stijn Smet, 'Freedom of Expression and the Right to Reputation: Human Rights in Conflict', 26 *American University International Law Review* (2010), 183–236 (in which I discuss preferential framing effects in the Court's defamation case law).

130 In the ECHR context, however, the right that does not appear in front of the ECtHR may very well have a *procedural* edge, due in particular to the operation of the Court's margin of appreciation doctrine. Indeed, the Court has held that, in conflicting human rights cases, the state's margin of appreciation is in principle wide. As a result, the Court requires strong reasons before it will substitute its substantive judgment for that of the domestic courts. This plays in favour of the right that has prevailed in the domestic proceedings. See *Fernández Martínez v Spain* [2014] ECHR 615, para 123 and 125; *Von Hannover (No. 2)*, *supra* note 28 at para 107. In the text, however, I am not concerned with procedural aspects, including the impact of the margin of appreciation. I am, rather, concerned with substantive balancing. There, the statement that conflicting human rights deserve equal respect implies that neither should have an edge over the other due to the outcome of domestic proceedings.

131 *Axel Springer*, *supra* note 28 at para 87. See also *Von Hannover (No. 2)*, *supra* note 28 at para 106 (decided on the same day as *Axel Springer*).

132 See *contra* Dean Spielmann and Leto Cariolou, 'The Right to Protection of Reputation under the European Convention on Human Rights', in Dean Spielmann *et al.* (eds), *The European Convention on Human Rights, A Living Instrument – Essays in Honour of Christos L. Rozakis* (Bruylant, 2011), 584 (arguing, in the context of the Court's defamation case law, that this 'assumption is debatable' since there is in their view 'no reason in principle why the outcome of the Court's analysis would depend on how an application is framed, particularly given the nature of the Court's examination that involves precisely the application of the same principles concerning freedom of speech').

judicial decisions.[133] It may, therefore, prove difficult to establish whether preferential framing effects have any practical impact on the adjudication of human rights conflicts.

One promising way to nevertheless test the hypothesis that preferential framing occurs in human rights reasoning is by analysing case law on a specific conflict under both relevant human rights provisions. If preferential framing effects have a concrete impact on human rights adjudication, bringing the same conflict under different human rights provisions should have a demonstrable effect on the outcome. The defamation case law of the ECtHR is particularly suited to test this hypothesis, for various reasons. First, it involves a conflict between freedom of expression and the right to reputation that has – depending on the outcome of domestic proceedings – been brought before the ECtHR under both relevant provisions (Articles 10 and 8 ECHR, respectively). Second, the case law is sufficiently vast to allow for a (rudimentary) statistical analysis. Third, the relevant case law has gone through a number of evolutions that, if the hypothesis holds, should have a demonstrable impact on the strength of preferential framing effect.

Defamation in the case law of the ECtHR

The defamation case law of the ECtHR has been the site of important evolutions. The text of Article 8 ECHR does not explicitly include a right to honour or reputation, unlike Article 17 ICCPR (International Covenant on Civil and Political Rights), for instance. As a result, the ECtHR initially considered reputation to be a private interest that was, under the ECHR, not protected as a matter of human right. In the Article 10 cases of *Radio France v France* and *Chauvy v France*, the Court started shifting position, explicitly stating that Article 8 ECHR includes a right to reputation.[134] *Chauvy* was particularly crucial, as in that case the Court for the first time found that defamation cases entailed a human rights conflict between freedom of expression and the right to reputation. Depending on the results of the domestic proceedings, these cases could now be brought to Strasbourg under either Article 8 (if the domestic courts ruled in favour of freedom of expression) or Article 10 (if the domestic courts ruled in favour of the right to reputation).

In assessing the hypothesis that preferential framing effects tend to skew the Court's reasoning in conflicting human rights cases, it is thus particularly useful

133 But see *infra* note 137 and accompanying text on the ECtHR taking explicit countermeasures in *Axel Springer AG v Germany* and *Von Hannover v Germany (No. 2)*. The Court was presumably influenced by the thoughts of one of its judges – Judge Françoise Tulkens – on the dangers of preferential framing. Judge Tulkens was part of the Grand Chamber that ruled on both cases. In her extrajudicial writings, she had already expressed concerns over the existence of framing effects in the Court's case law. See De Schutter and Tulkens, *supra* note 102.

134 *Radio France and Others v France* [2004] ECHR 127, para 31; *Chauvy and Others v France* [2004] ECHR 295, para 70.

to examine the outcome of defamation cases in Strasbourg. A statistical analysis of the relevant judgments, divided according to the invoked article, will allow us to compare the outcome under each article numerically. The statistical analysis will offer us an indication of the occurrence of preferential framing effects in the Court's defamation case law. It will be complemented by a qualitative assessment of the substantive reasoning of the ECtHR in key defamation judgments.

Statistical analysis of the Court's defamation case law

Two defining moments in the defamation case law of the ECtHR steer the (rudimentary) statistical analysis I provide below (Table 5.1). The first defining moment is the *Chauvy* judgment, in which the Court first acknowledged that defamation cases entail a conflict between freedom of expression and the – newly established – right to reputation. Acknowledgement of the existence of a human rights conflict in defamation cases brought the risk of preferential framing into play: without a human rights conflict, there is of course no threat of preferential framing in its adjudication. The Court's judgment in *Chauvy* therefore offers the temporal starting point of the statistical analysis.

The second defining moment is the Grand Chamber judgment of *Palomo Sánchez and Others v Spain*, in which the Court introduced a new, deferential approach to conflicts between the right to reputation and freedom of expression. The Grand Chamber judgment in *Palomo Sánchez* followed the distress signal sent by the Chamber in *Karakó v Hungary*. In *Karakó*, the Court had expressed its concerns over potential preferential framing effects in its defamation case law:

> the purported conflict between Articles 8 and 10 of the Convention ... is one of appearance only. To hold otherwise would result in a situation where – if both reputation and freedom of expression are at stake – the outcome of the Court's scrutiny would be determined by whichever of the supposedly competing provisions was invoked by an applicant.[135]

I argued in Chapter 1 that the Court's identification of the problem in *Karakó* may have been accurate, but its solution unacceptable. The existence of human rights conflicts cannot and should not be denied. Instead, such conflicts should be resolved in a manner that treats the human rights at stake with equal respect. As noted earlier,[136] in subsequent judgments the Grand Chamber of the Court would recognise the salience of this point:

> the outcome of the application should not, in principle, vary according to whether it has been lodged with the Court under Article 10 ... or under

135 *Karakó v Hungary* [2009] ECHR 712, para 17.
136 *Supra* note 133 and accompanying text.

> Article 8 ... Indeed, as a matter of principle these rights deserve equal respect.[137]

In the meantime,[138] however, the Court took an additional measure with an indirect impact on (potential) preferential framing effects. In *Palomo Sánchez*, the Court ruled:

> If the reasoning of the domestic courts' decisions concerning the limits of freedom of expression in cases involving a person's reputation is sufficient and consistent with the criteria established by the Court's case-law, the Court would require strong reasons to substitute its view for that of the domestic courts.[139]

With *Palomo Sánchez* the Court switched to a more procedural approach to tackling defamation cases, and the conflict between human rights they involve. The Court's new, procedural approach should lead it to increasingly find no violation of the invoked right, given that the Court is now more likely to defer to the balance struck by the domestic courts.[140] Because the domestic courts will have struck this balance *against* the human right invoked at the ECtHR, the Court's deferential approach has an indirect impact on (potential) preferential framing effects in its defamation case law.[141] The *Palomo Sánchez* judgment should thus mark the start of a second time period of the statistical analysis.

Table 5.1 reflects the outcome (violation – no violation) of all defamation judgments of the Court between *Chauvy* and the cut-off date of the analysis (15 February 2016). A total number of 168 judgments were released in that time frame. The first time period, between *Chauvy* and *Palomo Sánchez*, contained 102 judgments: 94 under Article 10, and 8 under Article 8. The second time period, between *Palomo Sánchez* and the cut-off date of the analysis, contained a further 66 judgments: 55 under Article 10, and 11 under Article 8. In the first time period, the Court found a violation in 76 of the 94 Article 10 cases and no violation in the remaining 18. The Court found a violation in 5 of the 8 Article 8 cases and no violation in the remaining 3. In the second time period,

137 *Axel Springer*, *supra* note 28 at para 87. See also *Von Hannover (No. 2)*, *supra* note 28 at para 106.

138 That is, between *Karakó* and *Axel Springer/Von Hannover (No. 2)*.

139 *Palomo Sánchez*, *supra* note 17 at para 57. This principle was first introduced in the Chamber judgment in *MGN Limited v the United Kingdom* [2012] ECHR 993, para 150.

140 When the domestic courts have failed to balance in accordance with established criteria in the ECtHR's case law, the Court will either find a procedural violation of the relevant ECHR provision or engage in its own substantive balancing exercise. For an example of the former, see *Niskasaari and Otavamedia Oy v Finland* [2015] ECHR 609. For an example of the latter, see *Perinçek v Switzerland* [2015] ECHR 907.

141 De Schutter and Tulkens, *supra* note 102 at 202–203 (considering this a powerful argument in favour of an increased role for the margin of appreciation in conflicting human rights cases).

Table 5.1 Statistics ECtHR defamation case law

	Chauvy – Palomo Sánchez	
	Violation	**No violation**
Article 10	*76*	*18*
Article 8	*5*	*3*
	Palomo Sánchez – 15 February 2016	
	Violation	**No violation**
Article 10	*37*	*18*
Article 8	*6*	*5*

the Court found a violation in 37 of the 55 Article 10 cases and no violation in the remaining 18. The Court found a violation in 6 of the 11 Article 8 cases and no violation in the remaining 5.

Drawing clear conclusions from these results is difficult, mostly due to the relatively low number (19 in total) of judgments under Article 8. The results do, however, offer valuable indications. They indicate that – during both examined time periods – the invoked human right was at a clear advantage: the Court found a violation in the (vast) majority of Article 10 cases *and* in the majority of Article 8 cases, even if the margin is much smaller in respect of the latter. Recall that our working hypothesis is that preferential framing effects, if real, would lead the ECtHR to on average rule in favour of the human right that is directly invoked in front of it. This hypothesis appears to be corroborated by the results of the statistical analysis.

This might, however, not be as clear from the absolute numbers as it is from the relative figures. Take the first time period. Under Article 10, the ratio violation/no violation was roughly 4/1 in that time period, while it was 5/3 under Article 8. Alternative explanations for the results, for instance an abstract preference on the part of the Court in favour of freedom of expression, would have led to *inverse* results under both ECHR articles. We would thus have noted a ratio of 1/4 violations/no violations under Article 8. For an abstract preference in favour of freedom of expression to be the *only* variable to explain the results, we should have noted – in absolute numbers – 20 no violations for the 5 Article 8 violations in the first time period. Instead, there are only 3. An abstract preference for freedom of expression can thus not explain the results, at least not taken alone. Instead, preferential framing effects appear – at least in part – responsible for the results.

This hypothesis is further corroborated by the results of the second time period. Here, the ratio violation/no violation is markedly narrower. Under Article 10, it is 2/1 (as opposed to 4/1 during the first time period). Under Article 8, it is 6/5 (as opposed to 5/3 during the first time period). Especially in relation to Article 10, under which we have a sufficient number of judgments to draw somewhat reliable conclusions from, the figures of the second time period corroborate the hypothesis that the Court's switch to a more deferential approach in *Palomo*

Sánchez has an indirect impact on preferential framing effects in its defamation case law. As anticipated, the 'success rate' of the directly invoked human right is markedly lower under the second time period than under the first (2/1 *versus* 4/1 for Article 10 claims). Since the Court's approach to balancing – from more substantive to more procedural/deferential – is the only variable to have changed between both time periods, it must be assumed to explain the results.[142] Yet, because the ratio remains 2/1 – and thus well above 1/1 – preferential framing effects plausibly persist.

These results are, however, inconclusive. In particular, the low total number of judgments under Article 8 bars us from either confirming or rejecting, with confidence, the hypothesis that preferential framing effects influence the outcome of defamation cases at the ECtHR. The results do, however, offer some support for the hypothesis. Moreover, an additional second hypothesis could be added to provide a more complete explanation of the results. This additional hypothesis would seek to explain the difference in results (in both absolute and relative numbers) under Articles 10 and 8. It seems unlikely that preferential framing effects alone would be responsible for the results in Table 5.1, since they cannot explain the marked difference in the ratio violation/no violation under Articles 10 and 8 (4/1 and 2/1 *versus* 5/3 and 6/5). Bearing in mind that the total amount of Article 8 cases may simply be too small to draw any conclusions from, one additional factor could explain the difference: an abstract preference for freedom of expression over the right to reputation on the part of the Court. Alone, such an abstract preference does not explain the results in Table 5.1. But the same goes for preferential framing effects. *Combined*, however, preferential framing effects and an abstract preference for freedom of expression on the part of the Court do provide a coherent explanation for the results.[143]

142 The impact of the margin of appreciation on the manner in which the ECtHR tackles human rights conflicts can also be observed in relation to other conflicts. On the conflict between freedom of expression and the right to private life of public figures, for instance, compare *Ojala and Etukeno Oy v Finland* [2014] ECHR 36 with *Lillo-Stenberg and Sæther v Norway* [2014] ECHR 59 (in both cases, the ECtHR defers to the reasoning of the domestic courts and concludes that there has been no violation of the invoked human right – freedom of expression and the right to private life, respectively).

143 It should be noted, however, that an alternative hypothesis – which is not testable – is available. The statistical analysis provided in the text only examines ECtHR *judgments*, not *decisions*. The reason for this is that all Court judgments are published, while this is not the case for its decisions. Therefore, systematic analysis of the latter is difficult to achieve. Yet, it is at least conceivable that the Court is more likely to declare Article 8 claims inadmissible as manifestly ill-founded than Article 10 claims. This alternative hypothesis could theoretically explain two things. First, the relative lack of Court judgments under Article 8 in Table 5.1. Second, the difference in ratio violation/no violation under Articles 10 and 8. When combined with the outcomes of hitherto unknown decisions, the results in Table 5.1 might conceivably show an abstract preference on the part of the Court for freedom of expression, *without* preferential framing effects being needed to offer a coherent explanation of the results. If significantly more Article 8 claims would be declared manifestly ill-founded than Article 10 claims, an abstract preference for freedom of expression *alone* could,

A brief qualitative analysis of the Court's defamation case law[144]

Although the results of the above statistical analysis support the hypothesis that preferential framing effects occur in the ECtHR's defamation case law, they remain inconclusive. The statistical results can, however, be further corroborated by qualitative analysis of the Court's defamation case law. Skewing of the Court's judicial reasoning in defamation cases, *i.e.* preferential framing in favour of the invoked human right, is particularly obvious in the Court's assessment of the damage suffered by the human rights in conflict. In both Article 10 and Article 8 judgments, the Court tends to only determine the damage suffered by the directly invoked human right. It generally fails to assess, or even mention, the damage suffered by the other human right at stake. This is consistent with the hypothesis that the Court's defamation case law is subject to preferential framing effects. Indeed, when the Court only determines the damage suffered by the invoked human right, it is more likely to rule in favour of that right (especially when the damage is serious). In the absence of countervailing arguments, given the 'invisibility' of the damage suffered by the other human right at stake, alternative solutions simply do not appear on the Court's radar.

These and other preferential framing effects can primarily be seen at work in the Court's Article 10 case law on defamation. Throughout its rich history, the Court has infused that case law with a plethora of factors, relevant to the resolution of particular cases. One such factor is the status of the person whose reputation has allegedly been damaged. The Court distinguishes between several categories of plaintiffs in defamation proceedings, linking different limits of acceptable criticism to these categories.[145] Politicians are required to demonstrate a higher degree of tolerance to criticism than ordinary citizens, since a politician 'inevitably and knowingly lays himself open to close scrutiny of his every word and deed'.[146] The level of acceptable criticism is also wider for public servants than for private individuals.[147] But because public servants do not lay themselves open to close scrutiny to the same extent as politicians do, and because they 'must enjoy public confidence . . . free of undue perturbation if they are to be successful in performing their tasks', the range of acceptable criticism against them is less broad than for politicians.[148] With regard to public figures, the Court has consistently held that

combined with the switch to a deferential approach in *Palomo Sánchez*, explain the results in Table 5.1. Yet, as already indicated, this hypothesis is untestable, given that the Court's decisions are not systematically made public. Since I have offered a coherent explanation for the available results by drawing on a combination of preferential framing effects and an abstract preference for freedom of expression, the burden should be on others to prove otherwise.

144 This section is partly based on Smet, *supra* note 129 (offering a more detailed substantive analysis of the Court's defamation case law).

145 *Lingens v Austria* [1986] ECHR 7, para 42.

146 Ibid.

147 *Nikula v Finland* [2002] ECHR 324, para 48.

148 Ibid.; *Lešník v Slovakia* [2003] ECHR 124, para 53.

when private individuals enter the public arena they lay themselves open to public scrutiny and should therefore display a higher degree of tolerance to criticism.[149] Finally, the Court has held that strictly private individuals should be awarded the greatest protection from defamatory statements, because they do not specifically lay themselves open to public scrutiny.[150]

By introducing a distinction between different categories of plaintiffs and requiring that certain persons exhibit a higher degree of tolerance to criticism than others, the Court creates an excellent opportunity for careful consideration of cases involving a conflict between freedom of expression and the right to reputation. Theoretically speaking, the Court's reasoning could be expected to take the following form. Categories of persons who willingly and knowingly lay themselves open to public scrutiny will expect the possibility of criticism. As a result, the impact of defamatory statements on their reputation is less profound and more easily mitigated. Therefore, the limits of acceptable criticism are wider with regard to these persons. Conversely, the impact of defamatory statements on the reputation of persons who do not lay themselves open to public scrutiny will be greater and less easily mitigated. Therefore, the level of acceptable criticism with regard to these persons is more limited.

In practice, however, the Court does not live up to these theoretical expectations. In Article 10 cases involving defamation of politicians, the foundation of the Court's reasoning invariably rests on the principle that the limits of acceptable criticism are wider with regard to politicians. When an Article 10 case involves defamation of a private individual, however, the Court rarely builds its analysis on the converse assumption that the level of acceptable criticism is more limited with regard to private individuals. The Court thus succumbs to preferential framing effects. Rather than looking at factors that have an impact on the strength of the applicant's argument for freedom of expression *and* the plaintiff's right to reputation, the Court focuses its attention on freedom of expression alone.

Similar preferential framing effects can be seen at work in the Court's assessment, also under Article 10, of the tone and form of allegedly defamatory statements. Take *Gavrilovici v Moldova*, for instance, a case involving the conviction of a private individual who was sentenced to five days in detention for having supposedly called the president of the regional council a fascist.[151] In that case, the Court took the particular circumstances in which the insulting remark had been uttered into account. The applicant was accused of making the statement during a heated exchange, immediately after he was told that the regional council would stop providing financial aid for the medical transportation of his chronically ill wife and son. The Court ruled that, even if the disputed remark had indeed been uttered by the applicant, he was clearly in a state of despair and anger, circumstances under which the effect on the reputation of the plaintiff must have been minimal,

149 See, for instance, *Bodrožić v Serbia* [2009] ECHR 978, para 54.
150 See, for instance, *Tammer v Estonia* [2001] ECHR 83, para 68.
151 *Gavrilovici v Moldova* (15 December 2009), para 54.

because those present at the council meeting were aware of the tension and had heard (unspecified) provocative statements by the plaintiff.[152] The Court thus concluded that the applicant's freedom of expression had been violated.[153] Taken in isolation, *Gavrilovici* indicates careful reasoning on the part of the Court. Yet, under Article 10 the Court only uses arguments on the tone and form of speech in cases where the damage to the reputation is expected to be limited. It rarely uses them in the opposite sense, to find that greater damage was done to someone's reputation when speech was uttered through mass or print media. This is another indication that preferential framing effects to the benefit of the directly invoked human right – freedom of expression – are at work in the Court's defamation case law under Article 10.

Similar findings apply to the Court's Article 8 case law, where the right to reputation is invoked; and thus receives preferential treatment. Under Article 8, the Court also assesses the damage done to the conflicting human rights in a one-sided manner. The Court does so, for instance, in *A v Norway*, a case involving a newspaper article in which it was alleged that, due to his prior conviction, the applicant was the prime suspect in a murder investigation.[154] In that case, the Court found a violation of Article 8 after having established that the public interest nature of the publication did not justify the defamatory allegations. According to the Court, the publication represented a 'particularly grievous prejudice to the applicant's honour and reputation that was especially harmful to his moral and psychological integrity and to his private life'.[155] The Court failed, however, to examine the damage that would be done to freedom of expression by having the right to reputation prevail. Such a one-sided assessment of the impact on conflicting human rights is a substantial – and the most obvious – indication that the Court's case law is indeed subject to preferential framing effects.

Counteracting preferential framing effects

The statistical and substantive analyses presented above indicate that preferential framing effects influence the manner in which the ECtHR balances human rights. The Court tends to formulate and conduct its balancing exercise with, first and foremost, the invoked human right in mind. The other human right fades into the background, due in part to the 'verticalization' of human rights conflicts before the human rights court.

Importantly, preferential framing effects can be linked to the other practical obstacles to balancing human rights I have discussed throughout this chapter. Preferential framing flows from judges' subjective or intuitive preferences for the human right that is directly invoked in front of them (and the right holder that

152 Ibid. at paras 58–59.
153 Ibid. at paras 60–61.
154 *A. v Norway* [2009] ECHR 580.
155 Ibid. at paras 71 and 73.

appears before them). When judges intuitively or subjectively favour one of the human rights in conflict, it should not come as a surprise that they (unconsciously) frame the balancing exercise to the benefit of that right. Such preferential framing also has a direct impact on the coherence of the Court's case law on human rights conflicts, or rather the lack thereof. When the reasoning and outcome of the Court's judgments is – at least in part – shaped by the directly invoked human right, coherence across cases will inevitably suffer. Similar cases risk being decided differently on the basis of an arbitrary factor: the human rights provisions under which they are brought before the Strasbourg Court.

To counteract preferential framing effects, judges should evaluate the importance of and impact on *both* (or *all*) human rights at stake in a conflict. As ECtHR Judges Sajó and Tsotsoria note in their dissent to *Delfi v Estonia*, '[i]f one applies a balancing approach, then the other side of the balance must also be considered'.[156] This is a basic proposition, but one that is often neglected – or implemented half-heartedly – in the adjudication of human rights conflicts.

The structured balancing test I propose in Chapter 6 invites judges to engage in *genuine comparison* between human rights in conflict, thereby preventing preferential framing effects from taking hold. In the first phase of its application, the seven criteria that make up the structured balancing test need to be applied – by design – to both (or all) human rights in conflict, to determine the reasons in favour of (or against) each right. In the process, separate nets of arguments are woven in support of each of the human rights in conflict. In the second phase, the strength of these nets of arguments – and the reasons within them – is compared to determine which right should prevail under the specific circumstances. In strictly analytical terms, this is how the balancing process is supposed to function. In actual judicial practice, and especially in communicating the results of adjudication to the parties and the general public in judgments, both phases will likely be presented through integrated, deliberative reasoning. That, however, does not detract from the fact that – in the background – a test would be operating to nudge judges towards full consideration and genuine comparison of both (or all) human rights at stake in a given conflict.

Conclusion

In this chapter, I have discussed four key practical obstacles to the balancing of human rights: subjectivity in balancing, the impact of intuitive reasoning on balancing, lack of coherence of balancing decisions and preferential framing in the construction of balancing exercises. In evaluating the impact of these four practical obstacles, I have related each of them – either directly or indirectly – to the absence of a clear balancing methodology. Without a clear vision on how to execute it, balancing may strike judges as something they have to do, without

156 Dissenting opinion of Judges Sajo and Tsotsoria in *Delfi AS v Estonia* [2015] ECHR 586, para 39.

knowing how to do it well. Judges may be prone to 'follow their gut feelings', letting their subjective preferences and intuitions influence how they go about balancing. This, in turn, may lead to preferential framing in the construction of balancing exercises. The end result is, unsurprisingly, lack of coherence within and across balancing decisions.

I have posited that judges may benefit from decision aids that assist them in overcoming the practical obstacles to balancing. To that end, I propose a *structured* balancing test. Use of such a structured balancing test would minimise the influence of subjective preferences, nudge judges towards quasirationality, increase the coherence of judicial reasoning and eliminate preferential framing effects. Note that I do not claim to provide a miracle cure. Subjective preferences will be minimised, not eliminated. Judges will be nudged towards quasirationality, not pushed to pure analysis. And coherence will be increased, not achieved. The introduction of a structured balancing test is thus not a perfect solution. It may, however, be the best we can aim for in tackling hard cases on which reasonable disagreement persists and which confront judges with the dilemma of deciding which human right should prevail over the other.

Part III

Making balancing work for conflicts between human rights

6 A structured balancing test for human rights conflicts

Across the past two chapters, I identified and discussed a number of theoretical challenges and practical obstacles to balancing human rights. In evaluating the theoretical challenge of incommensurability, I adopted Jeremy Waldron's distinction between weak and strong incommensurability. I acknowledged that rational balancing is impossible in the face of strong incommensurability of human rights. Yet, such strong incommensurability will only rarely occur. Most instances of incommensurability are of the weak variety. Crucially, such weak incommensurability does not imply incomparability. Instead, it 'merely' entails the absence of a common metric to adequately express the relationship between items, such as human rights in conflict.

In Chapter 4, I argued that the challenge from weak incommensurability to balancing human rights can be overcome. This requires abandoning the scales metaphor of balancing, and the associated idea that rights have weight. Ultimately, both ideas do more to confound balancing than to elucidate it. I submitted that balancing should, instead, be conceived of as normative 'balancing as reasoning', as opposed to the rather mechanical 'balancing of interests'. I proceeded to outline the skeleton of a structured balancing as reasoning test, which enables comparative judgments on the strength of reasons in favour of – and against – human rights in conflict through the construction of nets of arguments. This, in turn, should allow judges to determine – with some measure of rational confidence – which of the human rights in conflict should prevail. Thus, the structured balancing test successfully tackles the challenge from weak incommensurability.

Yet, balancing not only faces theoretical challenges. Its application is also fraught with practical obstacles. I discussed four of those obstacles in Chapter 5. There, I made a number of key claims. I argued that subjectivity in the construction of balancing exercises is particularly prone to occur when courts – such as the ECtHR – resort to open ended *ad hoc* balancing. I submitted that the structured balancing test, conversely, minimises the impact of subjective preferences on judicial balancing by imposing structure through its limited set of balancing criteria. I further posited that the structured balancing test is a useful decisional aid to nudge judges away from intuitive reasoning and towards quasirationality in balancing. The test thereby aims to restrict overzealous reliance by judges on their intuitions, in constructing and conducting balancing exercises. I moreover argued that the need for a subjective or intuitive moment at the very heart of judicial balancing can be avoided by focusing on the construction of nets of arguments, as opposed to Aleksander Peczenik's chains of arguments. Whereas the latter's reliance on sequential reasoning inevitably entails an intuitive or subjective moment as the 'ultimate argument' in balancing, the former's reliance on mutually supportive reasons avoids the need for such a subjective or intuitive moment. I finally explained how, in human rights law, courts such as the ECtHR are prone to skew balancing exercises to the benefit of the human right that is directly invoked in front of them. The other human right at stake in a human rights conflict, conversely, fades into the background. Such 'preferential framing', I showed, has a genuine impact on the resolution of human rights conflicts. I argued that use of the structured balancing test, which invites judges to make reflective arguments, should prevent preferential framing effects from taking hold.

Ultimately, however, I concluded that the structured balancing test does not provide a miracle solution. It will not render balancing of human rights perfectly rational, objective and coherent. Instead, the structured balancing test aims for more modest goals. It aims to minimise the impact of judges' subjective preferences (not eliminate them), nudge judges towards quasirationality in balancing (not push them towards pure analysis) and increase coherence in judicial reasoning (not achieve it). Exactly how the structured balancing realises these aims, I have not yet explained in detail. Doing so is the purpose of this chapter. Throughout this chapter, I explain the structured balancing test in detail, both in theory and in practice. I first describe the structured balancing test and its seven criteria in theoretical terms. Afterwards, I explain how the test could function in practice by applying it to the human rights conflict in the ECtHR case of *Palomo Sánchez and Others v Spain*.

The structured balancing test, in theory

The structured balancing test I propose in this chapter is inspired by normative 'balancing as reasoning', as opposed to the rather mechanical 'balancing of interests'.[1] The test aims to avoid objections raised against literal metaphors

1 Kai Möller, *The Global Model of Constitutional Rights* (Oxford University Press, 2012), 137–140. For discussion, see Chapter 7 'Alternative approaches to balancing: Möller and Barak'.

of balancing rights,[2] interests[3] or values.[4] Such metaphors inevitably conjure up the image of a set of scales, the idea of weight and the associated challenge of incommensurability (*i.e.* the lack of a common metric to weigh rights against each other). To avoid those negative connotations, I propose a structured balancing test that abandons the scales metaphor and does away with the idea of weight altogether.

The 'balancing as reasoning' test I have in mind enables comparative judgments on the strength of reasons in support of – and against – human rights in conflict.[5] To identify those reasons, I propose a multi-factorial test, composed of an exhaustive list of seven criteria: a value criterion, an impact criterion, a core-periphery criterion, an additional rights criterion, a general interest criterion, a purpose criterion and a responsibility criterion.[6] I first introduced these criteria in

2 Steven Greer, '"Balancing" and the European Court of Human Rights: A Contribution to the Habermas-Alexy Debate', 63 *Cambridge Law Journal* (2004), 412 (describing how it 'is common-place for judges to seek to resolve conflicts between … "human" rights … by "balancing" one against the other'). Balancing of rights is also part of the terminological register of the ECtHR. See, for instance, *Appleby and Others v the United Kingdom* [2003] ECHR 222, para 40; *Von Hannover v Germany (No. 2)* [2012] ECHR 228, paras 100, 106 and 108; *Fernández Martínez v Spain* [2014] ECHR 851, para 79; *Evans v the United Kingdom* [2007] ECHR 265, para 90.

3 Stavros Tsakyrakis, 'Proportionality: An Assault on Human Rights?', 7 *International Journal of Constitutional Law* (2009), 470 (referencing Justice Frankfurter's and Justice Harlan's view that balancing tests weigh interests); Patrick McFadden, 'The Balancing Test', 29 *Boston College Law Review* (1988), 625 (explaining that judges have admitted – both in their extrajudicial writing and in their opinions – that they balance interests). The ECtHR also often refers to the need to balance interests in conflicting human rights cases. See, for instance, *Palomo Sánchez and Others v Spain* [2011] ECHR 1319, para 54; *Pfeifer v Austria* [2007] ECHR 935, para 49; *Odièvre v France* [2003] ECHR 86, para 49. Note that the ECtHR uses the language of balancing of rights and balancing of interests interchangeably. See, for instance, *Evans, supra* note 2 at paras 83 and 90; *Fernández Martínez, supra* note 2 at paras 79 and 89.

4 Thomas M. Scanlon, 'Adjusting Rights and Balancing Values', 72 *Fordham Law Review* (2004), 1478–1479. The ECtHR has, under certain circumstances, also referred to the balancing of values. See, for instance, *Axel Springer AG v Germany* [2014] ECHR 1037, para 84; *MGN Limited v the United Kingdom* [2012] ECHR 993, para 142.

5 See Aleksander Peczenik, *On Law and Reason* (Kluwer Academic Publishers, 1989), 154 and 203; Kai Möller, 'Proportionality: Challenging the Critics', 10 *International Journal of Constitutional Law* (2012), 721. See also *Perinçek v. Switzerland* [2015] ECHR 907, para 228 (in which the ECtHR recognises the importance of examining 'the comparative importance of the concrete aspects of the two rights that were at stake').

6 The seven criteria are directly inspired by the case law of the ECtHR (as explained in the text: 'The seven criteria of the structured balancing test, in detail', and the work of several scholars. See, in particular, Eva Brems, 'Introduction', in Eva Brems (ed.), *Conflicts between Fundamental Rights* (Intersentia, 2008), 4–5; Eva Brems, 'Conflicting Human Rights: An Exploration in the Context of the Right to a Fair Trial in the European Convention for the Protection of Human Rights and Fundamental Freedoms', 27 *Human Rights Quarterly* (2005), 303–304; Donna J. Sullivan, Sullivan, 'Gender Equality and Religious Freedom: Toward a Framework for Conflict Resolution', 24 *New York University Journal of International Law and Politics* (1992), 821–823; Samantha Besson, *The Morality of Conflict: Reasonable Disagreement and the Law* (Hart Publishing, 2005), 445; Olivier De Schutter, as reflected in

Chapter 4. Further on in this chapter, I explain in detail what they entail and require. For now, I will briefly explain the idea behind each criterion. The summary that follows is intentionally crude. It aims to offer the reader a firm grasp on the essence of the test, before I delve into the details.

The seven criteria of the structured balancing test: an overview

The *value criterion* examines the abstract value, within a human rights system, of human rights in conflict. The underlying premise of the value criterion is that human rights with a higher abstract value should have an edge, in balancing, over other human rights. Yet, relative human rights are due equal respect. Therefore, their abstract value is, in principle, equal. Further on, I will insist that there are at least two important exceptions: the right to life and freedom from discrimination (on certain grounds).

The *impact criterion* evaluates two factors: the damage suffered by human rights in conflict, on the one hand, and the risk that such damage will actually occur, on the other. The latter factor is vital, in that it distinguishes damage that is certain from damage that involves a degree of speculation. The underlying premise of the impact criterion is that human rights that suffer more serious and more certain damage have an edge, in balancing, over human rights that suffer comparatively less serious and less certain damage.

The *core-periphery criterion* gauges whether the damage to human rights in conflict is located in a rather central or a rather peripheral aspect of the human rights at issue. The core-periphery distinction is best understood in terms of a continuum, as opposed to a binary dichotomy. An aspect of a human right can thus be located closer to (or farther removed from) that right's core or periphery. The underlying premise of the core-periphery criterion is that human rights that suffer damage in an aspect that is located closer to their core, have an edge – in balancing – over human rights that suffer damage in a rather peripheral aspect.

The *additional rights criterion* allows for more contextual consideration of a human rights conflict. It acknowledges that seemingly binary human rights conflicts may – in fact – be multipolar, *i.e.* conflicts in which additional human

Eva Brems, 'Recente Ontwikkelingen in de Rechtspraak van het Europees Hof voor de Rechten van de Mens', in Willem Debeuckelaere and Dirk Voorhoof (eds), *En Toch Beweegt het Recht* (die Keure, 2003), 243–244; Peggy Ducoulombier, *Les conflits de droits fondamentaux devant la Cour Européenne des Droits de l'Homme*, Ph.D. dissertation (University of Strasbourg, 2008), 559 and 566; Judith J. Thomson, *The Realm of Rights* (Harvard University Press, 1990), 89; Aharon Barak, *Proportionality: Constitutional Rights and Their Limitations* (Cambridge University Press, 2012), 350–351, 358–359 and 362; David Kosař, 'Conflicts between Fundamental Rights in the Jurisprudence of the Constitutional Court of the Czech Republic', in Eva Brems (ed.), *Conflicts between Fundamental Rights* (Intersentia, 2008), 376–377; Robert Alexy, 'On Balancing and Subsumption. A Structural Comparison', 16 *Ratio Juris* (2003), 436 and 446; Frank M. Coffin, 'Judicial Balancing: The Protean Scales of Justice', 63 *New York University Law Review* (1988), 23.

rights are involved. These additional human rights might be the rights of one (or both) of the parties to the original conflict. But they may also be the human rights of third parties. The idea behind the additional rights criterion is that, where additional human rights are in play, this has an inevitable bearing on the balancing exercise.

The *general interest criterion* also allows for a more contextual evaluation of human rights conflicts. Indeed, such conflicts should not automatically be reduced to binary oppositions between the interests of two individual parties. Often, resolution of human rights conflicts will have an impact on the general interest as well. The general interest criterion evaluates whether one (or all) of the human rights in conflict is (are) supported by a general interest. The idea behind the criterion is that, when the general interest is in play, this has an inevitable bearing on the balancing exercise.

The *purpose criterion* has, contrary to the preceding criteria, a rather limited field of application. It reflects the idea that certain human rights stand in function of other human rights, in the sense that one of their purposes is to ensure adequate protection of those other human rights. The purpose criterion is particularly relevant to the resolution of conflicts in which the best interest of the child is a primary consideration. Such conflicts often involve human rights that should, in principle, be exercised to the benefit – not detriment – of the best interest of the child.

The *responsibility criterion*, finally, infuses balancing with the correlative of human rights: duties. Under human rights law, however, such duties cannot be directly imposed on private individuals. The responsibility criterion therefore does not aim to enforce such duties *vis-à-vis* parties to a human rights conflict. Instead, it examines whether those parties have exercised their human rights in a responsible manner. This should, however, not be misunderstood as *carte blanche* to impose a 'less restrictive alternative' requirement on right holders in the exercise of their human rights. The scope of the responsibility criterion is, in short, rather restricted. It is particularly relevant to the resolution of conflicts involving freedom of expression, recognising that in human rights law, for example under Article 10 ECHR, free speech 'carries with it duties and responsibilities'.[7]

The (many) purposes of the structured balancing test

The seven criteria of the structured balancing test have not been chosen at random. They serve three primary purposes. First, they force judges to genuinely examine human rights conflicts from the perspective of both – or all – human rights at stake. This counteracts preferential framing effects in the judicial construction of balancing exercises. Second, the criteria encourage the elaboration of reflective arguments, which assess the strength of reasons in support of – and against – human rights in conflict. This, in turn, enables comparative judgments

7 Article 10 ECHR.

on the strength of those reasons.[8] Third, the criteria avoid unwarranted reduction of human rights conflicts to binary oppositions between two human rights. Instead, the criteria invite judges to assess human rights conflicts in a broader context. Certain criteria examine the relevance of other human rights, potentially held by third parties, and of the general interest. As a result, a more holistic picture of human rights conflicts emerges, as opposed to an artificial image in which one right is pitted against another in apparent isolation from the context in which the conflict has arisen.

The seven criteria of the structured balancing test are intended to 'work' together in the construction of nets of arguments in support of human rights in conflict, as illustrated in Figure 6.1. Comparison of the strength of reasons woven into nets of arguments enables judges to overcome the challenge from weak incommensurability. Application of the structured balancing test should allow judges to determine – with some measure of rational confidence – which human right should prevail under the circumstances of a given conflict.

Enabling comparative judgments on the strength of reasons in favour of – and against – human rights in conflict moreover reduces the impact of judges' subjective preferences and intuitions on balancing, while increasing the coherence and transparency of their reasoning.[9] Reliance on nets of arguments reduces subjectivity and intuition in balancing by avoiding the inevitability of an intuitive or subjective moment as the ultimate basis of balancing. The structured balancing test moreover invites judges to lay all relevant cards on the table.[10] But, importantly, the test does not aim to eradicate any and all intuitions from judicial reasoning. It does not force judges to engage in pure analysis, which looms as an unachievable aim. Instead, the structured balancing test nudges judges towards quasirationality in balancing.

The seven criteria of the structured balancing test in detail

Having provided a broad overview of the structured balancing test, I will now explain how its seven criteria should function, in theory and in practice. I will initially explicate the role of each criterion separately. Afterwards, I will illustrate how the structured balancing test, taken in its entirety, could function in practice, by applying it to a concrete human rights conflict. Throughout, it will become

8 Henry S. Mather, 'Law-making and Incommensurability', 47 *McGill Law Journal* (2002), 366.

9 See Chapter 5.

10 On the need for the law to provide 'transparent criteria as to how the weighing of legal rights should be achieved' and on how this is 'crucial if weighing is to amount to anything other than a purely subjective exercise in moral judgment', see Besson, *supra* note 6 at 448. On the need for openness in balancing and candour in legal reasoning, see Coffin, *supra* note 6 at 22–23; Daniel L. Shapiro, 'In Defense of Judicial Candor', 100 *Harvard Law Review* (1987), 731–750.

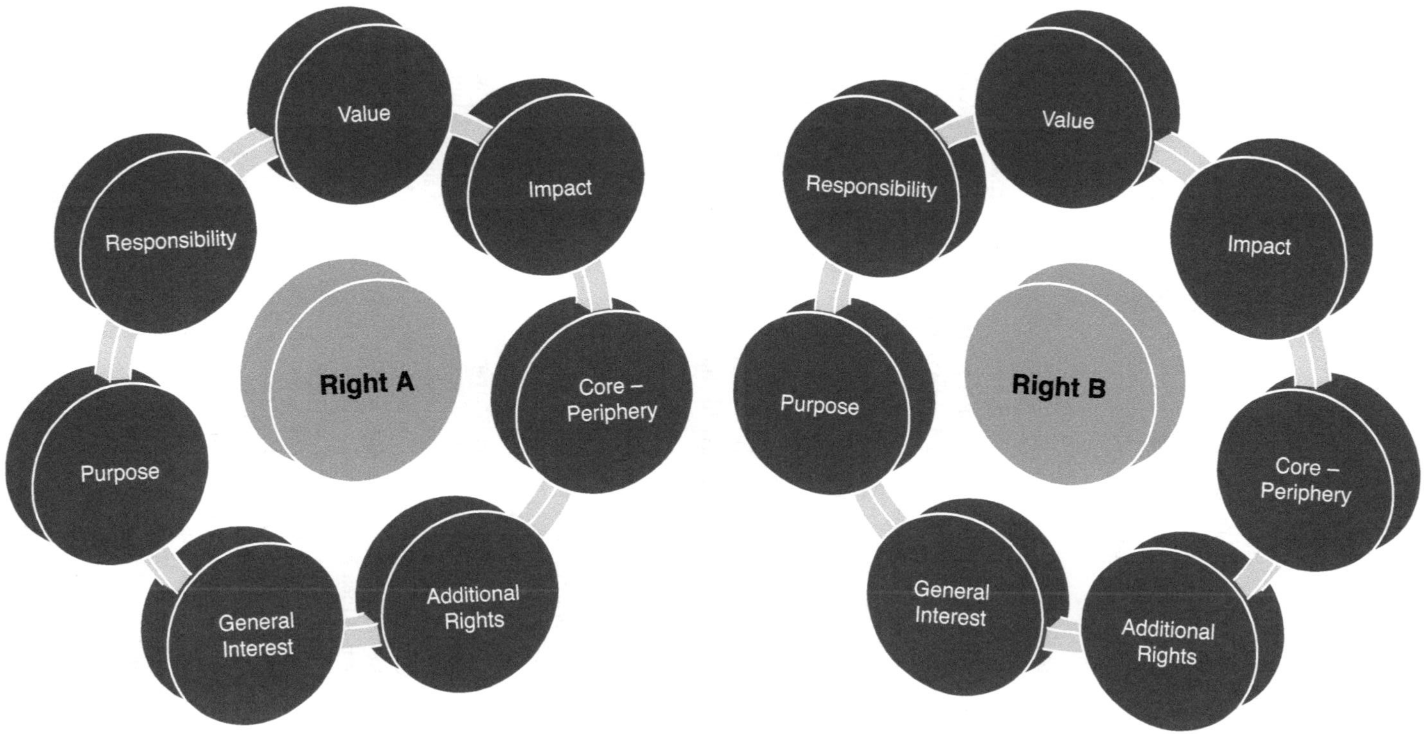

Figure 6.1 Graphic representation of the structured balancing test

clear that application of the test is not a purely technical exercise. On the contrary, it requires concerted normative argumentation.

In explaining each criterion of the structured balancing test separately, I will relate the seven criteria of the test directly to the ECtHR's case law on human rights conflicts, to demonstrate their practical relevance. In an important sense, the structured balancing test brings together elements that are already present in the Court's case law. It does not entail a complete overhaul of judicial reasoning on human rights conflicts. Instead, it provides a reconstructed account of the test already employed by one of Europe's highest courts. The test, in short, is firmly imbedded in human rights practice.

The value criterion

The value criterion evaluates the abstract value, within a human rights system, of human rights in conflict. The underlying premise of the value criterion is that there are strong reasons for resolving a human rights conflict to the benefit of the right that holds a – comparatively – higher abstract value within the human rights system.[11]

Refinement of the value criterion could be pursued along different lines of enquiry. One could, for instance, construct a purported hierarchy between human rights or suggest a 'soft ordering' among them.[12] This process would entail carefully outlining the rank of each human right within the human rights system as a whole.[13] I propose, however, to avoid that route. Not only is the construction

11 See also Besson, *supra* note 6 at 437–438 (referring to the qualitative priority some rights hold over others by virtue of the higher importance of the interests they protect, while pointing out that '[o]ne difficulty with [that] idea … is that all the duties a right may ground are not equally strong in relation to the interests protected by the right they are grounded on'). On the latter idea, *i.e.* that it is not because certain rights are more important than others that every duty associated with these rights is more important than any duty associated with other rights, see Jeremy Waldron, 'Rights in Conflict', 99 *Ethics* (1989), 515. It is for this reason that I do not advocate, in absolute terms, that certain human rights outrank others, but rather insist that their higher abstract value is only one of the factors to be considered in balancing such rights against other human rights.

12 Ducoulombier, *supra* note 6 at 521–525. See also Aharon Barak, 'Proportionality and Principled Balancing', 4 *Law and Ethics of Human Rights* (2010), 10 (arguing that not all rights are of equal importance and pointing towards the higher importance of the rights to life, human dignity, equality and freedom of expression).

13 Ducoulombier, *supra* note 6 at 521–525 (arguing, in the ECHR context, that Article 5 ranks highest among the relative rights, followed by Articles 9, 10 and 11, then Article 6, then Article 8 and finally Articles 1 and 3 of Protocol 1); Julian Rivers, 'Proportionality, Discretion and the Second Law of Balancing', in George Pavlakos (ed.), *Law, Rights and Discourse – The Legal Philosophy of Robert Alexy* (Hart Publishing, 2007), 178–179 (ranking the right to life higher than the right to physical integrity, which he in turn ranks higher than personal liberty, which he views as more important than the right to property; considering the ranking of privacy and equality more controversial).

of such hierarchies highly subjective.[14] In light of the indivisibility of human rights, it is also normatively undesirable.[15] Instead, I support the idea, endorsed by the ECtHR,[16] that human rights are due equal respect.[17]

Nevertheless, a number of human rights can be singled out as limited exceptions to the rule. In respect of these human rights, the value criterion finds its place in the structured balancing test. One such exception is freedom from discrimination.[18] Human rights law is – or should be – built on the fundamental premise that all individuals are equally entitled to human rights, regardless of, among others, their sex, race and religion.[19] In an important sense, equality is a prerequisite for the exercise and enjoyment of human rights. Granting all human rights equal respect in theory is pointless if and when discrimination is allowed to undercut equal enjoyment of human rights in practice. Therefore, freedom from discrimination should arguably hold principled higher value within the human rights system, at least where certain statuses are concerned. This is consonant with the human rights practice of, for instance, the ECtHR. In judging alleged discrimination on the basis of certain grounds, such as race, sex and sexual orientation, the ECtHR requires 'very weighty reasons' before a difference in treatment can be justified.[20] This 'strict scrutiny' arguably translates into a rebuttable presumption in favour

14 Theodor Meron, 'On a Hierarchy of International Human Rights', 80 *American Journal of International Law* (1986), 1–23.

15 Besson, *supra* note 6 at 444–445; Brems, 'Conflicting Human Rights', *supra* note 6 at 303.

16 See, for instance, *Axel Springer*, *supra* note 4 at para 87; *Von Hannover (No. 2)*, *supra* note 2 at para 106.

17 See Chapter 1.

18 Here, I restrict myself to providing some basic thoughts on human rights conflicts that involve freedom from discrimination. For more detailed discussion, see Stijn Smet, 'Conscientious Objection to Same-sex Marriages: Beyond the Limits of Toleration', 11 *Religion & Human Rights* (2016), 114- 139.

19 Article 2 (1) ICCPR; Article 2 (2) ICESCR; Article 14 ECHR. Note that, historically, the human rights project has been fraught with exclusionary assumptions about the 'human' in human rights law, whereby those who did not meet preconceived standards on – *inter alia* – rationality and autonomy, were excluded: non-whites, women, children, indigenous peoples, persons with a disability, etc. These historic exclusions have since, at least in human rights law theory, been largely corrected. The international human rights law regime is, today, a more inclusive project, founded on the fundamental equality of all individuals. For discussion, see Anna Grear, '"Framing the Project" of International Human Rights Law: Reflections on the Dysfunctional "Family" of the Universal Declaration', in Conor Gearty and Costas Douzinas (eds), *The Cambridge Companion to Human Rights Law* (Cambridge University Press, 2012), 17–35; Anna Grear, *Redirecting Human Rights: Facing the Challenge of Corporate Legal Humanity* (Palgrave Macmillan, 2010); Upendra Baxi, *The Future of Human Rights* (Oxford University Press, 2002), particularly at 27–29; Eva Brems, *Human Rights: Universality and Diversity* (Martinus Nijhoff Publishers, 2001), particularly at 18–21.

20 *D.H. and Others v the Czech Republic* [2007] ECHR 922, para 176; *Abdulaziz, Cabales, and Balkandali v the United Kingdom* [1985] ECHR 7, para 78; *Salgueiro Da Silva Mouta v Portugal* [1999] ECHR 176; *L. and V. v Austria* [2003] ECHR 20, para 45.

of freedom from discrimination, when it conflicts with other human rights.[21] This does not mean that freedom from discrimination automatically 'trumps' other human rights.[22] But it does mean that it should have a principled edge in balancing.[23]

Another exception, which I will consider in more depth, is the right to life. The right to life is generally considered to be 'a higher-ranking value' within the human rights system.[24] Awarding some sense of priority to the right to life is arguably justified, given that its enjoyment is a precondition for the enjoyment of all other human rights.[25] Without the right to life, other human rights do not make any sense. When the right to life conflicts with other human rights, courts should therefore arguably grant special – but not necessarily absolute – protection to the former. This is, in fact, what human rights courts already do in practice. An example from the domestic violence case law of the ECtHR illustrates the potential of the value criterion, as applied to the right to life. In *Opuz v Turkey*, a woman (Ms Opuz) who had suffered frequent abuse at the hands of her husband, was eventually murdered by him.[26] Confronted with the claim that the state had failed to take sufficient steps to protect Ms Opuz, the Turkish government argued that it 'could not be expected to separate the applicant and her husband and convict the latter while they were living together as a family, as this would amount to a breach of their rights under Article 8 of the Convention'.[27] The government thus argued on the basis of a human rights conflict.

In Chapter 2, I rejected this argument insofar as it implies that *Opuz* involved an intrapersonal conflict between Ms Opuz's right to life and her right to family life.[28] Here, I will deal with the other side of the government's argument: the claim that the case involved a conflict between Ms Opuz's right to life and her husband's right to family life. The Turkish authorities resolved that conflict to the

21 On rebuttable presumptions in the resolution of human rights conflicts, see Lorenzo Zucca, *Constitutional Dilemmas – Conflicts of Fundamental Legal Rights in Europe and the USA* (Oxford University Press, 2007). For discussion, see Chapter 7 – 'A non-balancing approach? Zucca on "constitutional dilemmas"'.

22 For discussion, see Maleiha Malik, 'Religious Freedom, Free Speech and Equality: Conflict or Cohesion?', 17 *Res Publica* (2011), 21–40.

23 For an application of this idea in judicial practice, see *Ladele v London Borough of Islington* [2009] EWCA Civ 1357 (on the refusal by a civil registrar to register same-sex partnerships and, thus, a conflict between freedom of religion and freedom from discrimination on the basis of sexual orientation).

24 *Odièvre*, *supra* note 3 at para. 45. See also *Pretty v the United Kingdom* [2002] ECHR 427, para 37 ('[t]he Court's case-law accords pre-eminence to Article 2 as one of the most fundamental provisions of the Convention'). See further Andrew Legg, *The Margin of Appreciation in International Human Rights Law – Deference and Proportionality* (Oxford University Press, 2012), 202–203.

25 *Pretty*, *supra* note 24 at para 37 ('Article 2 … safeguards the right to life, without which enjoyment of any of the other rights and freedoms in the Convention is rendered nugatory'). See also Legg, *supra* note 24 at 202–203.

26 *Opuz v Turkey* [2009] ECHR 870.

27 Ibid. at para 123.

28 See Chapter 2 – 'Public interest concerns masquerading as human rights rhetoric'.

benefit of the latter right, by refusing to separate the family. It is vital to note that, in doing so, the authorities were well aware of the threat posed by the husband, who had issued numerous death threats against his wife. Yet, the authorities refused to take protective measures. I submit that it is here, in evaluating the government's (in)actions, that the value criterion plays a key role. The value criterion provides a strong – nigh invincible – reason in favour of Ms Opuz's right to life, in the face of a real and immediate risk that her husband would murder her. Indeed, the ECtHR recognised as much in *Opuz* by ruling that Turkey had violated its positive obligation to protect Ms Opuz's right to life.[29]

The value criterion can only play such a decisive role, however, when 'the authorities knew or ought to have known at the time of the existence of a real and immediate risk to the life of an identified individual from the criminal acts of a third party'.[30] Indeed, conflicts between the right to life and other human rights necessarily entail an element of speculation or risk. A threat to the right to life will, when authorities become aware of a conflict, by definition be less than certain. The level of uncertainty involved determines whether or not the right to life should take on the nigh-invincible status it held in *Opuz*.

When the empirical circumstances of a given conflict do not disclose a real and immediate risk to the right to life of an identified individual, the value criterion should arguably not play a decisive role. On this point, another ECtHR – discussed in Chapter 1 – case is instructive. In *Osman v the United Kingdom*, the applicants claimed that the UK authorities had failed to protect the right to life of Mr Osman, who was killed by a former teacher of his son.[31] The applicants claimed that the UK police had sufficient indications that the teacher, who had become infatuated with Mr Osman's son, posed a real and imminent threat to the lives of both Mr Osman and his son (the latter had been wounded in the shooting). Yet, at the relevant time – *i.e.* before the shooting took place – that threat was necessarily speculative.

Finding that the risk was insufficiently substantiated, the ECtHR ruled in favour of the United Kingdom. The Court noted that the authorities were not only under an obligation to protect Mr Osman's life. They were also under an obligation to guarantee the right to personal liberty and the right to private life of the teacher. Because the authorities did not have sufficient empirical indications at their disposal based on which they knew or ought to have known that Mr Osman's life (and that of his son) were in real danger, they could not be blamed for refusing to infringe the teacher's human rights.[32] The level of speculation involved in the *Osman* case was simply too high to warrant a preventive detention order and sweeping house searches against the teacher.[33]

29 *Opuz*, *supra* note 26 at para 136.

30 Ibid. at para 129. See also *Osman v the United Kingdom* [1998] ECHR 101, para 116.

31 *Osman*, *supra* note 30.

32 Ibid. at paras 116 and 121–122.

33 Ibid. at para 121 ('the police must discharge their duties in a manner which is compatible with the rights and freedoms of individuals. In the circumstances of the present case, they

The *Osman* case thus illustrates the circumstances in which the right to life should not assume, simply by virtue of its higher value within the human rights system, nigh-invincible priority over other human rights. *Osman* also demonstrates that elements of speculation or risk can be a crucial factor in the balancing of human rights. Such elements are included in the impact criterion of the structured balancing test, to which I will now turn.

The impact criterion

The impact criterion evaluates two factors that are of immediate relevance to most – if not all – balancing exercises between human rights: the damage suffered by human rights in conflict and the likelihood that such damage will actually occur. The underlying premise of the first factor is that, all other things being equal, a human rights conflict should be resolved to the benefit of the right that suffers – or would suffer – the greatest damage.[34] Yet, merely determining the damage suffered by human rights in conflict is insufficient. Judges should also determine the likelihood that such damage will actually occur.[35] The underlying premise of the second factor is that, all other things being equal, a human rights conflict should be resolved to the benefit of the right that is most likely to suffer damage.

To operationalise both factors of the impact criterion, we require a scale on which the damage to human rights, as well as its likelihood, can be expressed. Given the differentiated nature of both factors, we require – in fact – two discrete scales: one on which the damage can be assessed and another on which its likelihood can be evaluated. Here, I have – quite clearly – found inspiration in Robert Alexy's balancing test, which I evaluate in detail in Chapter 7.

To assess the damage suffered by human rights, I propose we use a scale that lies somewhere in between Alexy's single triadic scale of 'light', 'intermediate' and 'serious' – which I consider to be too simplistic – and his nine-stage double triadic

cannot be criticised for attaching weight to the presumption of innocence or failing to use powers of arrest, search and seizure having regard to their reasonably held view that they lacked at relevant times the required standard of suspicion to use those powers or that any action taken would in fact have produced concrete results').

34 Alexy, *supra* note 6 at 436; Sullivan, *supra* note 6 at 821; Brems, 'Conflicting Human Rights', *supra* note 6 at 304; Thomson, *supra* note 6 at 89; Ducoulombier, *supra* note 6 at 559; Kosař, *supra* note 6 at 377. See, for instance, *Couderc and Hachette Filipacchi Associés v France* [2015] ECHR 992, para 87 (highlighting, in the context of publication of photographs of a public figure in a weekly magazine, the 'importance of assessing the seriousness of the intrusion into private life and the consequences of publication of the photograph for the person concerned').

35 Alexy, *supra* note 6 at 446; Coffin, *supra* note 6 at 23; Barak, *supra* note 6 at 362. See, for instance, *Bitto and Others v Slovakia* [2015] ECHR 667, para 111 ('The actual impact of the rent-control scheme is a particularly important factor in determining whether a fair balance has been struck between the interests at stake'). See also my discussion of *Osman v the United Kingdom*, *supra* note 30, in Chapter 2 – 'Unpacking the Three Pillars of the Definition'.

scale – which I find unworkable (see Chapter 7 for details). A more refined version of Alexy's single triadic scale should allow for a more detailed evaluation of the relevant damage. On such a more refined scale, differences in damage would be more pronounced, thereby offering clearer guidance in balancing. Alexy himself has hinted at the necessity of such refinement, for instance by speaking of 'very serious' or 'extremely serious' infringements.[36] I propose to not only add 'very serious', but also its mirror image 'very light' to Alexy's single triadic scale. The five stages of the scale on which the damage suffered by human rights may be evaluated, would thus be 'very serious', 'serious', 'moderate', 'light' and 'very light'. Although the development of such a scale inevitably involves some 'guesswork', my proposal arguably straddles the fence between allowing sufficient complexity for a reasonable evaluation of the damage suffered by a human right, without becoming so complex as to be unworkable.

As for the second set of scales, to evaluate the likelihood that the damage will actually occur, I propose – for reasons of symmetry – to also include five stages. These stages could be 'certain', 'a real and immediate risk',[37] 'reliable', 'maintainable' and 'unlikely'.[38] One may be tempted to argue for a sixth stage, such as 'merely speculative'. Throughout Part I of this book, however, I have argued that there cannot be a genuine human rights conflict when one of the human rights is merely speculatively at stake. Since it would signal the non-existence of a conflict, the stage 'merely speculative' has no place in a scale intended to assist in the resolution of *genuine* human rights conflicts.

The use of a double scale to evaluate the damage suffered by human rights in conflict and the likelihood that such damage will actually occur aims to infuse balancing with a necessary dose of rationality and objectivity. Obviously, mere inclusion of scales cannot hope to eradicate all intuitions and subjective preferences from judicial reasoning. But, as I explained in Chapter 5, that has never been the purpose. Instead, the structured balancing test aims to nudge judges towards quasirationality. In that respect, the primary purpose of the scales is to hand judges a decision aid to guide their normative judgments. At the very least, inclusion of the scales encourages judges to be transparent and candid in providing reasons in support of their judgments.

Room for reasonable disagreement will, nevertheless, remain. For one thing, the impact criterion will not always yield conclusive results. If one human right suffers 'certain' and 'serious' damage, while the other right suffers 'reliable' and 'light' damage, we would be hard pressed to find fault with the argument that the

36 Robert Alexy, 'Constitutional Rights, Balancing and Rationality', 16 *Ratio Juris* (2003), 139–140; Robert Alexy, 'Discourse Theory and Fundamental Rights', in Agustín José Menéndez and Erik Oddvar Eriksen (eds), *Arguing Fundamental Rights* (Springer, 2006), 28.

37 This particular stage relies directly on the Court's own case law. See, for instance, *Osman*, *supra* note 30 at para 116; *Huohvanainen v Finland* [2007] ECHR 205, para 98.

38 The five stages are partly taken from Robert Alexy's work, partly inspired by existing case law and partly the result of own insights.

former right is – in terms of impact – supported by stronger reasons. In other scenarios, however, application of the impact criterion will not be as clear-cut. Particularly when one of the human rights in conflict 'scores better' on the first scale, while the other 'scores better' on the second, drawing an unequivocal conclusion will not be straightforward. Understanding how a 'real and immediate risk' of 'serious' damage to one right relates to 'certain', but 'moderate' damage to another right, for instance, is difficult. We should recognise that, in certain situations, the impact criterion will not provide reasons in favour of either of the human rights in conflict. Instead, the results of its application will be indeterminate. Yet, we need not worry that this will be a general occurrence.

Instead, to maximise the potential of the impact criterion, we could introduce further normative arguments on how the reasons in favour of competing human rights differ in strength. A defensible argument could, for instance, be made in favour of preventing 'certain' damage, provided that it is sufficiently serious, over preventing 'unlikely' damage, even if it would be 'very serious'. For instance, if one right would suffer 'certain' and 'moderate' damage, while the other right would suffer 'very serious', but 'unlikely' damage, the former right is arguably supported by stronger reasons. Conversely, if one right suffers 'reliable' and 'light' damage, while the other right would suffer 'maintainable' and 'very serious' damage, the latter right is arguably supported by stronger reasons. Despite challenges in its application, the impact criterion will, once infused with appropriate normative arguments, often provide reasons on which a balancing exercise can be constructed, with some measure of rational confidence.

To evaluate the usefulness of the impact criterion to judicial practice, we should not linger in theoretical abstractions alone. Instead, we should also consider some practical examples. A first test case for the impact criterion is defamation, which involves a conflict between freedom of expression and the right to reputation.[39] In defamation cases, the likelihood that freedom of expression will suffer damage is always 'certain'. Protection of the right to reputation invariably requires measures that have a direct impact on free speech (an injunction order prohibiting publication, an order to publish an apology, an award of civil damages, a criminal conviction, etc.). The likelihood that the right to reputation will suffer damage, conversely, is not necessarily 'certain'. Because effects on a person's reputation depend on subjective interpretation, both by the person concerned and the publication's audience, the likelihood of damage will rather tend to involve 'a real and immediate risk' or be 'reliable'.

In defamation cases, the likelihood of damage to the right to reputation moreover depends on the status of the person concerned. Politicians, for example, are in a powerful position that allows them to decrease the likelihood that their reputation will suffer lasting damage as the result of a critical publication, for

39 Stijn Smet, 'Freedom of Expression and the Right to Reputation: Human Rights in Conflict', 26 *American University International Law Review* (2011), 183–236.

instance by demanding a right to reply.[40] Politicians moreover know that their actions will be subjected to public scrutiny. As a result, they are expected to show a higher degree of tolerance to criticism than private individuals.[41] These elements can be translated in terms of the impact criterion: speech will generally cause less damage to politicians' right to reputation than that of private individuals. Whereas the former are expected to show greater tolerance and are in a position that may allow them to mitigate the damage done to their reputation, neither of those protective factors apply to private individuals.

The damage of defamatory speech to the right to reputation moreover depends on the nature and tone of said speech. When speech takes the form of satire – a cartoon, for instance – the right to reputation suffers less grave damage than if the same accusation would be levelled in an objective and serious tone. This distinction is justified by the fact – well known to both the subject of the speech and the public at large – that satire by definition relies on exaggeration and provocation. The veracity of allegations has a further impact on the extent of the damage done to the right to reputation. When speech involves factually correct – and proven – allegations, the right to reputation suffers less damage than when speech takes the form of false allegations. In the former scenario, it is arguably the subject of the publication who has damaged her own reputation by engaging in illicit acts (corruption, for instance). In the latter scenario, conversely, her reputation suffers as a direct result of the false allegations made against her.

All these principles can be operationalised in a number of ways. One particularly promising avenue, I posit, is to start from a baseline assumption that damage to the right to reputation may range from 'very light' (for instance in the case of factually supported criticism, expressed in moderate terms, against a politician), over 'light' (for instance in the case of the same factually supported criticism, but expressed in harsh terms), to 'moderate' (for instance in the case of value judgements against a politician, expressed in harsh terms), and 'serious' (for instance in the case of allegations of a criminal offence against anyone, without proof and in the absence of a court judgment or prosecution), all the way up to 'very serious' (for instance in the case of grave insults of a private individual).[42]

The damage done to freedom of expression, conversely, may range from 'moderate' (for instance in the case of an order to publish an apology), over 'serious' (in the case of interferences that may have a chilling effect on speech,

40 See *Niskasaari and Others v Finland* [2010] ECHR 1063, para 75.

41 For the principle, see *Lingens v Austria* [1986] ECHR 7, para 42; *Lindon, Otchakovsky-Laurens and July v France* [2007] ECHR 836, para 46.

42 For concrete examples, see the ECtHR case law analysis presented in Smet, *supra* note 39. See, for a recent example, *Haldimann and Others v Switzerland* [2015] ECHR 215, para 52 ('the report in question did not seek to criticise the broker personally but highlighted certain commercial practices employed within his profession ... The impact of the report on the broker's personal reputation was therefore limited').

such as an injunction or an award of civil damages)[43] to 'very serious' (for instance in the case of prior censorship or a criminal conviction).[44] I submit that damage done to free speech should never be labelled 'light' or 'very light'. Given the central importance of free speech in a democratic society and because restrictive measures always carry the potential to chill speech, such measures should not be taken lightly. This is, of course, a normative argument that is open to reasonable disagreement. As such, it illustrates how application of the structured balancing test leaves ample room for – requires, even – normative arguments.

Having explored the impact criterion in the context of defamation, let us move on to another conflict: that between a religious employer's freedom of religion and the right to private life of its employee, who has been dismissed for breaching religious principles. Take, for instance, the case of a church organist and choir master who is dismissed when his church discovers that he has left (but not divorced) his wife and is living with another woman.[45] In cases like these, the likelihood that the human rights in conflict (would) suffer damage can be labelled 'certain'. Indeed, the employee's dismissal necessarily causes damage to his right to private life, while barring a religious employer from dismissing that employee (or forcing her to reinstate or compensate him) necessarily causes damage to her religious freedom.

The extent of the damage, however, depends on the circumstances. According to the ECtHR, an employee's ability to find a new job is of immediate relevance to the balancing exercise.[46] If and when an employee may easily find a new job, this is considered to mitigate the damage done to her right to private life. Yet, the dismissal itself will necessarily have damaged her right to private life. Its effects may be mitigated, but the damage itself cannot be undone. Immediate dismissal for actions taken in one's private life is – when compared to disciplinary measures, for instance – a relatively grave sanction. Therefore, I posit, such damage should at least be labelled 'moderate'. Depending on the aspect of private life at stake for the employee, it may be labelled as moderate' or 'serious', if the employee can easily find a new job, and 'serious' or 'very serious', if she will struggle to find a new job.

Evaluating the damage suffered by the religious employer's freedom of religion is more difficult. How one classifies it arguably depends on one's views on the importance of religious autonomy. If one considers religious autonomy to be a crucial aspect of religious freedom, possibly combined with constitutional

43 On 'chilling effects' on speech and the freedom of expression case law of the ECtHR, see Ronan Ó Fathaigh, 'Article 10 and the Chilling Effect Principle', *European Human Rights Law Review* (2013), 304–313.

44 For examples, see *Cumpǎnǎ and Mazǎre v Romania* [2003] ECHR 273, para 115; *Dupuis and Others v France* [2007] ECHR 5563, paras 46 and 48; *Niskasaari*, *supra* note 40 at para 77; *Axel Springer*, *supra* note 4 at para 109.

45 *Schüth v Germany* (23 September 2010).

46 See, for instance, ibid. at para 73.

arguments on the separation of church and state, any damage it suffers arguably should be classified as 'serious' (or even 'very serious'). If one focuses, instead, on the nature of a religious employer *qua* employer – and a powerful employer, at that – one could insist that it should be subject to similar constraints in employment policies as other employers. If one thereby downplays the religious autonomy argument, one could be led to classify the damage to freedom of religion as 'moderate'. Here, I will remain agnostic about the appropriate route to pursue. Instead, I recognise that arguments on religious autonomy confront judges with highly complex questions, the answers to which depend on the constitutional context within which judges operate.[47] This shows that, apart from requiring normative arguments, application of the structured balancing test is also influenced by contextual factors. My primary aim has been to indicate, through this brief discussion of religious autonomy, that the structured balancing test is sufficiently flexible to take such contextual factors on board.

A final example, on child care measures to protect children from abuse or neglect, serves to further illustrate the flexibility of the impact criterion. When a child is taken into care to protect her from established neglect or abuse by her parents, the likelihood of damage to the human rights in conflict is 'certain'. Both the child's rights to physical integrity and her parents' right to family life suffer damage. The damage itself should arguably be labelled 'very serious' with respect to the child, who has suffered abuse or neglect at the hands of her parents.[48] The damage to the parents' right to family life may *prima facie* seem 'very serious' as well, given that their child is taken away from them.[49] This damage can, however, be mitigated by the authorities. Child care authorities may take compensatory measures, such as granting access rights, limiting the duration of the order and foreseeing the future possibility of family reunification.[50] When such measures are put in place, the parents' right to family life suffers less serious (long-term) damage. That damage could thus more appropriately be labelled 'moderate'.

With the passage of time, however, the damage could increase. If compensatory measures are not effectively implemented, even though the circumstances allow

47 Compare, for instance, *Hosanna-Tabor Evangelical Lutheran Church and School v Equal Employment Opportunity Commission*, 132 S.Ct. 694 (2012) with *Fernández Martínez v Spain*, *supra* note 3. For discussion, see Ian Leigh, 'Balancing Religious Autonomy and Other Human Rights under the European Convention', 1 *Oxford Journal of Law and Religion* (2012), 109–125; Carolyn Evans and Anna Hood, 'Religious Autonomy and Labour Law: A Comparison of the Jurisprudence of the United States and the European Court of Human Rights' 1 *Oxford Journal of Law and Religion* (2012), 81–107; Mark Strasser, 'Making the Anomalous Even More Anomalous: On *Hosanna-Tabor*, the Ministerial Exception, and the Constitution', 109 *Virginia Journal of Social Policy and the Law* (2012), 400–449; Douglas Laycock, '*Hosanna-Tabor* and the Ministerial Exception', 35 *Harvard Journal of Law & Public Policy* (2012), 839–862.

48 For an example, see *K. and T. v Finland* [2001] ECHR 465, para 269. See also, *mutatis mutandis*, *Neulinger and Shuruk v Switzerland* [2010] ECHR 1053, paras 147–148.

49 *K. and T.*, *supra* note 48 at para 268; *N.P. v Moldova* [2015] ECHR 846, para 65.

50 Ibid.

for it, the parents' right to family life once more suffers 'serious' or 'very serious' damage: they risk losing lose all contact with their child, as well as the prospect of ever being reunited with her.[51] At the same time, if and when parents take sincere steps to remove the threat of abuse or neglect, the likelihood that the child's right to physical integrity would suffer future damage becomes less certain. If parents take the necessary measures, that risk may even become 'unlikely'. This should have a direct effect on the balancing exercise. The flexible nature of the impact criterion allows judges to take such evolving circumstances into account in balancing human rights.

The core-periphery criterion

The core-periphery criterion examines whether damage is done to a core or a peripheral aspect of human rights in conflict. The underlying premise of the criterion is that there are stronger reasons for ruling in favour of a right that suffers damage to a core aspect than for ruling in favour of a right that suffers damage to a peripheral aspect.[52] In order to fully grasp the intricacies of the core-periphery criterion, we need to delve into the concepts of the core and periphery of human rights.

The core of human rights can be conceived of in different ways. A first view is supported by proportionality scholars. They insist that the concept of the supposed core of a human right does not add anything that is not already captured by the proportionality principle.[53] In their view, a right's core can only be understood in relative terms: it cannot be defined in the abstract, but only identified as the result of a concrete balancing exercise.[54] On the relativist view, then, a right's core does not have an independent meaning. For that reason, several proportionality scholars have abandoned the concept altogether, arguing that it is practically useless and/or only serves to confuse matters.[55]

51 For examples, see ibid. at para 277; *Ageyevy v Russia* [2013] ECHR 432, paras 144 and 151. See also, *mutatis mutandis*, *Görgülü v Germany* [2004] ECHR 89, para 48.

52 Kosař, *supra* note 6 at 376; Brems, 'Conflicting Human Rights', *supra* note 6 at 303–304; Barak, *supra* note 6 at 362. See, for instance, *National Union of Rail, Maritime and Transport Workers v the United Kingdom* [2014] ECHR 366, para 87 ('If a legislative restriction strikes at the core of trade union activity ... more is required to justify the proportionality of the resultant interference ... with the exercise of trade union freedom. Conversely, if it is not the core but a secondary or accessory aspect of trade union activity that is affected ... the interference is, by its nature, more likely to be proportionate as far as its consequences for the exercise of trade union freedom are concerned.').

53 Robert Alexy, *A Theory of Constitutional Rights* (Oxford University Press, 2002), 193–196; Matthias Klatt and Moritz Meister, *The Constitutional Structure of Proportionality* (Oxford University Press, 2012), 67–68; Gerhard van der Schyff, *Limitation of Rights – A Study of the European Convention and the South African Bill of Rights* (Wolf Legal Publishers, 2005), 166.

54 Ibid.

55 Julian Rivers, 'Proportionality and Variable Intensity of Review', 65 *Cambridge Law Journal* (2006), 184–187; van der Schyff, *supra* note 53 at 167.

The proportionality view on the (supposed) core of human rights can be contrasted to an absolutist conception, on which a right's core is the inalienable aspect that lies at the very heart of the right.[56] On the absolutist conception, the core of a human right is absolute. Its infringement can never – under any circumstances – be justified.[57] In other words, 'there is no balance to talk about in the first place'.[58] The main obstacle for the absolutist view is, of course, that it presupposes that courts are able to define a right's core in abstract terms. Indeed, the absolutist conception can only function if a right's core can be identified independently of the specific circumstances of a given case. Yet, in the specific context of the ECHR, at least, it has proven difficult – if not impossible – to independently define the core of all human rights.[59]

An absolutist conception of the core of human rights moreover ignores the fact that – in human rights practice – there will nearly always be circumstances under which even a core aspect of a human right can justifiably be overridden.[60] This certainly transpires from the case law of the ECtHR. Although the Court sometimes speaks of the 'very essence', the '(very) substance' or the 'very heart' of human rights, it does not grant these 'cores' absolute protection.[61] Instead, it subjects them to proportionality analysis.[62] The Court has for instance ruled that measures that 'cannot be regarded as disproportionate to the legitimate aim pursued … [do] not, *therefore*, impair the very essence of the applicant's right'.[63] The Court has also noted that when there is 'a reasonable relationship of proportionality between the means used and the aim pursued … the restriction in question [does] not impair the very essence of the applicant's right'.[64] In light of existing human rights practice, and given the definitional problems involved, it seems unrealistic to maintain that the core of human rights can truly be absolute.

But this does not mean that the concepts of core and periphery of human rights would be irrelevant to the resolution of human rights conflicts. There is,

56 Tsakyrakis, *supra* note 3 at 492–493.

57 Ibid.; Besson, *supra* note 6 at 445 (stating that the core of a fundamental right is in principle absolute, but immediately adding that, in reality, it can be weighed and balanced against other rights when a certain threshold of infringement of those other rights is attained).

58 Tsakyrakis, *supra* note 3 at 493.

59 Rivers, *supra* note 55 at 186–187.

60 Klatt and Meister, *supra* note 53 at 67–68; Besson, *supra* note 6 at 445.

61 See, among many authorities, *Young, James and Webster v the United Kingdom* [1981] ECHR 4, para 57; *Appleby*, *supra* note 2 at para 47; *Sørensen and Rasmussen v Denmark* [2006] ECHR 24, para 54; *Hasan and Chaush v Bulgaria* [2000] ECHR 511, para 62.

62 See, among many other examples, *Young, James and Webster*, *supra* note 61; *Sørensen and Rasmussen*, *supra* note 61; *Röman v Finland* [2013] ECHR 90; *Prince Hans-Adam II of Liechtenstein v Germany* [2001] ECHR 467; *Leyla Şahin v Turkey* [2005] ECHR 819. See also van der Schyff, *supra* note 53 at 140.

63 *Prince Hans-Adam II*, *supra* note 62 at para 69 (emphasis added). See also the concurring opinion of Judge Costa in ibid. (criticising the majority's use of the word 'therefore', because he prefers an absolutist approach to the very essence of the right at issue (the right to access to court under Article 6 ECHR)).

64 *Leyla Şahin*, *supra* note 62 at paras 159 and 161.

I aim to show, genuine value in incorporating both concepts in balancing, even when cores are not conceived of in absolute terms. I posit that the core and periphery of human rights are best conceived in terms of a continuum, rather than a binary dichotomy. This continuum is, in turn, best imagined in the shape of a circle. The circle itself represents a human right, for instance freedom of expression. Within the circle, certain aspects lie closer to its centre – that is, closer to the core of the right – whereas others are located closer to its outer edges – that is, closer to the periphery of the right. Political speech, for instance, is located closer to the core of freedom of expression than commercial speech. Yet, political speech is not an absolute aspect of freedom of expression. It can be overridden under certain circumstances. Nevertheless, locating political speech closer to the core of freedom of expression than commercial speech expresses the idea that an interference with the former will require stronger justificatory reasons than an interference with the latter.[65]

This general idea can be utilised in balancing human rights, since it enables comparative arguments on reasons in favour of – or against – human rights in conflict. If all other things are equal, a conflict between human right A, which suffers damage to one of its more central aspects, and human right B, which suffers damage to one of its more peripheral aspects, should arguably be resolved to the benefit of human right A.

For the core-periphery criterion to function in practice, however, we require at least some idea of where different aspects of a human right should be located within that right. The standard to which we should aspire may not be as exacting as for the identification of a right's core on the absolutist conception thereof, given that the consequences are less critical. But we nevertheless require some guidance. The identification exercise is, necessarily, contextual. Different (human rights) courts, operating in different (human rights) systems, may favour distinct approaches. In the ECHR context, the ECtHR's case law provides some guidance on the core and periphery of a number of human rights.[66]

The Court considers, among others, the following aspects to be located closer to the core of the human rights at issue: sexual identity, the protection of health data and the right to the protection of one's image under the right to private life;[67] religious autonomy under freedom of religion;[68] political speech under freedom

65 Brems, 'Conflicting Human Rights', *supra* note 6 at 304.

66 For an overview of the Court's relevant case law, see Janneke Gerards, 'Pluralism, Deference and the Margin of Appreciation Doctrine', 17 *European Law Journal* (2011), 112–113; Sébastien Van Drooghenbroeck, *La proportionnalité dans le droit de la convention européenne des droits de l'homme: prendre l'idée simple au sérieux* (Bruylant, 2001), 408–471.

67 *Dudgeon v the United Kingdom* [1981] ECHR 5, para 52; *Z. v Finland* [1997] ECHR 10, para 95; *Biriuk v Lithuania* [2008] ECHR 1528, para 39; *Von Hannover v Germany (No. 2)* [2012] ECHR 228, para 96; *Couderc and Hachette Filipacchi Associés v France*, *supra* note 34 at para 85.

68 *Schüth*, *supra* note 45 at para 58; *Fernández Martínez*, *supra* note 2 at para 80.

of expression;[69] the right to form an association and the individual freedom not to join an association under freedom of association;[70] the right to access to education under the right to education;[71] and the right to vote and the right to stand for elections under the right to free and fair elections.[72]

The Court's case law on more peripheral aspects of human rights yields comparably scarcer results. Nevertheless, the Court arguably considers, among others, the following aspects to be located farther away from the core of human rights: tax surcharges under the right to a fair trial;[73] professional exchanges and the donation of embryos to scientific research under the right to private life;[74] commercial speech under freedom of expression;[75] secondary strike action and obstruction of traffic under freedom of assembly;[76] and the label accorded to one's association under freedom of association.[77] In the literature, some additional proposals can be found, for instance on the 'right to give birth at home'[78] as a peripheral aspect of the right to private life.[79]

A concrete example from the ECtHR's case law may illustrate how the core-periphery criterion could be of value to balancing practice. In *Biriuk v Lithuania*, a private individual's HIV status was published in a newspaper. *Biriuk* thus involved a conflict between the right to private life and the right to freedom of expression. One of the crucial factors in the ECtHR's ruling on the case is best understood in terms of the core-periphery criterion. In *Biriuk*, different aspects of the human rights in conflict were at stake. In respect of the right to private life, the Court held that

> protection of personal data, not least medical data, is of fundamental importance to a person's enjoyment of his or her right to respect for private and family life as guaranteed by art. 8 of the Convention ... especially ... as regards the protection of the confidentiality of a person's HIV status.[80]

69 *Lingens*, *supra* note 41 at para 42.
70 *Demir and Baykara v Turkey* [2008] ECHR 1345; *National Union of Rail, Maritime and Transport Workers v the United Kingdom*, *supra* note 52 at para 86.
71 *Catan and Others v Moldova and Russia* [2012] ECHR 1827, para 140.
72 *Ždanoka v Latvia* [2006] ECHR 994, para 104.
73 *Jussila v Finland* [2006] ECHR 996, para 43.
74 *Michaud v France* [2012] ECHR 2030, para 92; *Parrillo v Italy* [2015] ECHR 755, para 174.
75 *Ashby Donald and Others v France* [2013] ECHR 28, para 39.
76 *National Union of Rail, Maritime and Transport Workers v the United Kingdom*, *supra* note 52 paras 77 and 88; *Kudrevičius and Others v Lithuania* [2015] ECHR 906, para 97.
77 *Gorzelik and Others v Poland* [2004] ECHR 73, para 105.
78 *Ternovszky v Hungary* [2010] ECHR 2028, para 22.
79 Janneke Gerards, 'The Scope of ECHR Rights and Institutional Concerns – The Relationship between Proliferation of Rights and the Caseload of the ECtHR', in Eva Brems and Janneke Gerards (eds), *Shaping Rights in the ECHR: The Role of the European Court of Human Rights in Determining the Scope of Human Rights* (Cambridge University Press 2013), 84–106.
80 *Biriuk*, *supra* note 67 at para 39.

The Court thus considered the protection of health data to be a rather core aspect of the right to private life. With regard to the newspaper's freedom of expression, conversely, the Court found that

> the publication of the article in question, the purpose of which was apparently to satisfy the prurient curiosity of a particular readership and boost the defendant's commercial interests, cannot be deemed to contribute to any debate of general interest to society.[81]

The Court thereby intimated that sensationalist publications with a purely commercial interest are located in the periphery of freedom of expression.

Biriuk thus involved a conflict between a more central aspect of one human right (the right to private life) and a more peripheral aspect of another human right (freedom of expression). The Court resolved the conflict to the benefit of the former right, chiefly because of the great disparity in importance of the aspects of the human right in conflict. *Biriuk* thereby underscores the relevance of the core-periphery criterion to the balancing of human rights: there were stronger reasons in favour of the right that suffered damage to one of its more central aspects than in favour of the other right, which would suffer damage to one of its more peripheral aspects.

In the absence of full judicial guidance on the core and periphery of human rights, however, there will inevitably be instances in which it is difficult – or impossible – to pinpoint the exact location of the relevant aspects of human rights in conflict. In those cases, the core-periphery criterion will be of less use, or even outright inapplicable. There will moreover be cases in which the location is roughly equal for both human rights in conflict: both more central, both more peripheral or both somewhere 'in the middle'. In those cases, the core-periphery criterion does not offer reasons in support of (or against) either of the human rights in conflict. In both scenarios, we must turn to other criteria for guidance.

The additional rights criterion

One of these other criteria, the additional rights criterion, encourages a more contextual approach to human rights conflicts, by moving beyond a strictly binary consideration thereof. The additional rights criterion assesses the relevance to balancing of other human rights, held by one of the parties to the primary conflict or by third parties.[82] In relation to a primary conflict between human right A of X and human right B of Y, the additional rights criterion thus

81 Ibid. at para 42.

82 Sullivan, *supra* note 6 at 823; Kosař, *supra* note 6 at 377; Brems, *supra* note 6 at 304; Barak, *supra* note 6 at 362; Thomson, *supra* note 6 at 89; Xiaobing Xu and George D. Wilson, 'On Conflict of Human Rights', 5 *Pierce Law Review* (2006), 47–48.

factors in the relevance of, for example, human right C of X and human right D of third parties, for instance X's relatives. If those additional human rights – that is, human rights C and D – would suffer damage if the conflict would be resolved in favour of human right B of Y, this has an inevitable impact on the balancing exercise.

The underlying premise of the additional rights criterion is, however, not as strict as that of the preceding criteria. Even if all other things are equal, that is if the other criteria do not – on balance – yield conclusive reasons in favour of the human rights in conflict, the additional rights criterion does not necessarily settle the conflict. Resolution of a human rights conflict should not be reduced to a game of numbers, in which the claim supported by the most human rights prevails. It is not because, in the above example, X's claim is supported by multiple human rights (A, C and D) that her position is *necessarily* stronger than Y's claim, which is only supported by one human right (B). Weak incommensurability of the human rights involved, including failure of their transitivity, precludes us from relying on simple arithmetic to decide the conflict. Even if all other things are equal, human rights A, C and D of X and third parties therefore do not necessarily 'trump' human right B of Y.

Nevertheless, the additional rights criterion *is* relevant to the balancing of human rights in conflict. It does say something about the strength of (one of) the parties' positions. Indeed, a party's position will logically be stronger if it is supported by multiple human rights than if it is only supported by one of those human rights. In our example, the reasons for finding in favour of X will logically be stronger if both her human rights A and C are at stake, instead of only her human right A ($A + C > A$). Similarly, if a ruling against human right A of X would cause damage to human right D of third parties, the reasons for ruling in favour of X are stronger than would be the case if human right D of those third parties would not be at stake ($A + D > A$). The additional rights criterion thus has an inevitable bearing on the balancing exercise, even if it should not – on its own – offer conclusive reasons in favour of the human rights that make up the primary conflict.

A few concrete examples may serve to illustrate the above points.[83] The additional rights criterion is, for instance, of immediate relevance when individuals are forced, under a closed shop agreement, to join a trade union against their personal convictions and opinions. Such situations entail a conflict between the (negative) freedom not to associate of these individuals and the (positive) freedom of association of the trade union (and its members). The additional rights criterion is of immediate relevance here, because individuals who are forced to join a trade union against their personal convictions and opinions not only suffer damage in their associational right. Their freedom of thought and religion and their freedom of expression are damaged as well. The ECtHR has recognised the salience of this point:

83 See, apart from the examples discussed in the text, *Couderc and Hachette Filipacchi Associés*, *supra* note 34 at para 129.

> [t]he right to form and to join trade unions is a special aspect of freedom of association ... the protection of personal opinions guaranteed by Articles 9 and 10 of the Convention is one of the purposes of the guarantee of freedom of association ... such protection can only be effectively secured through the guarantee of both a positive and a negative right to freedom of association.[84]

The additional rights criterion also proves relevant in other cases, including defamation cases that involve allegations that a criminal act has been committed, for which the person at issue has not (yet) been convicted. In such cases, as recognised by the ECtHR, the targeted person's right to presumption of innocence may be at stake, in addition to her right to reputation:

> [w]here ... there is question of attacking the reputation of individuals and thus undermining their rights as guaranteed in Article 8 of the Convention ... regard must be had to the fair balance which has to be struck between the competing interests at stake. Also of relevance for the balancing which the Court must carry out ... is that, under Article 6 § 2 of the Convention, everyone has the right to be presumed innocent of any criminal offence until proven guilty.[85]

Such defamation cases also allow us to grasp why the additional rights criterion does not necessarily offer conclusive reasons for the resolution of a human rights conflict. There is no reason to assume that – even if all other things are equal – the combination of a person's right to reputation and her presumption of innocence necessarily 'trumps' another's freedom of expression. Nevertheless, the presumption of innocence *is* a relevant factor to the balancing exercise, since it logically renders the position of the first person stronger than it would have been if only her right to reputation had been at stake.

As indicated, the additional rights criterion not only assesses the relevance to balancing of additional rights held by one of the parties to the primary conflict. It also evaluates the potential relevance of human rights held by *third parties*. The ECtHR case of *Odièvre v France* illustrates this second aspect of the additional rights criterion. *Odièvre* involved a conflict between a woman's right to know her origins, an aspect of her right to private life, and the right to private life of her mother, who had given birth anonymously (pursuant to which the applicant had been adopted). In its judgment, the ECtHR recognised that not only the human rights of the applicant and her mother were at stake in the conflict, but also those of third parties:

84 *Sørensen and Rasmussen*, *supra* note 61 at para 54. See also *Young, James and Webster*, *supra* note 61 at para 57.

85 *Alithia Publishing Company Ltd and Constantinides v Cyprus* [2008] ECHR 420, para 63.

> [i]n addition to that conflict of interest [between the human rights of the applicant and those of her mother], the problem of anonymous births cannot be dealt with in isolation from the issue of the protection of third parties, essentially the adoptive parents, the father and the other members of the natural family. The Court notes in that connection that the applicant is now 38 years old, having been adopted at the age of four, and that non-consensual disclosure could entail substantial risks, not only for the mother herself, but also for the adoptive family which brought up the applicant, and her natural father and siblings, each of whom also has a right to respect for his or her private and family life.[86]

As before, those additional rights do not *decisively* settle the conflict. But they *are* relevant factors to the balancing exercise, since they provide reasons in favour of one of the human rights in conflict (and thus against the other). Just how relevant they are, will become clear in Chapter 8, when I apply the structured balancing test to *Odièvre*.

A final set of cases in which additional rights hold direct relevance to balancing, are child custody cases. The primary conflict in such cases often pits the right to family and private life of one parent against the same right of the other parent. Yet, the best interest of the child is, in principle, the primary consideration for the resolution of the conflict.[87] Indeed, the best interest of the child is often the decisive factor for the resolution of human rights conflicts that revolve around the rights of the child. The best interest of the child is, in that sense, crucially distinct from other 'additional rights'. To accurately express the *decisive* nature of the child's best interest in the balancing exercise, I will deal with it under a separate criterion: the purpose criterion. But first, I will explain the role of the general interest criterion.

The general interest criterion

Along with the additional rights criterion, the general interest criterion incorporates the broader context behind a human rights conflict in balancing. The general interest criterion evaluates, in particular, whether the human rights in conflict are supported by a relevant general interest.[88] The underlying premise of the general interest criterion is that there are stronger reasons for finding in favour of a human right supported by a general interest than for the same human right, unsupported by a general interest. As with the additional rights criterion, however, the general interest criterion does not necessarily provide conclusive reasons for the resolution

86 *Odièvre*, *supra* note 3 at para 44. See also *Röman*, *supra* note 62 at para 51.

87 *Hokkanen v Finland* [1994] ECHR 32, para 58; ECtHR, *Ignaccolo-Zenide v Romania* [2000] ECHR 25, para 94.

88 Brems, 'Conflicting Human Rights', *supra* note 6 at 304; Ducoulombier, *supra* note 6 at 566.

of a conflict, even when all other things are equal. Where relevant, the general interest *does* strengthen the position of (one of the) human rights in conflict. But it does so without saying everything there is to say about the *comparative* strength of those human rights, *i.e.* their strength in relation to each other.

In order to operationalise the general interest criterion, I further suggest a distinction between two kinds of general interests. On the one hand, a general interest may directly express part of what is at stake in a human rights conflict, in terms of value to society. In conflicts that involve freedom of expression, for instance, when a publication deals with a topic of public interest, the conflict extends beyond the two parties directly involved (for example, an investigative journalist and an allegedly corrupt politician). Instead, it also holds great relevance to society at large.[89] When speech serves the general interest by informing the public about issues of public concern, the position of freedom of expression in a human rights conflict should thus be strengthened, for instance *vis-à-vis* the right to reputation of the subject of the publication. On the other hand, however, a general interest may *not* directly express the societal value of the human rights in conflict. Budgetary considerations and legal certainty, for instance, can be relevant factors in the resolution of human rights conflicts, but they express a different kind of general interest than the societal value of speech on issues of public concern.

In keeping with the argument of Chapter 1 that human rights hold special normative force over the public interest, I submit that the first kind of general interest should offer stronger reasons in the resolution of human rights conflicts than the second kind of general interest. Differentiating the strength of the reasons involved allows us to acknowledge that general interests may be relevant to the balancing of human rights, while keeping a sense of rights as strong.[90] The kinds of general interests that would normally be 'subordinated' to human rights should, I posit, act as less strong reasons in balancing than the kinds of general interests that directly express the societal value of (one of) the human rights in conflict.

Human rights law seems to support the dual approach to the general interest suggested here. The ECtHR has, for instance, held, in a case concerning allegedly defamatory statements made by an expert witness against the prosecutor in the course of a trial, that

> [t]he parties' freedom of expression in the courtroom is not unlimited and certain interests, such as the authority of the judiciary, are important enough

89 Brems, 'Conflicting Human Rights', *supra* note 6 at 304.

90 On the paradox of recognising that non-rights considerations can help resolve a conflict of rights under a conception of rights as 'being directly opposed to concerns like utility … and social good', see Eugene Rice, 'Solving Human Rights Conflicts by Dissolving Them: The Failure of the Dissolution Strategy', 29 *Social Theory and Practice* (2003), 562. I believe my approach, viewed in light of the conception of rights proposed in Chapter 1, successfully addresses Rice's concerns.

> to justify restrictions on this right. Nonetheless, the Court refers to its case-law to the effect that it is only in exceptional circumstances that restriction … of for example defence counsel's freedom of expression can be accepted as necessary in a democratic society … For the Court, similar considerations should apply in respect of statements made by witnesses testifying before a court.

The authority of the judiciary – which belongs to the second kind of general interest I have identified above – thus provides a relatively weak reason against freedom of expression. This is in line with what I have proposed.

A few concrete examples further illustrate how the general interest criterion functions. I have already indicated that informing the public about matters of public concern serves a general interest that directly expresses the societal value attached to free speech.[91] Courts are generally highly protective of speech on matters of public interest,[92] because 'news media affords the public one of the best means of discovering and forming an opinion of the ideas and attitudes of political leaders'.[93] When freedom of expression conflicts with, for instance, the right to reputation or the right to private life, its position in a balancing exercise will be strengthened when the speech concerns a topic of public interest, given the societal value attached to said speech. Conversely, when speech does *not* contribute to a debate of public interest, but instead aims – for instance – at sensationalism, the position of freedom of expression in the conflict will be comparably weakened.[94]

Another example of a general interest that represents the societal value attached to human rights in conflict, confirming the salience of the general interest criterion, can be found in *Odièvre*:

> [t]here is also a general interest at stake, as the French legislature has consistently sought to protect the mother's and child's health during pregnancy and birth and to avoid abortions, in particular illegal abortions, and children being abandoned other than under the proper procedure.[95]

91 See *contra* Zucca, *supra* note 21 at 127. Zucca interprets the public's right to know as 'only the right of each individual to receive information', not as a general interest. Yet, for similar reasons to those offered in Chapter 2, I consider the public's 'right' to be informed to represent a general interest, rather than an aggregation of individual rights. See Chapter 2 – 'Human right or public interest? On human rights rhetoric, aggregation and speculation'.

92 See, among many authorities, *Observer and Guardian v the United Kingdom* [1991] ECHR 49; *Axel Springer*, *supra* note 4; *Verein gegen Tierfabriken Schweiz (VgT) v Switzerland (No. 2)* [2009] ECHR 1025; *Dalban v Romania* [1999] ECHR 74; *Centro Europa 7 S.r.l. and Di Stefano v Italy* [2012] ECHR 974.

93 *Centro Europa 7 S.r.l. and Di Stefano*, *supra* note 92 at para 131.

94 See *Von Hannover v Germany* [2004] ECHR 294, paras 63–65 and 76–77; *Biriuk*, *supra* note 67 at paras 42–43; *Ashby Donald*, *supra* note 75 at para 39.

95 *Odièvre*, *supra* note 3 at para 45. But see dissenting opinion of Judges Wildhaber, Sir Nicolas Bratza, Bonello, Loucaides, Cabral Barreto, Tulkens and Pellonpää in ibid., para 9 ('[a]s regards the general interest, the Court relied, *inter alia*, on the need to avoid illegal abortions

A particularly important example of the second kind of general interest, apart from the example of protecting the authority of the judiciary discussed above, is the need to ensure legal certainty. In the paternity case *Röman v Finland*, for instance, the ECtHR recognised that

> [a] person has a vital interest, protected by the Convention, in receiving the information necessary to uncover the truth about an important aspect of his or her personal identity and eliminate any uncertainty in this respect ... On the other hand, a putative father's interest in being protected from claims concerning facts that go back many years cannot be denied. Finally, in addition to that conflict of interest, other interests may come into play, such as those of third parties, essentially the putative father's family, and *the general interest of legal certainty*.[96]

Legal certainty assumes particular salience to the resolution of human rights conflicts when legislators have introduced bright line rules to tackle a conflict.[97] In such situations, legal certainty plays an inevitable role in subsequent adjudication of the conflict in concrete cases. If courts like the ECtHR were to overrule the balance struck by the legislator, the general interest in legal certainty would be jeopardised. Yet, because legal certainty does not express the societal value attached to either of the human rights in conflict, I submit that it should act as a relatively weak reason in the resolution of human rights in conflict. Only if the strength of other reasons in favour of the human rights in conflict is roughly equal may the general interest in legal certainty cast the die in favour of the human right that categorically prevails under national legislation. In spelling out the structured balancing test, I thus favour contextual balancing of the judicial kind over categorical balancing of the legislative kind.

One final point I should stress in relation to the general interest criterion, concerns the need to avoid 'double counting' in its application. The risk exists that the societal value of human rights in conflict would be counted twice under the structured balancing test: once here, under the general interest criterion, and once under the core-periphery criterion. Think of political speech, for instance. The strength of political speech in the balance with other human rights could be expressed with reference to its value to the public at large (general interest criterion). But political speech could also be identified as located close to the core of freedom of expression (core-periphery criterion). The risk thus arises that the same factor would be counted twice in balancing.

... However, it should be noted that at present there is no reliable data to support the notion that there would be a risk of an increase in abortions, or even of cases of infanticide, if the system of anonymous births was abolished').

96 *Röman*, *supra* note 62 at para 51 (emphasis added). See also *Laakso v Finland* [2013] ECHR 44, paras 45–46.

97 Ibid.; *Evans*, *supra* note 2 at para 89.

One way to ward against such double counting is to *combine* both criteria, where relevant. Courts could, for instance, express the idea that political speech lies closer to the core of freedom of expression with reference to its importance to the general interest, *i.e.* to inform the public about matters of political concern. Conversely, courts could clarify that commercial speech lies closer to the periphery of freedom of expression, because the societal value associated to speech in the public interest is missing. An alternative way to prevent double counting is to *separate* the core-periphery criterion from the general interest criterion, for instance by interpreting the former narrowly. Application of the core-periphery could then be limited to expressing the centrality of human rights to the person exercising them (*e.g.* political speech as crucial for politicians), while the general interest criterion would be reserved to express the societal importance of human rights (*e.g.* speech in the public interest). Given the rather artificial nature of the 'separation strategy', the former strategy arguably offers a better perspective to prevent double counting in balancing exercises between human rights in conflict.

The purpose criterion

The purpose criterion operationalises the idea that certain human rights stand in function of other human rights, in the sense that one of their purposes is to ensure adequate protection of those other rights. The scope of application of the purpose criterion should, however, be rather limited, given that it is at odds with the principle that all human rights deserve equal respect on their own terms. Human rights should thus, in principle, not be defined in function of (protection of) other rights. There are, nevertheless, a few exceptions. In discussing the value criterion, I have argued that the right to life, for instance, holds a higher abstract value within the human rights system, because its enjoyment is the prerequisite for the enjoyment of all other human rights. Here, under the purpose criterion, I will add another exception: the best interest of the child.

The purpose criterion is particularly relevant to the resolution of conflicts between human rights in which the best interest of the child is a primary consideration. Such conflicts may take different forms. They may be binary, *i.e.* between the human rights of the child and those of her parents (*e.g.* in certain child care cases or education cases).[98] They may be triadic, *i.e.* between the human rights of the child, those of one parent and those of the other parent (*e.g.* in custody cases, international abduction cases, certain child care cases and certain paternity cases).[99] Or they may be multipolar, *i.e.* between the human rights of the child, those of her parents and those of third parties, including adoptive parents,

98 See, for instance, *K. and T.*, *supra* note 48; *K.A. v Finland* [2003] ECHR 27; *Folgerø and Others v Norway* [2007] ECHR 546.

99 See, for instance, *Sommerfeld v Germany* [2003] ECHR 341; *Neulinger and Shuruk*, *supra* note 48; *Vojnity v Hungary* [2013] ECHR 131; *Mikulić v Croatia* [2002] ECHR 27.

step-parents or foster care 'parents' (*e.g.* in adoption cases, certain paternity cases and certain child care cases).[100]

Although the above conflicts take on different forms, they share one common element: 'the best interest of the child must be the primary consideration' in balancing the human rights involved.[101] Judicial inquiry into these conflicts focuses on the best interest of the child, because of the nature of the relationship between the child's human rights and those of the other parties to the conflict. The human rights of the other parties, for instance the child's parents, arguably have a dual function. On the one hand, they offer protection to these parties' own interests. On the other hand, however, they also stand *in function of* the human rights of the child, in the sense that their exercise is (to be) geared towards protection of the best interest of the child.

This dual approach to the child's best interest is incorporated in the United Nations Convention on the Rights of the Child (UNCRC), which provides that

> States Parties shall respect the responsibilities, rights and duties of parents ... the members of the extended family or community ... or other persons legally responsible for the child, to provide ... appropriate direction and guidance in the exercise by the child of the rights recognized in the present Convention,[102]

while simultaneously insisting that '[i]n all actions concerning children ... the best interests of the child shall be a primary consideration'[103] and noting that '[t]he best interests of the child will be [the] basic concern [of the child's parents and legal guardians]'.[104]

100 See, for instance, *Görgülü, supra* note 51; *Krisztián Barnabás Tóth v Hungary* [2013] ECHR 132; *Aune v Norway* [2010] ECHR 1994.

101 *Neulinger and Shuruk, supra* note 48 at para 134. See also *Sommerfeld, supra* note 99 at paras 62 and 64; *K. and T., supra* note 48 at para 154; *Krisztián Barnabás Tóth, supra* note 100 at para 32; *Görgülü, supra* note 51 at para 41; *Kearns v France* [2008] ECHR 1, para 79.

102 Article 5 UNCRC.

103 Article 3 (1) UNCRC.

104 Article 18 (1) UNCRC. See also Article 9 (1) UNCRC ('States Parties shall ensure that a child shall not be separated from his or her parents against their will, except when competent authorities subject to judicial review determine, in accordance with applicable law and procedures, that such separation is necessary for the best interests of the child. Such determination may be necessary in a particular case such as one involving abuse or neglect of the child by the parents, or one where the parents are living separately and a decision must be made as to the child's place of residence'); Article 14 UNCRC ('1. States Parties shall respect the right of the child to freedom of thought, conscience and religion. 2. States Parties shall respect the rights and duties of the parents and, when applicable, legal guardians, to provide direction to the child in the exercise of his or her right in a manner consistent with the evolving capacities of the child'); Article 27 CRC ('1. States Parties recognize the right of every child to a standard of living adequate for the child's physical, mental, spiritual, moral and social development. 2. The parent(s) or others responsible for the child have the

The dual approach to the best interest of the child is also present in the ECtHR's case law. In *Görgülü v Germany*, for instance, the Court stressed that

> in the balancing process, particular importance should be attached to the best interests of the child which, depending on their nature and seriousness, may override those of the parents. In particular, a parent cannot be entitled under Article 8 of the Convention to have such measures taken as would harm the child's health and development.[105]

Similarly, in *Folgerø and Others v Norway* the Court described the right of parents to ensure that their child's education takes place in conformity with their religious and philosophical convictions *in function of* the child's own right to education:

> [i]t is in the discharge of a natural duty towards their children – parents being primarily responsible for the "education and teaching" of their children – that parents may require the State to respect their religious and philosophical convictions. Their right thus corresponds to a responsibility closely linked to the enjoyment and the exercise of the right to education.[106]

The purpose criterion operationalises the idea, firmly embedded in human rights law, that the best interest of the child should be the primary consideration in balancing the child's human rights against the human rights of others, when the purpose of those other human rights is directly tied to the protection of the human rights of the child.[107]

The responsibility criterion

The final criterion of the structured balancing test, the responsibility criterion, infuses balancing with the correlative of human rights: duties. It does so by evaluating the responsibilities of persons in the exercise of their human rights.[108]

primary responsibility to secure, within their abilities and financial capacities, the conditions of living necessary for the child's development').

105 *Görgülü, supra* note 51 at para 43.

106 *Folgerø, supra* note 98 at para 84 (in which the Court described the right to education of Article 2 of Protocol 1 as 'a whole that is dominated by its first sentence'; the first sentence of the article protects the right to education, whereas its second sentence protects parents' right to ensure that their child's education takes place in conformity with their own religious and philosophical convictions).

107 See also Michel Levinet, 'La conciliation du droit à l'instruction de l'enfant et de l'obligation de respecter les convictions religieuses des parents, à la lumière de la Convention européenne des droits de l'homme', *Revue trimestrielle des droits de l'homme* (2011), 481–498 (arguing in favour of granting the right to education of the child priority when it conflicts with the right of parents to respect for their religious convictions).

108 De Schutter, *supra* note 6 at 244.

Yet, as indicated earlier, the responsibility criterion should be interpreted narrowly. Judges should, in particular, not require that right holders exercise their rights in the manner that causes least damage to the human rights of others. Under human rights law, adherence to a 'less restrictive alternative' requirement may be demanded of states.[109] But it should not be imposed on right holders.[110]

Nevertheless, the responsibility of certain right holders, most notably the media and its members in the exercise of freedom of expression, *can* be a relevant factor in balancing human rights.[111] Human rights law, in Article 10 ECHR for example, explicitly recognises that the exercise of freedom of expression 'carries with it duties and responsibilities'.[112] The responsibility criterion is intended to take these duties and responsibilities into account. Its application should, however, not go beyond the requirement that journalists and other members of the media act 'in good faith in order to provide accurate and reliable information in accordance with the ethics of journalism' when publishing statements that may cause damage to someone's right to reputation, presumption of innocence or right to private life.[113]

The responsibility criterion, in short, allows courts to factor in elements such as whether or not journalists have taken sufficient steps to verify their information, presented a distorted view of reality and made statements intended as a gratuitous personal insult or attack.[114] The responsibility criterion should, however, patently *not* be utilised to impose content or style restrictions on journalists, in the sense that they could have phrased their message in a manner that would have caused less damage to the human rights of others. Since it is almost always possible to

109 On the role of 'less restrictive alternatives' in the Court's case law, see Eva Brems and Laurens Lavrysen, '"Don't Use a Sledgehammer to Crack a Nut": Less Restrictive Means in the Case Law of the European Court of Human Rights', 15 *Human Rights Law Review* (2015), 139–168.

110 See also the partly dissenting opinion of Judge David Thór Björgvinsson in *MGN Limited*, *supra* note 4 at para 4 ('at least some of the principles applied by the House of Lords are not relevant in the balancing exercise. I refer in this regard to Baroness Hale's opinion that it was "not necessary to publish any further information" ... The test implied in that opinion is the wrong one. From the point of view of journalistic discretion in the presentation of a legitimate story, it is the restriction on freedom of expression that must be justified by reference to "necessity" and not the publication as such').

111 *Egeland and Hanseid v Norway* [2009] ECHR 622, para 59; *Axel Springer*, *supra* note 4 at para 82.

112 Article 10 (2) ECHR.

113 *Cumpănă and Mazăre*, *supra* note 44 at para 102; *Novaya Gazeta and Borodyanskiy v Russia* [2013] ECHR 251, para 40. See also, using a slightly different formulation, *Axel Springer*, *supra* note 4 at para 93; *MGN Limited*, *supra* note 4 at para 141 (both referring to the requirement of journalists to act 'in good faith and on an accurate factual basis and provide "reliable and precise" information in accordance with the ethics of journalism'). See further *Couderc and Hachette Filipacchi Associés*, *supra* note 34 at paras 138–139.

114 See, for instance, *Cumpănă and Mazăre*, *supra* note 44 at para 103; *Axel Springer*, *supra* note 4 at para 82; *Kwiecień v Poland* [2007] ECHR 4, para 54; *Europapress Holding D.O.O. v Croatia* [2009] ECHR 1613, paras 66–68; *Mahmudov and Agazade v Azerbaijan* 2008] ECHR 1739, para 40; *Oberschlick v Austria (No. 2)* [1997] ECHR 38, para 33.

present one's message in less damaging terms, imposing such a 'less restrictive alternative' requirement on journalists and other members of the media will inevitably eradicate all room for exaggeration and provocation in the exercise of freedom of expression. In that sense, courts like the ECtHR should strictly adhere to the principle that

> it is not for this Court, nor for the national courts ... to substitute their own views for those of the press as to what technique of reporting should be adopted by journalists ... [since] Article 10 ... protects not only the substance of the ideas and information expressed, but also the form in which they are conveyed.[115]

A deeply troubling evolution in the ECtHR's case law on human rights conflict, in this respect, is the Court's increasing reliance on 'less restrictive alternative' reasoning in certain freedom of expression cases.[116] The Court has, for instance, held in *PETA Deutschland v Germany* that 'the applicant has not established that it did not have other means at their (*sic*) disposal of drawing public attention to [its message on cruelty against animals]'[117] and in the defamation case *Ciuvică v Romania* that 'les termes employés par le requérant n'étaient pas indispensables pour la communication de son message'.[118] Imposing such duties on right holders in the exercise of their freedom of expression is profoundly at odds with the Court's broader free speech case law, in which it offers strong protection to statements that 'offend, shock or disturb'[119] and leaves room for exaggeration and provocation.[120]

The structured balancing test in practice

Thus far, I have discussed the structured balancing test in rather fragmented terms, explaining each of the seven criteria of the test separately. When applied to a given human rights conflict, each criterion may or may not yield reasons

115 *Jersild v Denmark* [1994] ECHR 33, para 31; *Stoll v Switzerland* [2006] ECHR 476, para 146.

116 See, apart from the examples offered in the text, *Ricci v Italy* [2013] ECHR 926, para 55 ('Si le requérant souhaitait ouvrir un débat sur un sujet d'intérêt primordial pour la société, tel que le rôle des médias télévisés, d'autres voies, qui ne comportaient aucune violation de la confidentialité des communications télématiques, s'ouvraient à lui'). See further the dissenting opinion of Judge Loucaides in *Öllinger v Austria* [2006] ECHR 665 ('[i]f the applicant's aim was to contest the legality of this provocative gathering, the proper way to do so was indisputably through legal means or peaceful demonstrations against the authorities who allowed the gatherings, and certainly not through a confrontation in a cemetery on All Saints' Day').

117 *PETA Deutschland v Germany* [2012] ECHR 1888, para 50.

118 *Ciuvică v Romania* [2012] ECHR 551, para 55.

119 *Handyside v the United Kingdom* [1976] ECHR 5, para 49.

120 *Prager and Oberschlick v Austria* [1995] ECHR 12, para 38.

in favour of – or against – the human rights at stake. Once their strength is determined, these reasons can be linked in the construction of nets of arguments. Under the structured balancing test, one net of arguments is constructed for each of the human rights in conflict. By comparing the strength of those nets, and the reasons woven into them, judges should be able to determine – with some measure of rational confidence – which of the human rights in conflict should prevail. This, in a nutshell, is how the structured balancing test functions in theory. Here, I will apply the test to the ECtHR case of *Palomo Sánchez and Others v Spain* to illuminate how it could function in practice.

The ECtHR case of *Palomo Sánchez* was introduced earlier, in Chapter 5, where I critiqued the balancing exercise conducted by the majority of the Court's Grand Chamber. I will briefly recall the facts of the case here. *Palomo Sánchez* involved a conflict between the freedom of expression of trade union representatives, on the one hand, and the right to reputation of two of their fellow employees and a human resources manager, on the other. In the context of a labour dispute with the company that employed them, the trade union representatives had reported on court proceedings in their newsletter. The cover of the newsletter featured a cartoon of the human resources manager sitting behind a desk, with a person on all fours underneath of it (only his legs visible). From the cartoon, it was clear that the person beneath the desk was offering sexual services to the resource manager. Two of the company's employees were drawn in front of the desk, waiting in line to sexually please the resource manager. Inside, the newsletter contained two articles in which the trade union representatives vehemently denounced the two employees on the cover for having testified in favour of the company in the court proceedings. After the newsletter was spread through the trade union's bulletin boards, located on the company's premises, the trade union representatives were dismissed on grounds of serious misconduct.

In its judgment, the majority of the ECtHR's Grand Chamber ruled that the dismissal did not violate the right to freedom of expression. I critiqued the majority's reasoning in Chapter 5. Here, I will briefly summarise its main points. The majority identified a number of elements as particularly relevant to the balancing exercise. The majority first pointed out that the cartoon and articles contained 'criticism and accusations, not directly against the company but against the two non-salaried deliverymen and the human resources manager'.[121] The majority then noted 'that the extent of acceptable criticism is narrower as regards private individuals than as regards politicians or civil servants acting in the exercise of their duties'.[122] Although the majority considered the publication to be 'at least a matter of general interest for the workers of the company',[123] it brushed aside the trade union aspect of the case, finding that 'the applicants' trade union

121 *Palomo Sánchez, supra* note 3 at para 71.
122 Ibid.
123 Ibid. at para 72.

membership did not play a decisive role in their dismissal'.[124] Instead, the majority emphasised that 'the existence of ... a matter [of general interest] cannot justify the use of offensive cartoons or expressions, even in the context of labour relations'.[125] The majority held that, on the contrary, 'certain manifestations of the right to freedom of expression that may be legitimate in other contexts are not legitimate in that of labour relations'.[126]

The majority further noted that 'in addition to being insulting, the cartoon and texts in issue were intended more as an attack on colleagues for testifying before the courts than as a means of promoting trade union action *vis-à-vis* the employer'.[127] The majority also considered it relevant that 'the remarks did not constitute an instantaneous and ill-considered reaction, in the context of a rapid and spontaneous oral exchange'.[128] 'On the contrary', the majority noted, 'they were written assertions, published in a quite lucid manner and displayed publicly on the premises of the company'.[129] The majority finally ruled that the cartoon and articles were particularly damaging to the subjects' right to reputation: '[an] attack on the respectability of individuals by using grossly insulting or offensive expressions in the professional environment is ... a particularly serious form of misconduct'.[130] Taking all the preceding elements together, the majority concluded that 'the measure of dismissal taken against the applicants was not a manifestly disproportionate or excessive sanction'.[131]

In Chapter 5, I criticised the majority judgment in *Palomo Sánchez* for leaving certain *prima facie* relevant balancing factors unaddressed, while downplaying the relevance of others. I linked these shortcomings to the open ended nature of the Court's balancing test, which invites a subjective selection of factors employed in balancing. Here, I aim to show how adjudication under the structured balancing test avoids these shortcomings. To illustrate the analytical structure of the test, I will first apply each of its seven criteria to the conflict in *Palomo Sánchez* separately. Application of the seven criteria will reveal the strength of the reasons in favour of – and against – the human rights in conflict in *Palomo Sánchez*. I will go on to explain that a comparative judgment on the strength of those reasons, linked in nets of arguments, supports an outcome in favour of freedom of expression. In applying the structured balancing test to *Palomo Sánchez*, I will thus be led to a different outcome than the one reached by the majority of the Grand Chamber.

The value criterion is irrelevant to *Palomo Sánchez*, given that the conflict involves human rights that, in principle, deserve equal respect. We can therefore disregard it. The same goes for the purpose criterion. Neither of the human rights

124 Ibid. at para 52.
125 Ibid. at para 73.
126 Ibid. at para 76.
127 Ibid. at para 74.
128 Ibid. at para 73.
129 Ibid.
130 Ibid. at para 76.
131 Ibid. at para 77.

in conflict in *Palomo Sánchez* serves to protect the other. The other five criteria of the structured balancing test, however, will prove of immediate relevance to the balancing exercise. I will examine those five remaining criteria in turn.

Under the impact criterion, we first need to evaluate the damage suffered by the human rights in conflict. In *Palomo Sánchez*, a number of key elements may guide that evaluation. Let us start with the damage suffered by the right to reputation. In relation to this right, one particularly relevant element is that the speech at issue was directed at private individuals, against whom 'the extent of acceptable criticism is narrower ... than as regards politicians or civil servants'.[132] Another relevant element is the insulting, crude and vulgar language used in both the cartoon and the articles, as well as the insinuations of sexual obedience implicit in the cartoon. When combined, those elements may tempt us to describe the damage suffered by the right to reputation as 'very serious'. This would certainly be in line with the majority judgment in *Palomo Sánchez*, which described the speech at issue as 'an attack on the respectability of individuals by using grossly insulting or offensive expressions in the professional environment [and] a particularly serious form of misconduct'.[133]

Yet, the majority arguably failed to take adequate account of a crucial countervailing element: the satirical nature of the speech at issue (this is particularly true of the cartoon).[134] Because the impugned speech took the form of satire (in part), the damage suffered by the right to reputation must be considered somewhat mitigated. Satirical speech aims, by its very nature, to exaggerate and provoke. The sexual obedience implied in the cartoon should, in that sense, of course not be taken literally. Instead, it was a metaphor for the obedience the employees had displayed towards the company, when asked to testify in its favour. This remains a serious allegation, but it is less serious than the literal meaning of the cartoon. The speech at issue in *Palomo Sánchez* moreover did not reach beyond the confines of the company. It was displayed, only, on bulletin boards on the company's premises. The impact of the speech on the employees' right to reputation was thus less grave than it would have been if the same cartoon and articles had featured, for instance, in a national newspaper. Nevertheless, the impact of the speech on the employees' right to reputation remained serious, given that the employees risked losing the esteem of their fellow colleagues. In that sense, the limited audience of the speech did not dramatically decrease the damage to the employees' right to reputation. Taking the above elements together, the damage to the right to reputation should, I posit, be labelled 'serious'.

On the damage suffered by freedom of expression, the majority judgment in *Palomo Sánchez* was surprisingly silent. The majority did not evaluate, in any sense, the damage done to freedom of expression. I venture that a subjective preference

132 Ibid. at para 71.

133 Ibid. at para 76.

134 See also the joint dissenting opinion of Judges Tulkens, David Thór Björgvinsson, Jočienė, Popović and Vučinić in ibid. at para 11.

for the right to reputation, in this particular case, led the majority to downplay or ignore arguments in favour of freedom of expression. In adjudicating the human rights conflict in *Palomo Sánchez*, the majority judges arguably fell prey to 'confirmation bias'. My hypothesis is that the judges had, fairly early on in their assessment, 'perceived' that the right to reputation should prevail. Afterwards, they focused on bolstering that intuitive conclusion by emphasising arguments that supported it, while ignoring or downplaying countervailing arguments. This explains why the majority judgment only evaluates the damage suffered by one of the human rights in conflict, while remaining silent on the damage suffered by the other right.

The dissenting judges, however, did pay specific attention to the damage done to free speech: '[a]s to the *seriousness of the sanction*, the applicants received … undoubtedly the harshest possible sanction that can be imposed on workers'.[135] The dissenters further pointed out that '[t]he imposition of such a harsh sanction on trade union members … is likely to have … a "chilling effect" on the conduct of trade unionists'.[136] Both elements are of immediate relevance to the evaluation, under the impact criterion, of the damage suffered by freedom of expression in *Palomo Sánchez*. Because the harshest possible sanction under labour law was imposed, and given the 'chilling effect' its imposition had on trade unions, the damage to free speech in *Palomo Sánchez* should arguably be labelled 'very serious'.

Having evaluated the damage suffered by the human rights in conflict in *Palomo Sánchez*, we can now move on to assessing the likelihood that said damage will actually occur. The damage suffered by freedom of expression is, under the circumstances, 'certain': the trade union representatives were dismissed, which *ipso facto* constituted the damage to their freedom of expression. As explained earlier, the likelihood that the right to reputation suffered actual damage is, by definition, less certain. In defamation cases, the likelihood of damage depends on subjective assessment by the targets of the speech at issue and by the audience that receives it. In *Palomo Sánchez*, that audience was composed of the employees of the company. Given the particular circumstances of the case – (1) the gravity of the acts depicted in the cartoon (even when taken metaphorically), (2) the allegations made in the accompanying articles, which contained crude and vulgar language and (3) the display of the newsletter on the premises of the company – the likelihood that the employees' right to reputation suffered actual damage arguably falls to be categorised as 'a real and immediate risk'. The likelihood may be less than certain, given that there is an inevitable element of subjective assessment involved, but the reputation of the employees in the eyes of their colleagues most likely suffered real damage.

To sum up, application of the impact criterion to the conflict in *Palomo Sánchez* yields the following results: freedom of expression suffered 'very serious' and 'certain' damage, while the right to reputation suffered 'a real and immediate risk'

135 Ibid. at para 15 (emphasis in original).
136 Ibid. at para 17.

of 'serious' damage. Taken in isolation, the impact criterion thus offers stronger reasons in support of freedom of expression than in support of the right to reputation.

The third criterion of the structured balancing test – the core-periphery criterion – is also instructive in balancing freedom of expression and the right to reputation in *Palomo Sánchez*. Both the majority judgment and the dissent in *Palomo Sánchez* are scarce in terms of arguments that may prove relevant to the core-periphery criterion. Nevertheless, the dissent provides some useful elements. The dissenting judges 'share[d] the view that "since trade unions play an important role, in that they express and defend ideas of public interest in professional and employment-related matters, their freedom to put forward opinions warrants a high degree of protection"'.[137]

The dissenting judges thus considered trade union freedom of expression to be located rather close to the core of freedom of expression. There is something to be said for this argument, given the parallel between press freedom and trade union freedom of expression in matters of public interest. Both the press and trade unions fulfil a 'watchdog' function in informing the public about matters of general interest. Yet, trade unions generally fulfil this role on a more limited scale, *i.e.* to the benefit of employees in a given company or sector, rather than society at large. Moreover, the 'watchdog' function of the press is intimately connected to free speech, whereas trade unions perform the same function in a variety of manners. Often, as in negotiations with employers, their 'watchdog' activities are not directly covered by freedom of expression. Trade union freedom of expression should therefore arguably not be located as close to the core of free speech as press freedom. But trade union speech is certainly more central to freedom of expression than, for instance, commercial speech, which is a rather peripheral aspect of the right. Thus, it seems fair to locate trade union freedom of expression closer to the core of free speech than to its periphery.

In locating the employees' right to reputation within their right to private life, a few observations can be made. Under prevailing ECtHR case law, the right to reputation is not considered as central to the right to private life as some of the core aspects highlighted earlier (*e.g.* protection of health data). When speech is in the public interest and does not reveal private information, the right to reputation should arguably be located away from the core of the right to private life. This, at least, is how the ECtHR appears to view the matter. The Court imposes a threshold requirement for the application of Article 8 ECHR, which protects the right to private life, in defamation cases:

> [i]n order for Article 8 to come into play … an attack on a person's reputation must attain a certain level of seriousness and in a manner causing prejudice to personal enjoyment of the right to respect for private life.[138]

137 Ibid. at para 5 (citing an article by Michael O'Boyle, former Registrar of the ECtHR).
138 *Axel Springer*, *supra* note 4 at para 83.

This indicates that the Court considers reputation to be, in principle, a less central aspect of the right to private life than the publication of photographs or health data. Indeed, in relation to the latter, the Court does not impose a similar threshold requirement.[139] The dissent in *Palomo Sánchez* usefully points out that '[t]he harsh criticism did not relate to the intimacy of the individuals or to other rights pertaining to their private lives'.[140] Here, we find a reason against locating the employees' right to reputation close to the core of their right to private life. Yet, we should also recall that the criticism at issue was directed at private individuals. Unlike politicians or public figures, private individuals have fewer options at their disposal to counter speech that allegedly damages their reputation. They moreover do not hold public functions, for which they can expect to be – and are used to being – publicly scrutinised. Taking these countervailing factors into account, there may be cause to locate the employees' right to reputation closer to the core of their right to private life than would be the case for politicians or public figures, in respect of speech that does not reveal private information.

We are, in short, confronted with competing arguments on the location of the employees' right to reputation within their right to private life. One argument pulls in the direction of the core of the right (the publication concerned private individuals). The other argument pushes away from the right's core (the publication did not reveal intimate or private information). In light of these competing arguments, it seems sensible to locate the employees' right to reputation somewhere 'in the middle' of the right to private life. Yet, given the serious nature of the allegations and in light of the vulgar language and images used, we arguably have cause to locate the employees' right to reputation – *in casu* – more towards the core-side of the continuum than to the periphery-side.

Application of the core-periphery criterion to the conflict in *Palomo Sánchez* thus yields less clear results than the impact criterion. Both trade union freedom of expression and the employees' right to reputation are, *in casu*, located somewhere 'in the middle' of the human rights in conflict, but closer to the core-side than to the periphery-side of the continuum. Arguably, the core-periphery criterion does not offer reasons in favour of, or against, the human rights in conflict. Or, in other words, the criterion offers equally strong reasons in favour of both rights.

139 Compare *Von Hannover*, *supra* note 94 at para 103 (holding that the publication of photographs is 'an area in which the protection of the rights and reputation of others takes on particular importance, as the photos may contain very personal or even intimate information about an individual or his or her family'); *Biriuk*, *supra* note 67 at para 39 ('protection of personal data, not least medical data, is of fundamental importance to a person's enjoyment of his or her right to respect for private and family life as guaranteed by Article 8 of the Convention ... especially ... as regards the protection of the confidentiality of a person's HIV status').

140 Joint dissenting opinion of Judges Tulkens, David Thór Björgvinsson, Jočienė, Popović and Vučinić in *Palomo Sánchez*, *supra* note 3 at para 12.

The fourth criterion of the structured balancing test – the additional rights criterion – plays to the advantage of freedom of expression. For the trade union representatives, not only was their freedom of expression at stake in *Palomo Sánchez*, their freedom of association was also at play. The trade union representatives were dismissed for exercising their freedom of expression *in the context of* labour disputes. Their dismissal moreover resulted in the *de facto* disbanding of their trade union. Despite the clear link between freedom of expression and freedom of association in *Palomo Sánchez*, the majority judgment largely ignored the trade union aspect of the case. The majority did start off by acknowledging that 'the facts of the present case are such that the question of freedom of expression is closely related to that of freedom of association in a trade-union context'.[141] Immediately afterwards, however, it brushed aside freedom of association in the balancing exercise, curiously noting that 'the applicants' trade union membership did not play a decisive role in their dismissal'.[142] On this point, the dissenting judges vehemently criticised their colleagues in the majority: '[b]oth in assessing the facts and in balancing the interests at stake, the majority give scant consideration to the fact that the applicants were members of a trade union, or that they were expressing professional and employment-related claims'.[143]

The trade union representatives' associational rights may not have been decisive in the balancing exercise. But they were at least a relevant factor within it. The fact that the trade union representatives had exercised their freedom of expression in the context of labour disputes *strengthens* their free speech claim. To fully appreciate this argument, one need only consider the same cartoon and articles being put on the company's bulletin board by an employee who was not a trade union representative, but simply wished to express his discontent at the testimony given by his colleagues. This other employee would have been in a comparatively weaker position than the trade union representatives in *Palomo Sánchez*. Indeed, the latter's trade union freedom lent context and support to their speech. The additional rights criterion thus provides a reason – inconclusive, when considered in isolation – in support of freedom of expression.

The fifth criterion – the general interest criterion – is of particular relevance in cases, like *Palomo Sánchez*, that involve speech in the public interest. Both the majority judgment and the dissent acknowledge that the speech in *Palomo Sánchez* addressed a matter of public interest.[144] As noted earlier, speech aimed at informing the public serves a general interest that directly expresses what is at stake in the conflict, in terms of value to society. Even if the intended public was rather limited in *Palomo Sánchez*, the debate to which the speech contributed was 'not a purely

141 *Palomo Sánchez*, *supra* note 3 at para 52.

142 Ibid.

143 Joint dissenting opinion of Judges Tulkens, David Thór Björgvinsson, Jočienė, Popović and Vučinić in ibid. at para 4.

144 *Palomo Sánchez*, *supra* note 3 at para 72; Joint dissenting opinion of Judges Tulkens, David Thór Björgvinsson, Jočienė, Popović and Vučinić in ibid. at para 12.

private one [but] at least a matter of general interest for the workers of the company'.[145] The general interest criterion thus provides a reason in favour of freedom of expression. Yet, given the limited audience of the speech at issue, that reason is arguably less strong than it would have been if similar statements had been published in the press, in the context of a debate of interest to society at large.

The seventh and final criterion of the structured balancing test – the responsibility criterion – is arguably the most controversial. In ruling against freedom of expression, the majority in *Palomo Sánchez* was heavily invested in arguments on the responsible exercise of free speech. The majority characterised the cartoon and articles as 'insulting' and 'intended more as an attack on colleagues for testifying before the courts than as a means of promoting trade union action *vis-à-vis* the employer'.[146] If accurate, this depiction would lend support to a finding in favour of the right to reputation. An argument could then be made that the trade union representatives had exercised their freedom of expression irresponsibly. As rightly pointed out in the dissent, however, the majority's characterisation of the speech at issue was not supported by the facts of the case. Instead, it '[amounted] to speculation' and was a direct result of the majority '[dissociating] the impugned texts from their context'.[147]

There seems to be no reason, other than perhaps unwarranted reliance on subjective preferences on the part of the majority, to assign a certain intention – to launch a personal attack on colleagues – to the trade union representatives. Their main intention was, according to their submissions, to protect trade union interests. There are no convincing reasons, available in the facts, to unequivocally hold that the speech at issue was instead intended as a gratuitous personal attack on the employees concerned. That being said, it remains true that the trade union representatives chose poor – insulting, crude and vulgar – language to express their opinion. They could, without a doubt, have expressed the same opinion in less vigorous terms. As I argued earlier, however, the responsibility criterion should not be employed to impose a 'less restrictive alternative' requirement on right holders, since doing so would eradicate any room for exaggeration and provocation in the legitimate exercise of freedom of expression. Obviously, the tone and content of the speech at issue *are* relevant factors to balancing, but they should be – and have already been – factored into account under the other criteria of the structured balancing test. The responsibility criterion therefore arguably does not provide additional reasons in favour of – or against – the human rights in conflict in *Palomo Sánchez*.

Having evaluated each of the seven criteria of the structured balancing test separately, I am now in a position to bring the identified reasons together in the

145 *Palomo Sánchez, supra* note 3 at para 72.
146 Ibid. at para 74.
147 Joint dissenting opinion of Judges Tulkens, David Thór Björgvinsson, Jočienė, Popović and Vučinić in ibid. at para 13.

construction of nets of arguments in favour of the human rights in conflict in *Palomo Sánchez*. A number of criteria have proven irrelevant to the balancing exercise: the value criterion, the purpose criterion and the responsibility criterion. Of the remaining four criteria, the core-periphery criterion provided equally strong reasons in favour of both rights. The result of the balancing exercise thus depends on the other three criteria: the impact criterion, the additional rights criterion and the general interest criterion.

Comparison of the reasons identified under these criteria reveals that – under all three – stronger reasons were found in favour of freedom of expression than of the right to reputation. The damage done to freedom of expression was found to be 'very serious' and 'certain', while there was a 'real and immediate risk' of 'serious' damage to the right to reputation. In other words, the right to reputation suffered comparably less serious damage than freedom of expression, which was moreover less likely to occur. The position of freedom of expression in the balance was further strengthened by the relevance of additional rights – the trade representatives' freedom of association – and of the general interest – informing the employees of the company on a matter of general interest. In and of themselves, these latter reasons would not have been decisive.[148] When combined with the reasons under the impact criterion, however, they allow us to construct a coherent judgment in favour of freedom of expression:

> Because (A) freedom of expression suffered more damage, which was moreover more likely to occur (impact criterion), (B) the trade union representatives' freedom of association was also at stake (additional rights criterion) and (C) the speech at issue contributed to a debate of general interest (general interest criterion), (D) without amounting to a gratuitous personal attack on the employees (responsibility criterion), the human rights conflict in *Palomo Sánchez* should have been resolved to the benefit of freedom of expression.

Conclusion

In this chapter, I have proposed a structured balancing test, aimed at overcoming the theoretical challenges and practical obstacles to balancing human rights identified in Chapters 4 and 5. After detailing the test in theory, I illustrated how it could function in practice by applying it to a concrete human rights conflict. For analytical purposes, I distinguished two phases in explaining the workings of the test. I first applied its seven criteria separately. I then brought the reasons drawn from application of the criteria together in the construction of a comparative judgment in favour of freedom of expression.

148 See *supra* 'The seven criteria of the structured balancing test in detail', 'Additional rights criterion' and 'General interest criterion'.

In actual judicial practice, application of the structured balancing test would, of course, not take on the analytical form it has assumed in this chapter. Actual judgments are written in a distinct linguistic style, whereby judges are motivated by their responsibility towards the parties to the case, the court on which they serve and society at large. Judges write in response to parties' arguments. They utilise the broader case law of the court on which they serve – and that of others – as a frame of reference. And for legitimacy reasons, their writing style is tailored to persuade the parties and society at large of the validity of the judgment they have rendered. I, conversely, have had one single aim in mind in this chapter: to demonstrate the analytical power of the structured balancing test. That power rests in the test's ability to assist judges in structuring and conducting balancing exercises to resolve human rights conflicts. In that sense, the structured balancing test would be operating in the background in judicial practice, as a decision aid that guides judges in balancing. Comparative arguments that result from application of the test would still need to be 'translated' – if you will – into judicial language, fit for communication to the parties and society at large.

Despite its analytical power, however, the structured balancing test has its limits. The test may be able to overcome the challenge from weak incommensurability. But it is powerless in the face of strong incommensurability. When comparability cannot be obtained, the structured balancing test does not provide a solution to a human rights conflict. Instead, judges will be confronted with a genuine dilemma. Such dilemmas – and the strong incommensurability they entail – are the subject of Chapter 8. There, I will explore the limits of the structured balancing test. First, however, I will evaluate the strength of the structured balancing test against alternative balancing tests, as well as one purported alternative to balancing.

7 Alternative (non-)balancing approaches

To make balancing work in judicial practice, I proposed a structured balancing test in the previous chapter. The test is designed to overcome the challenge from incommensurability (Chapter 4), while counteracting practical obstacles to balancing (Chapter 5). It does so by enabling comparative judgments on the strength of reasons in favour of – and against – human rights in conflict. Such comparative judgments are rendered possible through the construction and comparison of nets of arguments, woven with reference to a limited set of balancing criteria. Use of the structured balancing test should allow judges to decide, with some measure of rational confidence, which human right should prevail in a given conflict.

Yet, there are, of course, other balancing tests out there. And important *non-balancing* approaches to human rights conflicts have been proposed as well. In this chapter, I situate my structured balancing test among the most salient alternative approaches – both of the balancing and non-balancing kind – to human rights conflicts: the non-balancing approach of Lorenzo Zucca, on the one hand, and the balancing approaches of Robert Alexy, Kai Möller and Aharon Barak, on the other. In evaluating the alternatives, I explain why the structured balancing test I propose may well prove superior.

A non-balancing approach? Zucca on 'constitutional dilemmas'

Among potential alternative approaches to human rights conflicts, Lorenzo Zucca has arguably put forth one of the more detailed *non-balancing* approaches. In his *Constitutional Dilemmas*, Zucca depicts balancing as 'a helpful tool for the resolution of a well-defined number of cases, which do *not* include genuine conflicts of FLRs [fundamental legal rights]'.[1] Instead, Zucca argues, genuine conflicts between fundamental rights should be decided by prioritising certain values over others,[2] which boils down to 'stating the prevalence

1 Lorenzo Zucca, *Constitutional Dilemmas – Conflicts of Fundamental Legal Rights in Europe and the USA* (Oxford University Press, 2007), 169 (emphasis added).
2 Ibid. at 24.

of one right over another'.[3] In short, Zucca favours 'a rule based solution' to human rights conflicts.[4] Unfortunately, the precise content of this rule based solution remains somewhat obscure throughout Zucca's work. Nevertheless, Zucca does offer some important indications by arguing in terms of 'rebuttable presumptions'[5] and proposing, for instance, that press freedom be granted qualified priority over privacy, when both are in conflict.[6]

At first glance, Zucca's account of conflicts between fundamental rights squarely contradicts the position I have favoured over the course of the past four chapters: human rights conflicts should be defused, minimised through compromise or resolved through balancing. But the real disagreement between Zucca and myself arguably does not concern any of those steps, and balancing in particular, at all. Instead, it lies in our different conceptions of human rights and, concomitantly, our diverging definitions of conflicts between human rights. Whereas Zucca conceives of all fundamental rights as rules,[7] I have argued that relative human rights, at least, function as principles.[8] Somehow, Zucca deduces from his conception of fundamental rights as rules that genuine conflicts between them must be defined narrowly (but, interestingly, not excluded altogether). The notions of 'normative inconsistency' and 'strong incommensurability' are central to Zucca's narrow definition of conflict.[9] The definition of human rights conflicts I provided in Chapter 2 is, quite simply, broader than Zucca's. It not only encompasses instances of normative inconsistency and strong incommensurability, but also those of incompatible duties and weak incommensurability.

This, it turns out, has fundamental consequences, for Zucca does not reject balancing outright.[10] Rather, he argues that 'the idea of balance seems more apt

3 Ibid. at 86.
4 Ibid. at 134.
5 Ibid. at 168.
6 Ibid. at 141. Note that Zucca's turn to *rebuttable* presumptions is not entirely in line with his earlier argument on prioritising certain values over others or 'stating the prevalence of one right over another'.
7 Ibid. at 25.
8 See Chapter 1 'The proportionality view: (conflicts between) human rights are not special'.
9 Zucca, *supra* note 1 at 52 and 85–86. The notion of 'tragedy' also appears to play a role in Zucca's conception of fundamental rights conflicts, but its precise place is somewhat unclear. Zucca only refers to a 'tragedy' when he discusses physician assisted suicide as an example of what he considers to be *genuine* conflicts between fundamental rights. He fails to invoke the notion when he discusses another example of genuine conflict: that between free press and privacy. *Compare* ibid. at 142–167 (particularly at 160–162) *with* 114–141.
10 Zucca *is* critical of balancing, but the primary explanation he offers for his critical stance is puzzling. In explaining '[w]hat is wrong with balancing', Zucca identifies the problem in terms of public interests overriding fundamental rights. He argues that, by allowing this to happen, balancing 'fails to respect the priority of FLRs [fundamental legal rights]'. Yet, this is merely an argument as to why rights should not be balanced against the public interest. Zucca does not explain why rights should not be balanced against other rights (apart from noting that this '[does] not take FLR [fundamental legal rights] conflicts seriously'). See ibid. at 90 and 132.

to avoid conflicts rather than adjudicate them'.[11] Zucca particularly notes that balancing is appropriate for the resolution of what he terms 'spurious conflicts',[12] *i.e.* conflicts between fundamental rights that do not involve normative inconsistencies.[13] Crucially, my definition of human rights conflicts encompasses such 'spurious conflicts'. As it turns out, the argument I have advanced in Chapter 6 – that human rights conflicts can and should be resolved through a structured balancing test (when they cannot be defused or minimised through compromise) – is not *really* incompatible with Zucca's approach. Our disagreement, rather, is located elsewhere. Whereas Zucca conceives of balancing as a useful tool to *avoid* conflicts between weakly incommensurable human rights, I posit that balancing *resolves* such conflicts. Because our disagreement is rather conceptual, I will leave Zucca's work aside for now and refer the reader (back) to the core arguments of Chapters 1 and 2. I will, however, return to Zucca's 'constitutional dilemmas' in Chapter 8, where I discuss dilemmas, strong incommensurability and the limits of the structured balancing test of Chapter 6.

In the remainder of this chapter, I will situate my structured balancing test among alternative *balancing* approaches, as opposed to Zucca's purported non-balancing approach. To that end, I will first evaluate Robert Alexy's balancing test. Afterwards, I will briefly assess the balancing methodologies favoured by Kai Möller and Aharon Barak. Whereas I will prove rather critical of Alexy's test (while retaining some of its core elements), I will be more receptive to the approaches of Barak and Möller (while disagreeing with some of their core assumptions).

Alexy's balancing test: overly arithmetical and simplistic?

Among advocates of balancing, Robert Alexy has arguably given the concept most analytical thought. In deducing his (in)famous balancing test from the case law of the German Constitutional Court, Alexy has certainly dedicated great effort to demonstrating the purported rationality of balancing. Alexy has formulated a balancing test comprised of two Laws of Balancing and a Weight Formula. Combined, these purportedly allow for the rational weighing of competing principles (including constitutional and human rights). Yet, Alexy's balancing test arguably does not quite achieve the desired aim. *Qua* Weight Formula, it appears overly arithmetical in its operationalisation. *Qua* Laws of Balancing, conversely, it seems overly simplistic. It fails, in particular, to include important balancing factors. To fully grasp exactly *why* Alexy's balancing test ultimately fails to convince, we need a firm handle on it. To that end, I will describe the test in detail, before critiquing it.

11 Ibid. at 86.
12 Ibid. at 169.
13 Ibid. at 51.

Alexy's Laws of Balancing and Weight Formula

Alexy's balancing test might appear complicated to the uninitiated, but – at its core – it is actually quite simple. At the heart of Alexy's balancing test, rests his First Law of Balancing:

> [t]he greater the degree of non-satisfaction of, or detriment to, one right or principle, the greater must be the importance of satisfying the other.[14]

According to Alexy, the First Law of Balancing 'shows that balancing can be broken down into three stages', all of which are crucial to ensuring the rationality of balancing.[15] Alexy explains that

> [t]he first stage involves establishing the degree of non-satisfaction of, or detriment to, the first principle. This is followed by a second stage in which the importance of satisfying the competing principle is established. Finally, the third stage establishes whether the importance of satisfying the competing principle justifies the detriment to, or non-satisfaction of the first.[16]

Alexy equates the 'degree of non-satisfaction of or detriment to' a principle with the 'intensity of interference' therewith.[17] In what follows, I will use the latter, shorter term for ease of reference. In order to determine the 'intensity of interference' with a principle, as well as the 'importance of satisfying the competing principle', Alexy proposes the use of a triadic scale, which he deduces from the case law of the German Constitutional Court.[18] The triadic scale is composed of three stages: 'light', 'moderate' and 'serious'.[19]

In its most basic formulation, in which only the First Law of Balancing is in play, Alexy's balancing test proceeds as follows: the intensity of interference with the first principle is determined and compared to the importance of satisfying the competing principle. This comparison reveals which principle should prevail. Alexy recognises, however, that the First Law of Balancing alone is insufficient to rationally balance principles, since it does not take account of uncertainties. Such uncertainties arise when a case involves an element of speculation, potentiality or risk. In order to take these factors into account, Alexy introduces a Second Law of Balancing, which he terms the Epistemic Law of Balancing:[20]

14 Robert Alexy, *A Theory of Constitutional Rights* (Oxford University Press, 2002), 102.
15 Ibid. at 401; Robert Alexy, 'On Balancing and Subsumption. A Structural Comparison', 16 *Ratio Juris* (2003), 436–437.
16 Alexy, *supra* note 14 at 401.
17 Alexy, *supra* note 15 at 440.
18 Ibid. at 437–440.
19 Ibid. at 440.
20 Alexy, *supra* note 14 at 418.

> [t]he more heavily an interference in a constitutional right weighs, the greater must be the certainty of its underlying premisses (sic).[21]

The Second Law of Balancing comes with its own triadic scale, intended to express the reliability of the underlying premises. It is composed of the following classes: 'certain or reliable', 'maintainable or plausible' and 'not evidently false'.[22]

But that is (still) not all. Alexy further recognises that 'also the abstract weights [of principles] can play a role in balancing'.[23] Whenever the abstract weight of competing principles is different, this also needs to be expressed in balancing them against each other.[24] In short, the First and Second Laws of Balancing *and* the abstract weight of principles are all – in theory – relevant to the balancing of competing principles.[25] In order to operationalise such balancing, Alexy proposes a Weight Formula, which incorporates all three elements:

$$W_{i,j} = \frac{I_i \times W_i \times R_i}{I_j \times W_j \times R_j}$$

In the first half of the Weight Formula, (W) stands for concrete weight, (i) stands for the first principle and (j) for the second principle.[26] $W_{i,j}$ thus expresses the relationship between competing principles in terms of their weight in the concrete circumstances of a case.[27] The second half of the formula contains the factors that are, according to Alexy, necessary and sufficient to determine the concrete weights of competing principle. This part of the formula is expressed as an equation. The top part of the equation expresses the concrete weight of the first principle (i), while the lower part expresses the concrete weight of the second, competing principle (j). The remaining letters stand for the intensity of interference (I), the abstract weight of the principle (W) and the reliability of the underlying premises (epistemic reliability) (R), *i.e.* the certainty with which one can state that the effects on a principle will occur.[28]

Alexy resorts to an equation to express the relationship between competing principles (i) and (j) because it enables indirect comparison of their concrete weights. Under the Weight Formula, such indirect comparison is obtained by multiplying the relevant considerations – (I), (W) and (R) – for each principle and dividing the results for the first principle (i) by the results for the second

21 Ibid.
22 Alexy, *supra* note 15 at 447.
23 Ibid. at 446.
24 Ibid.
25 Ibid. at 448. Balancing and the Weight Formula of course only become relevant if the prior steps of the proportionality test, *i.e.* 'suitability' and 'necessity', have been unable to resolve the case at hand. I do not mention these other steps in the text, because I am – here – only concerned with Alexy's views on the balancing stage (proportionality *stricto sensu*).
26 Alexy, *supra* note 15 at 444.
27 Ibid.
28 Ibid. at 440 and 446.

principle (*j*). The outcome of the equation shows which principle should rationally prevail over the other, under the concrete circumstances.

The Weight Formula thus relies on mathematical operations: multiplication and division. In order to make the requisite calculations possible, we of course need numbers. To that end, Alexy proposes to represent his two Laws of Balancing in the Weight Formula by translating the elements of their respective triadic scales into numbers. The triadic scale of the First Law of Balancing – intensity of interference (*I*): 'light', 'moderate' and 'serious' – is represented by the following numbers in the Weight Formula: 2^0, 2^1 and 2^2 or 1, 2 and 4.[29] The triadic scale of the Second Law of Balancing – epistemic reliability (*R*): 'certain or reliable', 'maintainable or plausible' and 'not evidently false' – is represented by the following numbers in the Weight Formula: 2^0, 2^{-1}, 2^{-2} or 1, ½ and ¼.[30]

Alexy utilises coefficients 'to express the over-proportional growth of resistance of fundamental rights against infringements'.[31] The geometric sequences – 1, 2, 4 and 1, ½, ¼ – translate the idea that the concrete weight of a principle gets exponentially heavier the more serious the interference therewith is and the more reliable the underlying premises of the interference are (or, conversely, the idea that the concrete weight of a principle gets exponentially lighter the less serious the interference therewith is and the less reliable the underlying premises of the interference are).[32]

Because Alexy principally considers principles to be of equal abstract weight,[33] he generally does not utilise the full Weight Formula offered above. Instead, he usually disregards the abstract weights in balancing by omitting W_i and W_j from the equation. Because the abstract weights of competing principles are equal, they neutralise each other.[34] Thus, they can be left out of the equation. Hence, to balance conflicting human rights with Alexy's balancing test, the following version of the Weight Formula generally applies:

$$W_{i,j} = \frac{I_i \times R_i}{I_j \times R_j}$$

Now, how does this Weight Formula enable us, according to Alexy, to understand the rationality of balancing? Calculations under the Weight Formula have

29 Ibid. at 444.

30 Ibid. at 447.

31 Robert Alexy, 'Discourse Theory and Fundamental Rights', in Agustín José Menéndez and Erik Oddvar Eriksen (eds), *Arguing Fundamental Rights* (Springer, 2006), 28.

32 Alexy, *supra* note 15 at 446–447; Robert Alexy, 'The Construction of Constitutional Rights', 4 *Law & Ethics of Human Rights* (2010), note 37.

33 Alexy, *supra* note 15 at 440. But see Robert Alexy, 'Comments and Responses', in Matthias Klatt (ed.), *Institutional Reason: The Jurisprudence of Robert Alexy* (Oxford University Press, 2011), 328–329 (in which Alexy exceptionally argues that certain principles, for example human dignity, have higher abstract weight than others, for example the principle of private property).

34 Alexy, *supra* note 15 at 440 and 446–447.

three possible results: higher than, lower than and equal to 1. When the result is higher than 1, the concrete weight of the first principle (i) is higher than that of the second principle (j), for instance at 2/1.[35] In that scenario, the first principle prevails in the balancing test.[36] When the result is lower than 1, the concrete weight of the second principle (j) is higher than that of the first principle (i), for instance at 1/2.[37] In that scenario, the second principle prevails in the balancing test.[38] When the result is equal to 1, finally, there is a stalemate between both principles, for instance at 2/2.[39] Alexy argues that cases of stalemate signify 'structural discretion in balancing'.[40] A ruling court may, when confronted with a stalemate, refuse to overturn any earlier decision, be it a lower court ruling or a legislative act. In case of stalemate, that earlier decision is per definition 'not disproportionate'.[41]

In the absence of concrete examples, this all risks remaining somewhat abstract. To make things more concrete, let us therefore examine how the Weight Formula explains practical examples of balancing, according to Alexy. One example Alexy often invokes to illustrate the functioning of the Weight Formula, is the German *Titanic* Case. The case involved an article in a satirical magazine, *Titanic*, in which a paraplegic reserve officer was described as a 'born Murderer' and, in a later edition, as a 'cripple'.[42] In human rights terms, the *Titanic* Case entailed a conflict between the magazine's freedom of expression and the officer's right to reputation. In balancing the rights in conflict, the German Constitutional Court found in favour of the magazine's freedom of expression with regard to the statement of 'born Murderer', but against it with regard to the statement of 'cripple'.[43]

Alexy explains how the Weight Formula enables us to understand the outcome of the Constitutional Court's balancing exercise in the *Titanic* Case, by reconstructing that balancing exercise in terms of his two Laws of Balancing and Weight Formula. In doing so, Alexy ignores the abstract weights of the competing principles (presumably because he considers them to be equal). But he also disregards the relevance of (R_i) and (R_i), presumably because he considers the epistemic reliability to be identical with respect to both principles.[44] The only remaining factor, on which the entire balancing exercise thus hinges, is the intensity of interference:

$$W_{i,j} = \frac{I_i}{I_j}$$

35 Ibid. at 444.
36 Ibid.
37 Ibid.
38 Ibid.
39 Ibid. at 445.
40 Ibid. at 443; Alexy, *supra* note 14 at 411.
41 Alexy, *supra* note 15 at 443.
42 Ibid. at 438.
43 Ibid.
44 Ibid. at 437–438.

Alexy explains that, with regard to the statement of 'born Murderer', the Constitutional Court considered the interference with the magazine's freedom of expression to be 'serious', while it considered the interference with the officer's personality rights[45] to be 'moderate, perhaps even light', given the highly satirical context.[46] Alexy then substitutes 'serious' and 'moderate' for their corresponding numbers in the Weight Formula, *i.e.* respectively 4 and 2.[47] When we fill those into the (highly simplified) Weight Formula, the result is 4/2 = 2.[48] Because the result is higher than 1, the magazine's freedom of expression prevails.[49]

The outcome is different, however, with regard to the Constitutional Court's evaluation of the speech labelling the officer a 'cripple'. Alexy posits that the Constitutional Court considered that label to constitute a 'serious' interference with the personality rights of the officer.[50] The result of the equation under the Weight Formula therefore becomes 4/4 = 1. This is a case of stalemate, which explains why the magazine's constitutional complaint was unsuccessful with regard to its statement that the officer was a 'cripple'.[51] Thus, Alexy posits, reconstruction of the Constitutional Court's reasoning through the Weight Formula test demonstrates the rationality of the Court's balancing in the *Titanic* Case.

A critique of Alexy's balancing test

Alexy's balancing test, as just described, offers *prima facie* attractive prospects for the rationality of balancing. Most importantly, it appears to successfully tackle the challenge from incommensurability. According to Alexy, his Weight Formula shows how balancing overcomes incommensurability by enabling indirect comparability of competing principles.[52] Yet, Alexy's balancing test also has important drawbacks, which ultimately lead me to favour the more fluid and contextual balancing test of Chapter 6.

Alexy's balancing test qua *Weight Formula: overly arithmetical?*

Alexy's balancing test *qua* Weight Formula relies strongly on the 'rules of arithmetic'.[53] Alexy locates the solution to the incommensurability challenge in

45 In terms of the German Basic Law.
46 Alexy, *supra* note 15 at 31.
47 Ibid.
48 Ibid.
49 Ibid. at 32.
50 Ibid. at 31.
51 Ibid.
52 Alexy, *supra* note 15 at 442.
53 Ibid. at 448. See also Matthias Klatt and Moritz Meister, 'Proportionality – A Benefit to Human Rights? Remarks on the I•CON Controversy', 10 *International Journal of Constitutional Law* (2012), 694. For criticism of this approach to balancing (as part of his

the creation of a common scale, represented in the Weight Formula, on which competing principles can indirectly be compared. Both the abstract and concrete weight of principles are key components of the Weight Formula. My core objection to the Weight Formula image of balancing is that it remains 'stuck', if you will, in the logics of the scales metaphor of balancing and the idea that rights can somehow be weighed against each other (or against the public interest). In an important sense, Alexy's Weight Formula mirrors the scales metaphor, rather than abandoning it. Like the scales metaphor, the Weight Formula relies on an image of two – not more – competing principles that are weighed against each other; not literally, but figuratively with the use of a mathematical equation.

Translating balancing into a game of numbers is, however, not *required* for the application of Alexy's balancing test. Alexy has clarified that his Weight Formula is merely intended to *represent* or *illustrate* balancing exercises.[54] In fact, when 'intensity of interference' is the only relevant factor in a balancing exercise between competing principles, Alexy's balancing test can perfectly do without the use of numbers. 'Serious' outweighs 'light'. Clear enough. Alexy nevertheless admits that numbers play a central role in his balancing test. In explaining how the Weight Formula works, he, for instance, states that the 'concrete weight [of a principle] can only really be defined as a quotient in a numerical model which illustrates the structure of balancing'.[55] Indeed, the Weight Formula is pointless in the absence of numbers: '[e]ven crude, discrete scales ... cannot dispense with the allocation of numbers if the inferential structure of balancing is going to be expressed by the Weight Formula'.[56]

Yet, one could still maintain that the Weight Formula does no more – or less – than *express* or *illustrate* balancing. The real balancing, Alexy would surely insist, takes place without numbers. But is this really true? I posit that Alexy's balancing test can only do without numbers if the entire balancing exercise boils down to a comparison of the intensity of interference with competing principles. Only if the values for the other elements of the balancing test – abstract weight and epistemic reliability – are equal for both competing principles, and therefore irrelevant from the viewpoint of the Weight Formula, can Alexy's balancing test truly function without numbers. In that particular scenario, we do better to simply posit that a serious interference with one principle 'outweighs' a moderate interference with another principle, rather than completing the Weight Formula. It simply does not make sense to utilise an equation and numbers here. Both are redundant.

As soon as other balancing factors are relevant, however, it becomes much more difficult to apply Alexy's balancing test without actually entering the numbers into the Weight Formula. Arguably, 'obsession' with numbers even causes Alexy to

general critique of balancing), see Stavros Tsakyrakis, 'Proportionality: An Assault on Human Rights?', 7 *International Journal of Constitutional Law* (2009), 474.

54 Alexy, *supra* note 14 at 444.

55 Ibid.

56 Alexy, *supra* note 32 'The Construction of Constitutional Rights' at 31.

skew one of the two examples he routinely utilises to illustrate the rationality of balancing through his Weight Formula.[57] The example at issue concerns a judgment in which the German Constitutional Court upholds the constitutionality of a legislative prohibition on cannabis products (the Cannabis Case). Alexy maintains that the Cannabis Case 'allows one to grasp the interplay between the six elements which are relevant in order to determine the concrete weight of a principle in case of a collision of two principles'.[58]

In contrast with his discussion of the *Titanic* Case, however, Alexy does not restrict himself to simply translating the reasoning of the German Constitutional Court in the Cannabis Case into the corresponding numbers in the Weight Formula. Instead, he takes the somewhat bizarre turn of working *backwards* in explaining the Court's ruling. In the process, he ends up filling in the blanks in the Weight Formula so as to secure, with the benefit of hindsight, a rational explanation for the outcome in the Cannabis Case. Let me clarify what I mean by this.

In discussing the Cannabis Case, Alexy first states that '[t]he abstract weights of the colliding principles P_i [i.e. the constitutionally protected liberty to smoke cannabis products] and P_j [i.e. the protection of collective goods, especially public health] shall be considered as equal, which allows one to neglect them'.[59]

I would, of course, already take issue with that assumption, since it contradicts the argument of Chapter 1 that human rights hold special normative force over the public interest.[60] But let us remain within the logics of Alexy's principles theory, on which all principles are optimisation requirements and thus normally of equal abstract weight. In the Cannabis Case, on Alexy's argument at least, the applicable version of the Weight Formula is thus one in which only the intensity of interference and epistemic reliability are relevant:

$$W_{i,j} = \frac{I_i \times R_i}{I_j \times R_j}$$

In entering the relevant numbers into the equation, Alexy starts off by identifying two of the four variables – R_i and R_j – as positively established, either in fact or in the Constitutional Court's judgment. Alexy argues that '[i]f cannabis products are prohibited, the interference with P_i must be considered as certain. The value of R_i is therefore $2^0 = 1$.'[61] He then looks at 'R_j [,which] stands in our case for the reliability of the empirical assumption of the legislator that the prohibition of cannabis products was necessary in order to avoid dangers for

57 The second example, the *Titanic* case, has been discussed above. See *supra* notes 42–51 and accompanying text.

58 Alexy, *supra* note 15 at 448.

59 Ibid. at 447.

60 I am assuming, here, that the freedom to smoke cannabis products would indeed be protected by way of human rights.

61 Ibid.

collective goods, especially public health'.[62] Alexy notes that the Constitutional Court 'classes R_j as "maintainable"'; he thus assigns it the value $2^{-1} = \frac{1}{2}$.[63]

So far, so good. Up to this point, Alexy's analysis of the Cannabis Case 'merely' relies on identifying the relevant variables on the basis of empirical facts and the judgment of the German Constitutional Court. Alexy is, within his conception of balancing at least, doing no more – or less – than illustrating the purported rationality of balancing. In reconstructing the remainder of the Weight Formula, however, he takes a bizarre turn. Left with two blanks in the Weight Formula – I_i and I_j – on the intensity of interference with the competing principle, Alexy claims that

> [f]rom [the considerations listed immediately above] and the fact that the Court considered prohibition of cannabis products as constitutional, it follows that the interference with P_i is not of the highest degree. Its highest possible value is 2, that is [moderate]. This becomes clear by putting the following values into the Weight Formula: $1 = \frac{2 \times 1}{4 \times \frac{1}{2}}$.[64]

Alexy is, here, no longer *reconstructing* the German Constitutional Court's balancing exercise. Instead, he is actively *shaping* the Weight Formula to fit his needs:

> $W_{i,j}$ must not be more than 1, for if it exceeds 1 the prohibition would be unconstitutional. The Court, however, declares the prohibition constitutional. In this constellation the highest possible value which I_i can achieve is 2, that is, moderate, because I_j cannot achieve in the simple triadic model a higher value than 4, that is, [serious].[65]

Alexy completes the blanks in the Weight Formula with the numbers that happen to be needed to achieve the desired result: constitutionality. But it is far from obvious, to me at least, why the interference with individual freedom in the Cannabis Case would be 'moderate', at best, whereas the risk for public health would be 'serious'. In presenting this conclusion as inevitable under his Weight Formula, Alexy ignores an alternative explanation: perhaps his Weight Formula does not function satisfactorily. If blanks in the Weight Formula can simply be filled by entering the numbers needed to support a certain outcome, then the Weight Formula can explain just about anything. Instead of a useful vehicle to illustrate the rationality of balancing, it turns into a rhetorical device that inevitably confirms the presupposed rationality of balancing.

This points towards two important shortcomings of Alexy's balancing test *qua* Weight Formula. First, its focus on numbers leads even its most prominent

62 Ibid.
63 Ibid.
64 Ibid.
65 Ibid. at 448.

defender to subjectively enter the numbers needed to support a certain outcome. Rational reconstruction of judicial balancing is no longer the aim here. Rather, the aim has become a rather irrational defence of the Weight Formula. Second, the need for numbers, whenever more than one factor plays a role in balancing, conceals the inability of the Weight Formula to truly offer a rational reconstruction of balancing. In relation to the Cannabis Case, for instance, it is far from obvious that the case involved a stalemate, even if we accept Alexy's argument that one principle suffered a 'certain' and 'moderate' interference, while the other suffered a 'serious' and 'maintainable' interference. Without filling the corresponding numbers into a formula and insisting that they 'show' a stalemate (*i.e.* a result of 1), that conclusion hardly seems inevitable. One might as well argue that preventing 'serious' and 'maintainable' damage to public health is more important than avoiding 'certain', but 'moderate' damage to individual freedom. Or, for that matter, the other way around.

I suspect that Alexy's focus on numbers is linked to him taking the incommensurability challenge to balancing too literally. Alexy admirably attempts to reconstruct balancing, but he remains stuck in search of a – quite literal – common scale on which competing principles can be weighed. As I argued in Chapter 4, however, there is no reason to assume that comparability *requires* such a common scale. On the contrary, comparability – and therefore also weak commensurability – can be obtained by comparing reasons in support of human rights in conflict. On a 'balancing as reasoning' test, such as the one proposed in Chapter 6, the right supported by the strongest reasons should prevail. As shown in Chapter 6, such a test can well do without numbers, equations, weights, etc.

Alexy's balancing test qua *Laws of Balancing: overly simplistic?*

In critiquing Alexy's balancing test *qua* Weight Formula, I explained that it can only function without numbers when the only relevant factor in the balancing exercise is the intensity of interference with competing principles. Whenever that is the case, one may simply note the relevant 'values' – 'light', 'moderate' or 'serious' – instead of substituting them by numbers. In case of a human rights conflict, for instance, if one right suffers 'serious' damage and the other 'moderate' damage, one does need numbers to conclude that the first right should prevail (provided that intensity of interference is the *only* relevant factor).[66] This simple conclusion reveals a further drawback of Alexy's balancing test, which becomes clear once it is stripped of its mathematics: it appears to be overly simplistic.

Alexy's balancing test *qua* Laws of Balancing constructs conflicts of principles (including human rights) in strictly binary terms, in which the description of an

66 See, however, Grégoire C. N. Webber, 'Proportionality, Balancing, and the Cult of Constitutional Rights Scholarship', 23 *Canadian Journal of Law and Jurisprudence* (2010), 195 ('one should not assume that a light interference with one principle is of the same measure as a light interference with another principle').

interference as 'light', 'moderate' or 'serious' is moreover often the only factor to determine the outcome of the balancing exercise. To add some complexity to his balancing test, Alexy sometimes describes infringements more intricately, as 'very serious' or 'extremely serious'.[67] He thereby indicates that a more refined scale may be more appropriate, for instance in hard cases.[68] This refinement is certainly worth salvaging. In Chapter 6, I combined a more complex infringement scale with another of Alexy's core concepts: epistemic reliability.

Indeed, Alexy's Second Law of Balancing teaches us that not all infringements are certain. Instead, courts may be confronted with a *risk* of infringement, which can by definition only be assessed in terms that are less than certain. Whereas Alexy dedicates two separate laws of balancing to these core ideas on the severity and reliability of infringements, I combined them in a single criterion of the structured balancing test: the impact criterion. I moreover took Alexy's considerations on abstract weight into account by adding a value criterion, which – unlike in Alexy's argument – has an actual effect on the balancing of certain human rights, namely those that are considered to be of higher value within a human rights system. Yet, where the above exhausts Alexy's balancing test *qua* Laws of Balancing, I have gone further. I have submitted, in particular, that balancing requires additional refinement. Balancing, in short, also entails the examination of *other* factors.

This brings me to a central objection to Alexy's balancing test *qua* Laws of Balancing: it is arguably overly simplistic, in that it reduces conflicts to a binary opposition between two principles.[69] Indeed, Alexy acknowledges that 'the Law

67 Robert Alexy, 'Constitutional Rights, Balancing and Rationality', 16 *Ratio Juris* (2003), 139–140; Alexy, *supra* note 31 at 28.

68 Alexy has, in fact, proposed a more refined scale, building upon his 'basic' triadic scale. Alexy's double-triadic scale consists of nine stages: *ll*, *lm*, *ls*, *ml*, *mm*, *ms*, *sl*, *sm*, *ss*, in which *l* stands for 'light', *m* stands for 'moderate' and *s* stands for 'serious' (Alexy, *supra* note 15 at 445). According to Alexy, 'these nine classes are quite easy to understand' (ibid.). Alexy claims that '[e]verybody understands a statement such as "The infringement is light (*l*)" or a statement as "[t]he infringement is a serious moderate infringement"' (Alexy, *supra* note 14 at 31). With all due respect to Alexy, I fail to see what a 'serious moderate infringement' would consist of and find it particularly difficult to distinguish it from a 'light serious infringement', which would rank higher on Alexy's double-triadic scale. It is, in that respect, not all too surprising to note that no one – neither Alexy, nor his followers – have attempted to explain an instance of balancing with use of the double-triadic scale. Matthias Klatt and Moritz Meister, for instance, have described the double-triadic scale in their work, only to state that '[t]o simplify matters, we will only apply the basic triadic model here'. See Matthias Klatt and Moritz Meister, *The Constitutional Structure of Proportionality* (Oxford University Press, 2012), 12.

69 See also Webber, *supra* note 66 at 192 ('proponents of the principle of proportionality often prefer to simplify matters and assume only *two* "competing interests." Few rights-claims can fairly be so reduced, as the issues involved are often polycentric' (emphasis in original)). See further Thomas A. Aleinikoff, 'Constitutional Law in the Age of Balancing', 96 *Yale Law Journal* (1987), 1004 (explaining, in a different context, that the United States Supreme Court has 'not adequately explored the "mathematics" of balancing. As a way to avoid problems in calculation, it has generally – with little theoretical justification – adopted scaled-down equations that do not take account of all the possible interests').

of Balancing concerns exclusively the relation between ... two colliding principles'.[70] Obviously, intensity of interference is a relevant factor to the resolution of such conflicts, as is the reliability of the underlying premises. That is why I included both factors in the structured balancing test of Chapter 6. But I also insisted on the relevance of criteria that look *beyond* the binary nature of a particular human rights conflict and examine the broader context in which the conflict has arisen as well.

In Chapter 6, I particularly insisted on the inclusion of an additional rights criterion and a general interest criterion in the structured balancing test. These criteria respectively assess the relevance of *other* human rights (potentially even held by third persons) and of the general interest to the resolution of human rights conflicts. On Alexy's balancing test, which conceives of conflicts in terms of binary opposition between two principles, there appears to be no room for such more contextual considerations. In Alexy's balancing test, there is also no room for two other criteria that – I posited in Chapter 6 – should be part of a structured balancing test: the purpose criterion and the responsibility criterion. The purpose criterion examines whether one of the human rights in conflict stands in relation to the other(s), in the sense that one of its purposes is to ensure protection of the other human right(s). The responsibility criterion, finally, incorporates the correlative of rights – duties – to the extent that it is appropriate to demand a certain level of responsibility in the exercise of human rights.

None of these four more contextual criteria – the additional rights criterion, general interest criterion, purpose criterion, nor responsibility criterion – appear to have a bearing on Alexy's balancing test *qua* Laws of Balancing. Instead, his test focuses entirely on one criterion – at best, two – of my structured balancing test: the impact on human rights in conflict (and theoretically, but not – it seems – in practice, their value (abstract weight)). Compared to the structured balancing test of Chapter 6, Alexy's balancing test appears to take an overly narrow and simplistic approach to balancing human rights. In that respect, I posit, my contextual test may well prove superior.

Alternative approaches to balancing: Möller and Barak

In the previous section, I have been rather critical of Robert Alexy's approach to balancing, while salvaging some of his core underlying arguments on balancing. The opposite goes for the alternative balancing approaches of Kai Möller and Aharon Barak: I will prove rather receptive of Möller's and Barak's conception and operationalisation of balancing, while disagreeing with some of their core assumptions about balancing. In this section, I focus on the works of Möller and Barak, because they have arguably put forth the most developed alternative approaches to balancing (within proportionality analysis). Whereas Möller focuses on disentangling different theoretical conceptions of balancing, Barak

70 Alexy, *supra* note 15 at 441.

attempts to refine the operationalisation of balancing in judicial practice. In the process, both provide key insights on balancing, while relying on contestable assumptions.

In *The Global Model of Constitutional Rights*, Möller makes a number of claims that are principally objectionable from the viewpoint of the core arguments of this book.[71] In Chapter 1, in particular, I proved critical of Möller's contentions that: (1) everything that matters in constitutional law can and should be expressed in terms of 'autonomy interests'; and (2) therefore, we should abandon the idea that constitutional or human rights hold special normative force. On Möller's argument, the proportionality test rules supreme. I, conversely, have submitted that taking the special normative force of human rights seriously requires application of *different* tests to 'traditional' human rights cases (human right *versus* public interest), on the one hand, and human rights conflicts, on the other.

Yet, when it comes to balancing human rights, there is room for *rapprochement* to Möller's argument, since his objectives are aligned with mine. In balancing, I have posited, human rights in conflict are due equal respect. Although Möller and I strongly disagree on the scope of such equal respect in balancing – Möller would also extend it to balancing human rights against the public interest – as far as *human rights* are concerned, we start from the same baseline assumption. There is, in that respect, real value in evaluating Möller's thoughts on balancing.

As it turns out, Möller indeed provides a number of important insights on balancing, some of which have proven central to the development of Chapter 6's structured balancing test. Most importantly, Möller clarifies the precise meaning of balancing by disentangling four different concepts of balancing: balancing as 'autonomy maximization', 'interest balancing', 'formal balancing' and 'balancing as reasoning'.[72] According to Möller,

> the choice is not between any of [these] concepts in isolation … Rather we have to keep in mind that the four concepts relate to each other in the fashion of four concentric circles: each one includes the previous one.[73]

Möller's four concepts of balancing range from the more specific to the more general. They moreover function differently. Whereas balancing as 'autonomy maximization' and 'interest balancing' rely on the scales metaphor and the notion of weight, 'formal balancing' and 'balancing as reasoning' do away with the scales metaphor and are insensitive to the idea of weight.[74] Earlier in this book, I argued *against* reliance on the scales metaphor of balancing and the idea of weight.[75]

71 Kai Möller, *The Global Model of Constitutional Rights* (Oxford University Press, 2012).
72 Ibid. at 137–140.
73 Ibid. at 140.
74 Ibid. at 137–140.
75 See Chapter 4 and, in particular, 'The incommensurability challenge overcome'.

I have, thus, already rejected Möller's balancing as 'autonomy maximization' and 'interest balancing'.[76] The whole idea behind the structured balancing test of Chapter 6 has instead been to move *beyond* the scales metaphor of balancing and *abandon* the notion of weight. More interesting perspectives can, in that sense, be gleaned from Möller's 'formal balancing' and 'balancing as reasoning'.

Möller's 'balancing as reasoning' operates at the most general level, where balancing is 'simply … a matter of assessing the relative strength of reasons'.[77] Möller notes that 'balancing as reasoning' applies to all conflicts.[78] It is always appropriate.[79] The structured balancing test of Chapter 6 is intended to operationalise such 'balancing as reasoning'. The test is, in particular, designed to enable comparative judgments about the strength of reasons in favour of – and against – human rights in conflict. Yet, Möller would probably retort that I have moved beyond 'balancing as reasoning', which he understands in terms of moral argumentation to the effect that one interest is granted unconditional priority over the other(s).[80] The structured balancing test of Chapter 6 does not aim to establish such unconditional priority. Instead, it is a contextual test aimed at enabling judges to decide, with some rational confidence, which human right should prevail under the concrete circumstances of a given conflict. In that respect, the test is arguably a form of Möller's 'formal balancing', in which 'the correct moral argument requires a trade-off between the two values [but] is more complex than simply putting the respective interests on the scales, adjusting the weights and comparing them'.[81] I am content to acknowledge that, in theoretical terms, the contextual balancing test of Chapter 6 operationalises 'balancing as reasoning' in the particular form of 'formal balancing'. In *practical* terms, the test moreover shares important features with Aharon Barak's approach to balancing in constitutional rights practice.

In his *Proportionality – Constitutional Rights and Their Limitations*, Barak emphasises the 'moral' and 'normative' nature of balancing, much in the same vein as Möller.[82] Although Barak invokes the scales metaphor of balancing and the idea of weight, he goes to some lengths to explain that '[t]he scales do not actually exist'.[83] Barak notes, in particular, that

76 Note that Möller himself acknowledges that 'in most cases, formal balancing but not interest balancing is required', while retaining room for the concepts of balancing that I find objectionable: 'in some cases interest balancing and occasionally even autonomy maximization will be appropriate'. See Möller, *supra* note 71 at 143.

77 Ibid. at 139.

78 Ibid. at 140.

79 Ibid.

80 Ibid. at 140–141.

81 Ibid. at 141 and 143.

82 Aharon Barak, *Proportionality – Constitutional Rights and Their Limitations* (Cambridge University Press, 2012), 342 and 346.

83 Ibid. at 346.

> balancing is normative in nature … The solution is not by providing a permanent label of "weight" to each conflicting principle, but rather through shaping legal rules – the rules of balancing – that determine under which circumstances we may fulfill one principle while limiting another.[84]

In explicating his basic balancing rule, however, Barak is unable to truly let go of the scales metaphor and the concomitant idea of weight (presumably because he considers them necessary to conjure, in the reader, a workable image of balancing).[85] The basic balancing rule Barak formulates is, as a result, remarkably similar to Alexy's First Law of Balancing. Under the basic balancing rule, Barak posits,

> we are comparing the marginal social importance of the benefit gained by the limiting law and the marginal social importance of preventing the harm to the constitutional right caused by the limiting law. The question is whether the weight of the marginal social importance of the benefits is heavier than the weight of the marginal social importance of preventing the harm.[86]

But, Barak insists, measurement of the 'marginal social importance' of constitutional rights sets his balancing rule apart from – and presumably renders it superior to – Alexy's balancing test.[87] On the face of it, the difference seems negligible. But once Barak begins to explore the factors that are relevant to balancing in judicial practice, it becomes clear that he thinks of balancing in more contextual terms than Alexy. Barak not only notes the relevance of the weight and probability of realisation of the items in the balance[88] (the fairly obvious relevance of these factors he shares with Alexy), he also discusses the relevance of other factors. Barak notes that 'a right that constitutes a precondition to another right may be considered more important',[89] points towards 'the importance of [underlying] reasons within society's fundamental understanding of rights',[90] signals the relevance of 'additional rights'[91] and indicates that 'a limitation of the right's core differs from a limitation on the right's penumbra'.[92]

These other factors, all of which Barak considers relevant to balancing, correspond to the value criterion, the general interest criterion, the additional rights criterion and the core-periphery criterion, respectively, of the structured

84 Ibid.
85 Ibid. at 348–350.
86 Ibid. at 351.
87 Ibid. at 365.
88 Ibid. at 351 and 358.
89 Ibid. at 350.
90 Ibid. at 359.
91 Ibid. at 362.
92 Ibid.

balancing test of Chapter 6. There is, in short, significant congruence between Barak's approach to balancing and my structured balancing test. Yet, Barak does little more than briefly point towards the relevance of other factors to balancing.[93] He does not explain how these factors work, how they relate to each other, nor how they contribute to making balancing work in judicial practice. I, conversely, hope to have answered these key questions in Chapter 6. In an important sense, my structured balancing test arguably represents a more developed and operationalised – as well as somewhat modified – version of Barak's balancing test.

Conclusion

Alternative approaches to human rights conflicts – both of the balancing and the non-balancing kind – are certainly available. Yet, the structured balancing test of Chapter 6 is either congruent with or, in my opinion, superior to these alternatives. At first glance, my balancing argument appears incompatible with Zucca's purported non-balancing approach to human rights conflicts. Upon closer inspection, however, Zucca and I disagree not about the role of balancing, but on the conceptualisation of human rights and conflicts between them. Whereas Zucca views balancing as a useful tool to *avoid* conflicts between weakly incommensurable human rights, I consider it to be a method to *resolve* such conflicts.

By abandoning the scales metaphor of balancing and doing away with the notion of weight in the operationalisation of balancing, the structured balancing test of Chapter 6 arguably outperforms Alexy's arithmetical balancing test *qua* Weight Formula. By incorporating criteria that examine the broader context within which human rights conflicts arise, the test arguably also improves upon Alexy's balancing test *qua* Laws of Balancing. When considered in light of other balancing approaches, my structured balancing test arguably operationalises Möller's 'balancing as reasoning', in the specific form of 'formal balancing'. Moreover, it is congruent with some of Barak's insights on factors that are relevant to balancing.

Despite its advantages over alternative approaches to human rights conflicts, however, the structured balancing test inevitably has limitations. Through the construction of nets of arguments, which enable comparative judgments on the

93 Instead, Barak pays more attention to identifying an intermediate form of balancing: principled balancing rules that operate somewhere between the (highly abstract) basic balancing rule and (very specific) *ad hoc* balancing decisions. Once formulated/identified, these principled balancing rules can be applied to future cases. See ibid. at 368–369 and 542–544. I have not engaged with this idea in detail throughout this book. Instead, I have focused on making balancing work in individual cases. I have, however, indicated that more general balancing rules might indeed surface through repeated application of balancing to similar circumstances. Such balancing rules could then, as Barak posits, be applied to future cases. Identifying balancing rules is, however, not among the aims of this book. That aim can only be achieved – by judges or scholars – through concerted analysis of a sufficient number of coherent and transparent judicial balancing decisions. My aim is to enable the latter.

strength of reasons for (and against) human rights in conflict, it may be able to overcome the challenge from weak incommensurability, but it is powerless in the face of strong incommensurability (or incomparability). Where genuine dilemmas are in play, the structured balancing test will fail to provide a rational answer. Such genuine dilemmas, and the limits of the structured balancing test they reveal, are the focus of the last chapter of this book.

8 Human rights dilemmas and the limits of the structured balancing test

The structured balancing test of Chapter 6 is designed to overcome the challenge from weak incommensurability to the balancing of human rights. It aims to enable comparative judgments on the strength of reasons in support of human rights in conflict, despite the lack of a common metric to adequately express the relationship between those rights. In this, I have argued, the structured balancing test succeeds. But because the test focuses on enabling comparability of human rights, it is ineffectual in the face of strong incommensurability: the 'sort of incommensurability that can leave us paralysed, not knowing what to choose'.[1] By definition, strongly incommensurable rights are *incomparable*. Thus, where a conflict involves strongly incommensurable rights, the structured balancing test encounters its limits.

In order to explore those limits, I will assess – throughout this chapter – when exactly strong incommensurability between human rights obtains. Such strong incommensurability is particularly likely to occur, not in 'standard' human rights conflicts, but in genuine human rights dilemmas. In this chapter, I take a closer look at such dilemmas. Based on a rather broad definition of the notion 'dilemma' – as a particularly intense human rights conflict that involves an element of tragedy – I will identify two cases that may pose problems for the structured balancing test: *Odièvre v France* and *Evans v the United Kingdom* (both cases at the ECtHR). I aim to show that, whereas *Odièvre* can be resolved with use of the structured balancing test, *Evans* cannot. *Evans* thus confronts us with a rare case of strong incommensurability, a genuine human rights dilemma. Such a genuine dilemma cannot be resolved with even a semblance of rationality. But it can also not be escaped. A choice must be made. Given strong incommensurability, this choice will be *arational*. It will inevitably be based on subjective or intuitive preferences. Due to their relative lack of democratic legitimacy, I posit, courts should defer this arational choice to the legislator.

1 Jeremy Waldron, 'Fake Incommensurability: A Response to Professor Schauer', 45 *Hastings Law Journal* (1994), 815–816.

Human rights dilemmas: strong incommensurability and tragedy

Dilemmas are at the heart of Lorenzo Zucca's important work on human rights conflicts.[2] In Chapter 7, I explained that Zucca and I adhere to different conceptions of human rights and, concomitantly, adopt diverging definitions of conflicts between them. Zucca favours a narrow definition of conflicts between human rights, which he equates with 'constitutional dilemmas'.[3] According to Zucca, such constitutional dilemmas cannot be resolved through balancing.[4] I, conversely, favour a broader definition of human rights conflicts, which not only includes instances of strong incommensurability, but also those of weak incommensurability. In Chapters 4 and 6, I showed that such human rights conflicts *can* generally be resolved through balancing. Yet, I also foresaw – in Chapter 7 – a future need to return to Zucca's argument on 'constitutional dilemmas', to explore the limits of the structured balancing test.

Zucca is right to claim that his constitutional dilemmas, which entail strong incommensurability, cannot be resolved through balancing.[5] Since strong incommensurability precludes comparability, a core objective of Chapter 6's structured balancing test cannot be met in the face of strong incommensurability: no comparative judgments in favour of – or against – human rights in conflict can be made where strong incommensurability is in play. Instead, the rights in conflict are incomparable. To locate the limits of the structured balancing test, we should thus determine when, exactly, a human rights conflict entails strong incommensurability. Zucca's notion of 'constitutional dilemmas' provides an invaluable starting point for the analysis.

In discussing 'constitutional dilemmas', Zucca identifies four central characteristics of these dilemmas: (1) joint incompatibility of fundamental legal rights; (2) the existence of a (constitutional) tragedy, which 'lurks behind these types of conflicts'; (3) the inevitability of loss for one of the parties involved; (4) and the inability to determine one rational right answer to solve the case.[6] Characteristics 1 and 4 point towards the existence of strong incommensurability between human rights. Characteristics 2 and 3, conversely, emphasise the tragic nature of 'constitutional dilemmas'.[7] Two concepts – strong incommensurability and tragedy – thus lie at the heart of Zucca's definition of a dilemma.[8]

2 Lorenzo Zucca, *Constitutional Dilemmas – Conflicts of Fundamental Legal Rights in Europe and the USA* (Oxford University Press, 2007).

3 Ibid. at 52 and 85–86.

4 Ibid. at 169.

5 Ibid.

6 Ibid. at 26.

7 See also Silvina Alvarez, 'Constitutional Conflicts, Moral Dilemmas and Legal Solutions', 24 *Ratio Juris* (2011), 61–63 and 66–68.

8 See Jacco Bomhoff and Lorenzo Zucca, 'Evans v. UK, European Court of Human Rights – The Tragedy of Ms Evans: Conflicts and Incommensurability of Rights, *Evans* v. *the United*

In discussing Zucca's argument on dilemmas, David Martínez Zorilla provides further useful insights.[9] Martínez Zorilla explains that 'the expression "moral dilemma" is not normally used to refer to a case of (moral) normative conflict'.[10] Instead, he explains, 'the label is only used in situations of especially relevant or intense conflict'.[11] In other words, genuine dilemmas are rare. This corresponds to my earlier hypothesis that strong incommensurability rarely occurs and that, therefore, the structured balancing test is able to resolve most human rights conflicts (*i.e.* those characterised by weak, not strong incommensurability).

Martínez Zorilla further confirms the salience of strong incommensurability and tragedy to the definition of dilemmas. He submits, however, that there are two distinct streams in the literature: whereas the first focuses on the element of indeterminacy (*i.e.* strong incommensurability) in defining dilemmas, the second emphasises the element of tragedy.[12] In Chapters 4 and 6, I joined the first stream by arguing that the structured balancing test is able to overcome the challenge from weak incommensurability, but is ineffectual in the face of strong incommensurability. In essence, I consider weak incommensurability to be a state that obtains *prior to* an attempt at balancing human rights in conflict. Strong incommensurability, conversely, is the state that – in rare circumstances – obtains *after* balancing has failed. Those rare situations in which strong incommensurability obtains epitomise genuine human rights dilemmas. Such dilemmas are characterised by the inability to choose between human rights in conflict with even a semblance of rationality.[13]

On the account of human rights conflicts I present throughout this book, strong incommensurability is the true marker of genuine human rights dilemmas. Yet, I have just claimed that we can only learn about the existence of such strong incommensurability *after* we have attempted to balance human rights in conflict. In exploring the limits of the structured balancing test, we are thus faced with a problem: how do we identify circumstances in which strong incommensurability might obtain, in the first place? How do we begin to narrow down the search for genuine human rights dilemmas? In tracking the broad contours of a human rights dilemma, the second element highlighted by Zucca and Martínez Zorilla – tragedy – is arguably of central importance. The impression that a particular human rights

Kingdom, Fourth Section Judgment of 7 March 2006, Application No. 6339/05', 2 *European Constitutional Law Review* (2006), 430–431 and 441.

9 David Martínez Zorrilla, 'Constitutional Dilemmas and Balancing', 24 *Ratio Juris* (2011), 347–363.

10 Ibid. at 349.

11 Ibid.

12 Ibid. at 349–350. Martínez Zorrilla himself gives priority to the first element (see ibid. at 350).

13 Ibid. at 350. On the link between incommensurability and moral dilemmas, see Joseph Raz, *The Morality of Freedom* (Clarendon Press, 1986), 359.

conflict requires a tragic choice offers a rudimentary – but inconclusive – indication that sets us on the path towards identifying genuine human rights dilemmas.[14]

In exploring the limits of the structured balancing test, I will thus start off with a broad definition of dilemma: a human rights conflict that entails an element of tragedy. This broad definition allows us to identify concrete conflicts that *may* involve the second element: strong incommensurability. In order to determine whether or not that is the case, we need to apply the structured balancing test to these conflicts. If the test is able to resolve them, they do not involve a *genuine* human rights dilemma, since they are not marked by strong incommensurability. But if the structured balancing test fails to provide a solution, a genuine dilemma arises. Confronted with such genuine dilemmas, I posit, judges should defer to the legislator. Since genuine dilemmas cannot be resolved with even a semblance of rationality, their resolution should arguably be left to the democratically elected legislator, who enjoys greater legitimacy – in this respect, at least – than unelected judges.

Identifying potential dilemmas: human rights conflicts and tragedy

To locate the limits of the structured balancing test of Chapter 6, I aim to identify human rights conflicts that might entail a genuine human rights dilemma. The element of tragedy will guide the initial identification process. Once I have identified relevant cases, I will attempt to resolve them through the structured balancing test. If the test fails to solve a given case, this signals that the conflict at issue involves strong incommensurability. The case will thus entail a genuine dilemma, resolution of which lies beyond the grasp of the structured balancing test.

To make the discussion that follows both tangible and relevant to judicial practice, I will locate (potential) dilemmas in the case law of the ECtHR. When exploring the Court's vast case law in search of potential dilemmas, two particularly intense conflicts spring to mind: *Odièvre v France* and *Evans v the United Kingdom*.[15] Both Grand Chamber cases involved a human rights conflict in which

14 Cass Sunstein, 'Incommensurability and Valuation in Law', 92 *Michigan Law Review* (1994), 859.

15 Other potentially interesting cases relate to torture of terrorism suspects (*Gäfgen v Germany* [2010] ECHR 759), assisted suicide (*Pretty v the United Kingdom* [2002] ECHR 427; *Haas v Switzerland* [2011] ECHR 2422) and abortion (*A., B. and C. v Ireland* [2010] ECHR 2032; *R.R. v Poland* 2011] ECHR 828; *P. and S. v Poland* [2012] ECHR 1853). For discussion, see Daniel Rietiker, 'From Prevention to Facilitation? Suicide in the Jurisprudence of the ECtHR in the Light of the Recent *Haas v. Switzerland* Judgment', 25 *Harvard Human Rights Journal* (2012), 86 (describing *Haas v Switzerland* as involving a dilemma); Zucca, *supra* note 2 at 160–161 (describing physician assisted suicide as a constitutional tragedy); Janneke Gerards, '"Hard Cases" in Law', in Adriaan in 't Groen *et al.* (eds), *Knowledge in Ferment – Dilemmas in Science, Scholarship and Society* (Leiden University Press, 2007), 122 (describing the ECtHR abortion cases as moral dilemmas).

tragic choices were inevitable. They thus conform to the broad definition of dilemmas offered above.

Odièvre involved a conflict between a woman's right to know her origins and the right to decisional privacy of her mother, who had given birth to her anonymously. In its judgment, the Court referenced 'the ethical dilemma posed by the right to give birth anonymously',[16] while concurring Judge Rozakis emphasised 'the obvious dilemma' inherent in the case.[17] Indeed, in *Odièvre* there was no way to accommodate both rights. One party would inevitably suffer a tragic loss. Either Ms Odièvre would never know her biological origins or her mother would – *ex post facto* – see the very reason for her anonymous birth undermined.

Evans, a case I have discussed before, likewise entailed an inevitable and tragic loss. The case involved a conflict between Ms Evans' decisional privacy to become a genetic parent and the decisional privacy of her former partner, who had revoked his consent to use frozen embryos for IVF treatment. The tragic nature of the *Evans* case springs from the fact that Ms Evans had ovarian cancer. The IVF treatment at issue was – at the time[18] – presumed to be her last and only chance to become a genetic parent, given that her ovaries had already been removed. These unfortunate circumstances infused the conflict with the particular kind of intensity that rendered a tragic choice inevitable. Indeed, *Evans* has been repeatedly described as a dilemma, both in the Court's judgment and in the literature.[19]

In the remainder of this chapter, I will attempt to resolve the human rights conflicts in *Odièvre* and *Evans* with use of the structured balancing test. In doing so, I will explore the limits of the test, while further elucidating how it may function in judicial practice. I aim to demonstrate, in particular, that the structured balancing test is able to resolve the conflict in *Odièvre*, but not that in *Evans*. This finding will lead me to make two key claims. First, cases that appear to involve a dilemma – like *Odièvre* – may nevertheless be resolved with some measure of rational confidence. The conflict involved might be tragic, but it need not entail strong incommensurability. Therefore, the dilemma is merely apparent, not genuine. Second, other *prima facie* dilemmas – like *Evans* – will resist resolution

On cases that involve an ethical or moral dilemma to the parties, but do not involve a legal dilemma for courts, see Alvarez, *supra* note 7 at 64–68.

16 *Odièvre v France* [2003] ECHR 86, para 19.

17 Concurring opinion of Judge Rozakis in ibid.

18 Subsequent development, unbeknownst to the parties and the ECtHR at the time, have made it possible for Ms Evans to become a genetic parent after all. See Lorenzo Zucca, 'The Comedy of Mrs Evans', in Stijn Smet and Eva Brems (eds.), *Conflicts of Rights at the European Court of Human Rights* (Oxford University Press, forthcoming; manuscript on file with the author).

19 *Evans v the United Kingdom* [2007] ECHR 264, para 73 ('The dilemma central to the present case is that it involves a conflict between the Article 8 rights of two private individuals'); Bomhoff and Zucca, *supra* note 8 at 430–431; Lorenzo Zucca, '*Evans v United Kingdom*: Frozen Embryos and Conflicting Rights', 11 *Edinburgh Law Review* (2007), 447.

through the structured balancing test. These are the rare cases in which strong incommensurability obtains. They entail a genuine dilemma: a particularly intense human rights conflict that involves an element of tragedy and cannot be resolved with even a semblance of rationality.

Odièvre v France: the success of the structured balancing test

The *Odièvre* case at the ECtHR revolved around Ms Odièvre, whose biological mother had given birth to her anonymously, a possibility catered for under French law. At the age of 3, Ms Odièvre was adopted. More than two decades later, at the age of 25, she consulted her childcare file, thereby obtaining non-identifying information about her biological parents. The file included a description of her biological mother and father, as well as her mother's surname (but not her father's). The file further noted that her father, who was married to another woman, 'refuses to have anything to do with [the child] and says that he cannot take on this new burden'.[20] The file finally described the mother's attitude towards the impending abandonment of her daughter:

> [the mother] appears to have no will of her own and is content to go along with her partner's wishes. She has not visited her daughter at the clinic, saying that she does not wish to become attached. She did not see her daughter until today and greeted their separation with total indifference.[21]

At the age of 32, Ms Odièvre requested a court order for the release of further information about her origins: copies of birth, death and marriage certificates and civil-status documents.[22] She filed the request after she had discovered that her biological parents had three other children, all boys and all of whom they kept. Two of the children were moreover born after Ms Odièvre. Ms Odièvre claimed that 'now that she knew of her siblings' existence, she was entitled to seek an order for the release of information about her own birth'.[23] Her request was, however, refused. The French courts did not even examine Ms Odièvre's claim. Instead, the registrar informed her that she 'should consider applying to the administrative court to obtain, if possible, an order requiring the authorities to disclose the information, although such an order would in any event contravene the [legislation on anonymous births]'.[24]

No longer believing in the effectiveness of further court proceedings in France, Ms Odièvre brought her case to Strasbourg, where the Grand Chamber of the ECtHR ruled against her. In its judgment, the Court recognised that the case

20 *Odièvre*, *supra* note 16 at para 12.
21 Ibid.
22 Ibid. at para 13.
23 Ibid.
24 Ibid. at para 14.

involved a human rights conflict between Ms Odièvre's right to know her origins (as part of her right to private life) and the right to decisional privacy of her mother (also part of her right to private life).[25] The Court described the conflict as a 'dilemma', but nevertheless resolved it – with confidence – to the detriment of Ms Odièvre's human rights.[26]

Application of the structured balancing test to Odièvre

In what follows, I will apply the structured balancing test of Chapter 6 to the conflict in *Odièvre*. I aim to show, in particular, that the ECtHR judgment contains a number of arguments that, when organised in terms of the structured balancing test, support the Court's ruling in favour of the right to decisional privacy of the mother. Application of the structured balancing test will thus reveal that *Odièvre* does not involve a genuine dilemma. Instead, the human rights conflict inherent in the case can be resolved with some measure of rational confidence.

As before, in Chapter 6, I will break the application of the structured balancing test down into two distinct phases, strictly for analytical reasons. In a first phase, I apply the seven criteria of the test separately to identify reasons in favour of – and against – the human rights in conflict in *Odièvre*, as well as the strength of those reasons. Once I have examined the seven criteria separately, I move on to the second phase, in which I combine all relevant reasons by weaving them into nets of arguments. I conclude by comparing the strength of these nets of arguments. That comparative judgment provides a supportive structure for the ECtHR's ruling in *Odièvre*, in favour of the mother's human rights.

In the particular circumstances of the conflict in *Odièvre*, the value criterion and the responsibility criterion are either inapplicable or irrelevant. The value criterion is inapplicable, given that the conflict does not involve the right to life or freedom from discrimination. Instead, it involves two aspects of the right to private life, which should be treated with principled equal respect. The responsibility criterion is irrelevant, because the conflict does not involve rights that come with particular responsibilities, similar to those inherent in the exercise of freedom of expression. We can thus safely ignore both the value criterion and the responsibility criterion. Instead, we should turn our attention towards the five remaining criteria of the structured balancing test.

In applying the impact criterion to *Odièvre*, we need to evaluate two elements. First, we need to assess the damage suffered by the human rights in conflict. The damage to Ms Odièvre's right to know her origins appears – at first glance – 'serious'. Ms Odièvre was, after all, denied access to information about her origins. Yet, as pointed out by the ECtHR, the damage done to her human rights was mitigated: 'the applicant was given access to non-identifying information about

25 Ibid. at para 44.
26 Ibid. at para 19.

her mother and natural family that enabled her to trace some of her roots'.[27] Ms Odièvre was indeed not denied access to any and all information about her biological parents. She had learned the surname of her mother, obtained a physical description of her mother and father and was granted access to information that described the circumstances under which her mother had decided to give birth anonymously. Nevertheless, crucial pieces of information, including her place of birth, her mother's first name and the names of her father and siblings, remained inaccessible to Ms Odièvre. As a result, the damage done to her right to know her origins was merely mitigated, not erased. The damage was certainly not as serious as it would have been if Ms Odièvre had not been given any information about her origins. But the absence of key information should also not be underestimated. Ms Odièvre was given snippets of information, which gave her some, but not much insight into her origins. Taking both the mitigating circumstances and the importance of the absent information into account, the damage to Ms Odièvre's right to know her origins should arguably be labelled 'moderate'.

When we turn to examine the damage done to the mother's decisional privacy, we face an obstacle. Under the actual circumstances of the *Odièvre* case, the mother's decisional privacy was kept (largely) intact. There was thus no actual damage. In balancing her human rights against those of her daughter, we should therefore imagine a hypothetical scenario under which Ms Odièvre's request would have been granted. This would have entailed lifting her mother's request for secrecy. There would, moreover, not be any mitigating measures available to limit the damage done to the mother's decisional privacy. For all intents and purposes, her decisional privacy would be eradicated. As a result, the hypothetical damage done to the mother's right to decisional privacy may be labelled 'serious'. It arguably does not reach the extreme stage of 'very serious', which should be reserved for the most egregious human rights violations (such as racist violence or criminal convictions for fair comments on issues of public interest).

Still under the impact criterion, we should now evaluate the likelihood that the identified damage would actually occur. In *Odièvre*, the damage is – or would be – 'certain' with respect to both human rights in conflict. Ms Odièvre's right to know her origins effectively suffered damage as a direct consequence of the French authorities' decision to deny her access to information about her origins. Conversely, if Ms Odièvre's request had been granted, her mother's right to decisional privacy would inevitably have suffered damage. To sum up, application of the impact criterion yields the following reasons: the damage done to Ms Odièvre's right to know her origins is equally certain, but less serious than the (hypothetical) damage done to her mother's right to decisional privacy.

The next criterion of the structured balancing test – the core-periphery criterion – was the *locus* of strong disagreement between the majority and the minority of the ECtHR in *Odièvre*. The majority appeared to consider Ms Odièvre's right to know her origins to be located rather towards the periphery of her right to private

27 Ibid. at para 48.

life. The majority acknowledged that 'people have a right to know their origins', but noted that 'that right [is] derived from *a wide interpretation* of the scope of the notion of private life'.[28] The majority moreover compared Ms Odièvre's case to earlier cases, in which the Court had ruled that persons 'have a *vital* interest ... in receiving the information necessary to know and to understand their childhood'.[29] The majority concluded, however, that Ms Odièvre's situation differed from that in the earlier cases, finding that

> [t]he issue of access to information about one's origins and the identity of one's natural parents is *not of the same nature* as that of access to a case record concerning a child in care or to evidence of alleged paternity.[30]

In construing Ms Odièvre's right to know her origins as deriving from a 'wide interpretation' of the right to private life and as being 'not of the same nature' as the 'vital interest' at stake in other cases, the majority emphasised the rather peripheral status of Ms Odièvre's right (as compared to other, more core aspects of the right to private life). The dissenting judges, however, strongly disagreed. They submitted that a core right was at stake:

> certain aspects of the right to private life are peripheral to that right, whereas others form part of its inner core. We are firmly of the opinion that the right to an identity, which is an essential condition of the right to autonomy ... and development ... is within the inner core of the right to respect for one's private life.[31]

The dissent arguably presents the stronger argument here. Indeed, Ms Odièvre's right to know her origins is closely tied to her right to an identity. As such, there is cause to locate it closer to the core of her right to private life than to its periphery, where such rights as the right to give birth at home dwell.[32]

28 Ibid. (emphasis added).
29 Ibid. at para 42 (emphasis added).
30 Ibid. at para 43.
31 Dissenting opinion of Judges Wildhaber, Bratza, Bonello, Loucaides, Cabral Barreto, Tulkens and Pellonpää in ibid. at para 11.
32 See *Jäggi v Switzerland* (13 July 2006), para 37 ('the right to an identity, which includes the right to know one's parentage, is an integral part of the notion of private life. In such cases, particularly rigorous scrutiny is called for when weighing up the competing interests'). See also Samantha Besson, 'Enforcing the Child's Right to Know her Origins: Contrasting Approaches under the Convention on the Rights of the Child and the European Convention on Human Rights', 21 *International Journal of Law, Policy and the Family* (2007), 151 (interpreting the cited passage in *Jäggi* as confirming that 'the right to identity, and hence to know one's origins, belongs to the inner core of the right to respect for one's private life').

As far as the mother's human rights are concerned, however, both the majority and the minority remained silent. Neither attempted to locate the mother's right to decisional privacy within her right to private life. I will therefore venture my own attempt here. I posit that the mother's right to decisional privacy – given its centrality to the autonomous exercise of her right to private life – should be located closer to the core of the right than to its periphery. Since *Odièvre* involves a conflict between two rights that are located equally close to the core of the right to private life, application of the core-periphery criterion does not yield reasons in favour of – or against – the human rights in conflict in *Odièvre*. Or, in other words, it yields equally strong reasons in favour of both rights.

The additional rights criterion, conversely, does provide reasons in favour of one of the human rights in conflict in *Odièvre*. It provides some support – albeit limited – to the right to decisional privacy of the mother. The majority in *Odièvre* noted that the conflict was not limited to the human rights of Ms Odièvre and her mother. Instead, it allegedly also involved those of other persons:

> [i]n addition to that conflict of interest [*i.e.* between the applicant and her mother], the problem of anonymous births cannot be dealt with in isolation from the issue of the protection of third parties, essentially the adoptive parents, the father and the other members of the natural family. The Court notes in that connection that the applicant is now 38 years old, having been adopted at the age of four, and that non-consensual disclosure could entail substantial risks, not only for the mother herself, but also for the adoptive family which brought up the applicant, and her natural father and siblings, each of whom also has a right to respect for his or her private and family life.[33]

As correctly noted by the majority, the conflict in *Odièvre* was indeed not a binary one. We should, however, not overestimate the extent to which the human rights of all persons listed by the majority were actually at stake. It is, for instance, difficult to perceive how the right to private and family life of Ms Odièvre's adoptive family would be affected if Ms Odièvre – now an adult woman – were to obtain further information about her origins. No actual damage appears conceivable here. Moreover, as pointed out by the dissenting judges, 'there is nothing in the case file to suggest that [the adoptive parents] were opposed to [Ms Odièvre's] action'.[34] The majority's assumption that the adoptive parents' human rights were at stake in the conflict thus rested on mere speculation. Contrary to the majority's assertion, the human rights of the adoptive family are irrelevant to the balancing exercise in *Odièvre*.

Some of the other additional human rights enumerated by the majority are, however, of immediate relevance to the balancing exercise between the human rights of Ms Odièvre and those of her mother. The human rights of the biological

33 *Odièvre, supra* note 16 at para 44.

34 Dissenting opinion of Judges Wildhaber, Bratza, Bonello, Loucaides, Cabral Barreto, Tulkens and Pellonpää in ibid. at para 8.

father are of particular salience. Given that the biological father had unequivocally expressed his unwillingness to take care of Ms Odièvre after her birth, he would presumably object to having his identity disclosed some 30 years later. The father's right to private life was thus effectively at stake in the conflict. It functions as an additional right that strengthens the position of the mother's human rights in the balance with those of Ms Odièvre.

That leaves the right to private and family life of Ms Odièvre's siblings. Based on the facts of the case, it is difficult to assess how these rights might affect the balancing exercise. We have no information on the siblings' knowledge about Ms Odièvre, nor of their preferences. The siblings might not even have known about Ms Odièvre's very existence. On that hypothesis, it is impossible to determine the relevance of their human rights to the balancing exercise. Any evaluation would necessarily rest on pure speculation. But even if we assume that the siblings knew about Ms Odièvre's existence, we would be hard pressed to assess their preferences. Would they wish to meet Ms Odièvre or at least learn more about her? Or would they prefer to avoid any contact and object to Ms Odièvre learning more about them? Given the silence of the facts on this particular point, we simply do not know. Therefore, it seems prudent to not take the siblings' human rights into account at all. Otherwise, we risk imposing on them a view they may well not share.

Hence, the only additional right that offers reasons in favour of the human rights in conflict in *Odièvre* is the right to private and family life of the biological father. His human rights clearly play to the benefit of the mother's right to decisional privacy. Their relevance alone cannot, however, decide the case. As I noted in Chapter 6, balancing exercises should not be reduced to a game of numbers, in which the human right supported by the most additional rights prevails. The relevance of additional rights should, therefore, not offer conclusive reasons for the resolution of a conflict. Nevertheless, the human rights of the biological father offer a presumptive reason for resolving the conflict to the benefit of the mother's rights to decisional privacy. Along with other balancing reasons, it will be weaved into the nets of arguments I will construct once I have identified all relevant reasons.

One such reason is revealed by application of the general interest criterion to the conflict in *Odièvre*. The general interest played a prominent role in the ECtHR's majority judgment:

> [t]here is also a general interest at stake, as the French legislature has consistently sought to protect the mother's and child's health during pregnancy and birth and to avoid abortions, in particular illegal abortions, and children being abandoned other than under the proper procedure. The right to respect for life, a higher-ranking value guaranteed by the Convention, is thus one of the aims pursued by the French system.[35]

35 *Odièvre*, *supra* note 16 at para 45.

The reference to 'the right to respect for life' should arguably not be read as entailing a further human rights conflict (between Ms Odièvre's right to decisional privacy and the right to life). Since the 'right' in question was only speculatively at stake *and* because it was held by indeterminate individuals (potentially all newborns), the definition of genuine human rights conflicts – provided in Chapter 2 – is not met. Instead, the majority's reference to the 'general interest' at the start of the cited passage more accurately identifies what might also be at stake in *Odièvre*: protection of the value of life (*not* someone's specific right to life).

The dissenting judges, however, disputed the majority's assumption that the French system effectively protected the value of life:

> [a]s regards the general interest ... it should be noted that at present there is no reliable data to support the notion that there would be a risk of an increase in abortions, or even of cases of infanticide, if the system of anonymous births was abolished.[36]

The dissenting judges moreover compared the French system of anonymous births to systems adopted in other European countries, noting that

> [i]t has not been established, in particular by statistical data, that there has been a rise in the number of abortions or cases of infanticide in the majority of the countries in the Council of Europe that do not have legislation similar to that existing in France.[37]

To fully appreciate the salience of the majority's argument and the dissenting judges' retort, we must shortly venture into heretofore unexplored terrain: the subsidiary nature of the European human rights system.[38] Protection of human rights is, within the ECHR system, first and foremost the obligation of national states. Only when those states fail to abide by the standards imposed by the ECHR will the Court step in and find states in breach of the Convention. These standards, however, may be flexible. Indeed, if the idea of subsidiarity in human rights law has any substantive meaning, it entails that different states may tackle the same

36 Dissenting opinion of Judges Wildhaber, Bratza, Bonello, Loucaides, Cabral Barreto, Tulkens and Pellonpää in ibid. at para 9.

37 Ibid.

38 For detailed discussion, see Stijn Smet, 'When Human Rights Clash in "The Age of Subsidiarity": What Role for the Margin of Appreciation?', in Petr Agha (ed.), *Human Rights Between Law and Politics: The Margin of Appreciation in Post-National Contexts* (Hart Publishing, forthcoming 2017; manuscript on file with the author). See also Lech Garlicki, 'Judicial Deliberations: The Strasbourg Perspective', in Nick Huls *et al.* (eds), *The Legitimacy of Highest Courts' Rulings – Judicial Deliberations and Beyond* (T.M.C. Asser Press, 2009), 391.

problem in different ways, *without* thereby necessarily breaching human rights standards.[39] Where multiple viable avenues for human rights protection are available, the ECtHR would arguably need concrete evidence to the contrary before it could dismiss a state's argument that its particular system contributes to the protection of the general interest.

Under the particular circumstances of the *Odièvre* case, however, no such evidence existed. The dissenting judges merely referred to the *absence* of evidence. This seems insufficient to dismiss the French system of anonymous birth out of hand. In the absence of genuine countervailing evidence, the French system at least had the capacity to contribute to the protection of the value of life. Even if the extent to which that value was actually at stake remained uncertain, resolution of the conflict in *Odièvre* had a bearing on the general interest pursued by the French system of anonymous births. Once that premise is accepted, the general interest undeniably plays to the benefit of the mother's human rights. It may not decisively settle the conflict, but it does provide a presumptive reason in favour of the mother's right to decisional privacy.

The purpose criterion, finally, might *seem* relevant to the balancing exercise in *Odièvre*, but it is – in fact – not. As I explained in Chapter 6, the purpose criterion is of primary relevance when a human rights conflict centres on the rights of the child. The purpose criterion is of particular salience when a human rights conflict involves children, on the one hand, and persons responsible for them, on the other (*e.g.* parents, foster care families, etc.). In that context, the criterion expresses the idea that certain human rights stand in function of the rights of the child. The right of parents to educate their children in conformity with their own religious or philosophical beliefs, for instance, stands in function of the right to education of the child. The purpose of the former right is – at least in part – to ensure effective protection and fulfilment of the latter.

In the history that preceded the *Odièvre* case, there was surely a moment in which a potential human rights conflict arose between parents and child. Ms Odièvre was abandoned as a child by her parents. At the moment of abandonment, her right to family life arguably clashed with the right to decisional privacy of her

39 *Odièvre*, *supra* note 16 at para 49 ('[t]he Court observes ... that the States must be allowed to determine the means which they consider to be best suited to achieve the aim of reconciling [competing] interests'). The dissenting judges rejected the majority's argument. Instead, they argued that the 'fairest scrutiny was called for when weighing up the competing interests'. See the dissenting opinion of Judges Wildhaber, Bratza, Bonello, Loucaides, Cabral Barreto, Tulkens and Pellonpää in ibid. at para 11. If the argument by the dissenting judges were accepted, the assessment under the general interest criterion would, of course, change. If a narrow margin of appreciation (strict scrutiny) were to apply, France should indeed prove that its system effectively contributed to the reduction of abortions, particularly illegal ones, and of child abandonments outside the proper procedures. This indicates that the substantive arguments advanced in this book need to be combined with more procedural and institutional considerations, in applying the framework to human rights conflicts in a particular jurisdiction (see Introduction).

parents.[40] That particular conflict, however, was not at issue in the *Odièvre* case that reached Strasbourg. Instead, the case at the ECtHR entailed a conflict between the human rights of two adults. For Ms Odièvre, her right to family life was no longer in play. Rather, her right to know her origins was at stake. The adult Ms Odièvre's right clashed with the right to decisional privacy of her biological mother. But neither of those rights stands in function of the other. The child's best interest is – quite simply – irrelevant to the particular conflict at issue in *Odièvre*.[41] Therefore, the purpose criterion is, upon further reflection, inapplicable to the balancing exercise between Ms Odièvre's human rights and those of her mother.

Having applied the seven criteria of the structured balancing test to the human rights conflict in *Odièvre*, we can now weave the identified reasons into nets of argument. The basic structure of those nets is made up of the reasons identified under the impact criterion. In applying that criterion to the facts of the *Odièvre* case, I concluded that the human rights of Ms Odièvre had suffered 'certain' and 'moderate' damage, while the human rights of her biological mother would have suffered 'certain' and 'serious' damage (if Ms Odièvre's request had been granted). Application of the impact criterion thus yields slightly stronger reasons in favour of the mother's right to decisional privacy than Ms Odièvre's right to know her origins.

This intermediate conclusion is not altered by the core-periphery criterion. Indeed, the human rights in conflict in *Odièvre* are both rather core aspects of the right to private life. Thus, the core-periphery criterion does not offer reasons in favour of – nor against – either right. The additional rights criterion and the general interest criterion, conversely, offer clear reasons in favour of the mother's human rights. Although inconclusive in their own right, those reasons strengthen the basic structure of the net of arguments supporting the mother's right to decisional privacy. The value criterion, the responsibility criterion and the purpose criterion turned out to be irrelevant or inapplicable. They do not, therefore, provide reasons that may alter the results of the balancing exercise. In sum, application of the structured balancing test provides support to the majority judgment of the Grand Chamber in *Odièvre*. Since the biological mother's right to decisional privacy was supported by stronger reasons than Ms Odièvre's right to decisional privacy, the conflict was correctly resolved – by the majority of the Grand Chamber – to the benefit of the former.

In applying the structured balancing test to *Odièvre*, we are thus able to make a comparative judgment on the strength of the reasons supporting the human rights in conflict. We are able to decide, with some measure of rational confidence, which human right should prevail. Thereby, it has become clear that the *Odièvre*

40 One way to conceive of that conflict is that it was resolved to the best interest of Ms Odièvre when she was adopted by the Odièvre family.

41 Unsurprisingly, then, the majority judgment and dissent in *Odièvre* do not reference the best interest of the child at all, in relation to Ms Odièvre.

case did not entail a genuine dilemma. It might have involved an element of tragedy, but the human rights in conflict were not strongly incommensurable. The human rights in conflict in another ECtHR case, however, were. That case – *Evans v the United Kingdom* – illustrates the limits of the structured balancing test.

Evans v the United Kingdom: the limits of the structured balancing test

Unlike *Odièvre*, the ECtHR case of *Evans the United Kingdom* – which I have already discussed in earlier chapters – entailed a genuine dilemma: a particularly intense human rights conflict that is marked by an element of tragedy and strong incommensurability. Given the strong incommensurability involved, the conflict in *Evans* cannot be resolved through application of the structured balancing test. That is, at least, what the following analysis reveals.

Ms Evans, the person at the heart of the *Evans* case, wished to undergo IVF treatment in order to have a genetic child. Her former partner, however, withdrew his consent to the use of frozen embryos, which contained his genetic material. A few years earlier, when Ms Evans and her partner (referenced as 'J.' in the ECtHR judgment) were still together, they had undergone medical treatment to increase their chances of having genetic children. In the process, preliminary tests revealed that Ms Evans had serious pre-cancerous tumours in both ovaries. She was informed that her ovaries would have to be removed. She was also told that, because the tumours were growing slowly, it would be possible to first extract some eggs for *in vitro* fertilisation.

Ms Evans and J. decided to make use of that opportunity. They were informed that they would each have to sign a form consenting to the IVF treatment. In accordance with the applicable legislation, either partner could withdraw his or her consent at any time before the embryos were implanted in Ms Evans' uterus. Both partners signed the requisite form. Eleven of Ms Evans' eggs were subsequently harvested and fertilised with J.'s sperm. Six embryos were eventually created and consigned to storage. Afterwards, Ms Evans had an operation to remove her ovaries.

At the time, all relevant parties – Ms Evans, her partner and all courts that ruled on their case – assumed, based on medical opinions, that use of the stored embryos would be Ms Evans' last and only chance to have a genetic child.[42] Before the embryos could be implanted, however, Ms Evans and J. broke up. The latter subsequently withdrew his consent for further use and storage of the embryos. Ms Evans knew that she would, as a result, not be able to undergo the IVF treatment she desired. She instituted judicial proceedings, seeking an injunction order requiring J. to restore his consent. But the UK courts dismissed her claims.

42 Subsequent medical advances, however, have made it possible for Ms Evans to have a genetic child, after all. Since this eventuality was unknown and unforeseeable to the actors involved at the time, I will not address it further. For discussion, see Zucca, *supra* note 18.

The Court of Appeal, in particular, found that adopting the solution requested by Ms Evans would 'require a balance to be struck between two entirely *incommensurable* things'.[43]

Ms Evans then brought her case to the ECtHR, where the Grand Chamber of the Court ruled against her. The Court concluded that

> [a]s regards the balance struck between the conflicting … rights of the parties to the IVF treatment, the Grand Chamber, in common with every other court which has examined this case, has great sympathy for [Ms Evans], who clearly desires a genetically related child above all else. However, … it does not consider that [her] right to respect for the decision to become a parent in the genetic sense should be accorded greater weight than J.'s right to respect for his decision not to have a genetically related child with her.[44]

Earlier in its judgment, the Court had already described the *Evans* case as a dilemma:

> [t]he dilemma central to the present case is that it involves a conflict between the Article 8 rights of two private individuals: the applicant and J. Moreover, each person's interest is entirely irreconcilable with the other's, since if the applicant is permitted to use the embryos J. will be forced to become a father, whereas if J.'s refusal or withdrawal of consent is upheld the applicant will be denied the opportunity of becoming a genetic parent. In the difficult circumstances of this case, whatever solution the national authorities might adopt would result in the interests of one or the other parties to the IVF treatment being wholly frustrated.[45]

This particular passage emphasises the intense nature of the conflict in *Evans* ('entirely irreconcilable'), as well as the tragedy involved (any solution 'would result in the interests of one or the other parties … being wholly frustrated'). But although the domestic courts had invoked the notion of incommensurability, the ECtHR itself did not. The Court instead adopted the broad definition of dilemma provided above: a particularly intense conflict in which a tragic choice is inevitable. Whether *Evans* also entailed strong incommensurability, the decisive element of a *genuine* human rights dilemma, will be examined below.

Application of the structured balancing test to Evans

In applying the structured balancing test of Chapter 6 to *Evans*, we are bound to realise – fairly quickly – that several of its criteria are either inapplicable or irrelevant

43 *Evans, supra* note 19 at para 25 (emphasis added).

44 Ibid. at para 90.

45 Ibid. at para 73.

to the conflict at issue. The value criterion is inapplicable, given that the conflict in *Evans* pits two instances of the right to private life against one another, to which the value criterion does not apply. The additional rights criterion is irrelevant, because *Evans* concerns a strictly binary conflict between two individual right holders. No other – additional – rights were in play. The purposes for which the human rights in conflict were exercised did not, furthermore, stand in direct relation to each other, nor was the responsibility of the right holders in exercising their rights at issue. Thus, the purpose and responsibility criterion do not apply either. That leaves three potentially relevant criteria to the balancing exercise between Ms Evans' and J.'s right to decisional privacy: the impact criterion, the core-periphery criterion and the general interest criterion.

Under the impact criterion, the human rights in conflict in *Evans* suffered – or would have suffered – 'certain' damage. In the actual circumstances of the case, Ms Evans' right to decisional privacy suffered 'certain' damage. As a result of J.'s withdrawal of consent, Ms Evans was no longer able to pursue her decision to become a genetic parent. If J.'s consent had been restored by judicial order, conversely, *his* right to decisional privacy would have suffered equally 'certain' damage.

As for the extent of the damage, this arguably falls to be classified as 'serious' – or even 'very serious' – with regard to both human rights in conflict. In the actual circumstances of the case, Ms Evans was precluded from having a genetic child. She thereby saw her decisional privacy 'wholly frustrated', as the ECtHR put it.[46] But if the case had been decided differently by the UK courts, J. would have been forced to become a genetic parent against his express will, thereby also seeing his decisional privacy wholly frustrated.[47] The inevitable sacrifice involved in the conflict was recognised by the ECtHR:

> each person's interest is entirely irreconcilable with the other's, since if [Ms Evans] is permitted to use the embryos J. will be forced to become a father, whereas if J.'s refusal or withdrawal of consent is upheld [Ms Evans] will be denied the opportunity of becoming a genetic parent.[48]

Because resolution of the conflict in *Evans* necessarily entailed that the decisional privacy of one of the parties (not) to become a genetic parent would be eviscerated, the damage should be labelled equally 'serious' (or 'very serious') with respect to both human rights. Application of the impact criterion thus does not offer reasons in favour of – or against – the human rights in conflict: both (would) suffer 'certain' and 'serious' (or 'very serious') damage.[49]

46 Ibid. ('In the difficult circumstances of this case, whatever solution the national authorities might adopt would result in the interests of one or the other parties to the IVF treatment being wholly frustrated.').

47 Ibid.

48 Ibid.

49 I should note, however, that the *Evans* case shows that the results of structured balancing depend, at least in part, on how one qualifies the human rights in conflict. In the text, I have followed the ECtHR in characterising *Evans* as a conflict between two instances of the right

Turning to the core-periphery criterion, we are bound to conclude that the human rights at stake in the conflict were identical for both parties. Both Ms Evans and J. saw their right to decisional privacy (not) to become a genetic parent threatened. Since the rights in conflict were identical, they should – obviously – be located equally close to the core of the right to private life. Thus, the core-periphery criterion fails to offer reasons in favour of – or against – the human rights in conflict in *Evans*.[50]

That leaves us with the general interest criterion, on which the entire balancing exercise now hinges. Speaking directly to the relevance of this criterion, the ECtHR held in *Evans* that 'the case does not involve simply a conflict between individuals; the legislation in question also served a number of wider, public

to decisional privacy (on the decision (not) to become a genetic parent). See ibid. at para 90. But if one were to qualify the conflicting rights differently, the result of the structured balancing test may well change. If one, for instance, would qualify Ms Evans' and J.'s rights as, respectively, the right to become a genetic parent and the right *not* to become a genetic parent, one could very well debate whether the impact on both rights would still be equal. The damage to Ms Evans' right to become a genetic parent would be total, given that IVF treatment was her last opportunity to have a genetic child. The damage could thus be qualified as 'serious' (or 'very serious') and 'certain'. J.'s right not to become a genetic parent would suffer certain damage as well. But one could debate whether the damage is really of the same gravity as the damage suffered by Ms Evans' right. Indeed, 'all' J. would have to live with is the knowledge that there is a genetic child of his out there in the world. Seemingly, this does less serious damage to J.'s rights than the converse situation does to Ms Evans' right to have a genetic child. Thus, the application of the structured balancing test changes. Yet, we could re-qualify the rights to be balanced once more, this time as the right (not) to become a parent (in all possible senses, not necessarily genetic). In this scenario, nothing would change for J., but things *would* change for Ms Evans. Indeed, the damage done to her right to become a parent would certainly be less serious than the damage done to her right to become a *genetic* parent, given that she could – for instance – adopt a child. What I aim to demonstrate, here, is that it is vital to be aware of the importance of the qualification of the human rights in the balancing exercise. In keeping with the ECtHR's characterisation of the *Evans* case, I consider the balance to be struck in *Evans* as one between both parties' right to decisional privacy (not) to become a genetic parent. The application of the structured balancing test offered in the text is based on that premise. For a contrary view, see Eva Brems, 'Evans v UK: Three Grounds for Ruling Differently', in Stijn Smet and Eva Brems (eds), *Conflicts of Rights at the European Court of Human Rights* (Oxford University Press, forthcoming; manuscript on file with the author). Brems frames the conflict in *Evans* differently and defends a balancing outcome in favour of Ms Evans.

50 Note that, as indicated in the previous footnote, it is possible to contest the premise on which this relies, namely that the human rights in conflict in *Evans* were the respective parties' right to decisional privacy (not) to become a genetic parent. If one were to contest that premise, for instance by arguing that the rights to in conflict were the respective parties' right (not) to become a genetic parent, the reasons identified under the core-periphery criterion may well be different. Indeed, one could then plausibly argue that Ms Evans' right to become a genetic parent was located closer to the core of her right to private life than J.'s right *not* to become a genetic parent.

interests, in upholding the principle of the primacy of consent and promoting legal clarity and certainty, for example'.[51]

Insofar as 'the principle of the primacy of consent' relates to J.'s right to decisional privacy, it has already been incorporated under the impact criterion. There, I labelled the hypothetical damage done to J.'s right to decisional privacy as 'serious' (or 'very serious'), precisely because revoking his consent would eviscerate his decisional privacy. To avoid double counting, we should thus evaluate the Court's emphasis on 'the primacy of consent' in terms, not of J.'s rights, but of the general interest. The Court's reference to 'the principle of the primacy of consent' should thus be read in light of its subsequent emphasis on 'promoting legal clarity and certainty', a quintessential general interest.[52]

Under UK law, legal certainty in the context of IVF treatment was promoted by a bright line rule under which absolute priority was given to the primacy of consent of both partners. This plays to the benefit of J., who had withdrawn his consent. As I noted in Chapter 6, however, the general interest in legal certainty should provide less strong reasons in balancing human rights than more substantive, rights-oriented general interests (*e.g.* the societal value of freedom of expression on issues of public concern).[53] Nevertheless, the general interest in legal certainty operates as a (relatively weak) reason in favour of J.'s right to decisional privacy, and thus against Ms Evans' right to decisional privacy.

Yet, as I also noted in Chapter 6, reasons identified under the general interest criterion cannot – in and of themselves – decisively settle a human rights conflict.[54] Instead, they should be woven into nets of arguments along with *other* reasons. In *Evans*, no such other reasons could be found. All remaining criteria of the structured balancing test failed to yield reasons in favour of – or against – the human rights in conflict. This, I posit, signals the strong incommensurability of the human rights in conflict in *Evans*. The case entailed a particularly intense human rights conflict, under which a tragic choice was inevitable. In contrast to *Odièvre*, moreover, the structured balancing test failed to provide a solution to *Evans* that has even a semblance of rationality. Thus, the human rights conflict in *Evans* arguably constituted a genuine human rights dilemma.[55]

Despite the strong incommensurability involved, the tragic choice provoked by the circumstances of the *Evans* case could not be escaped. Given the failure of

51 *Evans*, *supra* note 19 at para 74.

52 The fact that the ECtHR referenced the *principle* of the primacy of consent indicates that it, also, was thinking first and foremost about the general interest in legal certainty (for all couples who jointly decide to undergo IVF treatment).

53 Chapter 6 – 'The seven criteria of the structured balancing test in detail'.

54 Ibid.

55 Zucca, *supra* note 2 at 26; Virgilio Afonso da Silva, 'Comparing the Incommensurable: Constitutional Principles, Balancing and Rational Decision', 31 *Oxford Journal of Legal Studies* (2011), 276 and 292. See also Dworkin, 'No Right Answer?', 53 *New York University Law Review* (1978), 31 ('[i]f there is no right answer in a hard case, this must be in virtue of some more problematic type of indeterminacy or incommensurability').

rational comparability, the inevitable choice between the human rights in conflict would be *arational*, based on subjective preferences or intuition.[56] Such an arational choice is 'permitted by reason', but is 'not made for any articulable reason yielding a judgment about the comparative merits of the available alternatives'.[57] The core aim of the structured balancing test – enabling a comparative judgment on the strength of reasons in favour of human rights in conflict – could thus not be achieved.

If and when an arational choice between human rights in conflict is inevitable, a human rights court such as the ECtHR is arguably not the appropriate body to make it. Instead, the subjective choice should be left to the legislator, who – in principle – enjoys greater democratic legitimacy.[58] Because the ECtHR was faced with a genuine dilemma between strongly incommensurable human rights in *Evans*, it acted prudently in deferring to the bright line rule adopted by the UK legislator, which at least had the benefit of providing legal certainty.[59] The alternative scenario, under which the ECtHR would have struck the balance in favour of Ms Evans, would inevitably have entailed moulding a subjective preference into law, imposed by an unelected judiciary.[60]

Conclusion

In this final chapter, I set out to explore the limits of the structured balancing test of Chapter 6. I hypothesised that those limits would be reached where a human rights conflict involves a genuine dilemma. To test the hypothesis, I first defined the notion of 'dilemma' broadly, as a particularly intense conflict that involves an element of tragedy. With that broad conception of a dilemma in hand, I identified two cases that might pose a challenge to the structured balancing test: *Odièvre v*

56 Henry S. Mather, 'Law-making and Incommensurability', 47 *McGill Law Journal* (2002), 366 ('[w]hen confronted with conflicting goods or instantiations that are rationally incommensurable, lawmakers ... can use intuition to make arational choices'). See also Waldron, *supra* note 1 at 816 ('if the choice problem [under strong incommensurability] is acute enough, the agent's behaviour will eventually reveal a preference for one consideration or another. However the strong incommensurability thesis holds that such a preference reveals only a particular preference or choice ... Different people will decide differently ... and nothing much in the way of reason can be adduced').

57 Mather, *supra* note 56 at 388.

58 It of course remains open to higher courts, like the ECtHR, to scrutinise the quality of the democratic decision-making process. If that process reveals deficiencies, for instance a failure to abide by procedural human rights standards, the ECtHR could still set aside the bright line rule adopted in the legislation at issue. Yet, that would be the result of procedural scrutiny, not substantive balancing. Since Parts II and III of this book focus on the latter, I do not discuss this alternative, procedural approach in the text.

59 See also Afonso da Silva, *supra* note 55 at 276, 292 and 300 (arguing in terms of "parity" or stalemate between both rights in the *Evans* case, which he claims is the ground for discretion in deciding).

60 See Zucca, *supra* note 19 at 448 (arguing that the dissenting judges' argument that Ms Evans' right should have been granted priority 'does not sound more than an entrenched preference').

France and *Evans v the United Kingdom*. Both cases confronted the ECtHR with a particularly intense conflict, in which a tragic choice was inevitable.

In applying the structured balancing test to *Odièvre*, I found that it provided a clear solution to the conflict, supported by convincing reasons. *Odièvre* therefore did not, I concluded, entail a *genuine* human rights dilemma. It did not present the ECtHR with a case of strong incommensurability. Such strong incommensurability *did* obtain, however, in *Evans v the United Kingdom*. The tragic conflict in *Evans* could not be resolved with use of the structured balancing test. This signals that the case entailed strong incommensurability. In the face of such strong incommensurability, only an *arational* choice between the human rights in conflict can be made. But because arational choices are inevitably based on subjective or intuitive preferences, I argued that courts should defer the decision to the legislator, which in principle enjoys greater democratic legitimacy.

Conclusion

When human rights conflict, judges face a dilemma: they are seemingly forced to make difficult choices between superior norms that deserve principled equal respect. To assist judges in tackling conflicts between human rights, I have developed – throughout this book – a framework for the adjudication of such conflicts. The framework is composed of three consecutive steps, ranging from the most to the least optimal approach to human rights conflicts. The first step – defusing conflicts between human rights – aims to remove the conflicts themselves, while keeping the human rights at stake within intact. Defusing conflicts enables judges to avoid any dilemmas in the adjudication of human rights conflicts. Whenever a conflict cannot be defused – *i.e.* whenever it is genuine – the second step of the framework comes into play. Under the second step, judges are encouraged to reach a compromise between human rights in conflict. This entails finding a solution under which competing human rights make mutual, but minimal sacrifices, so as to have them survive the conflict as intact as possible. Compromises, in other words, aim to minimise the impact of human rights conflicts.

Yet, in relation to most human rights conflicts, defusing proves impossible and reaching a compromise unviable. Instead, difficult choices between human rights have to be made. Judges have to decide, in particular, which human right should prevail over the other(s); and, concomitantly, which human right(s) should be sacrificed. To assist judges in making these difficult choices, I have proposed a decisional aid in the form of a structured balancing test. The structured balancing test aims to enable comparative judgments on the strength of reasons in favour of – and against – human rights in conflict. It relies on the construction of nets of arguments, into which reasons in favour of – and against – human rights in conflict are woven. These reasons, and their strength, are identified through application of a limited set of balancing criteria. By comparing nets of arguments woven in support of human rights in conflict, judges should be able to decide – with some measure of rational confidence – which human right should prevail in the concrete circumstances of a given conflict. Thus, the structured balancing test overcomes the challenge from weak incommensurability of human rights.

The structured balancing test is ineffectual, however, in the face of strong incommensurability. When strong incommensurability is in play, human rights are incomparable. Hence, the core aim of the structured balancing test – enabling comparative judgments – cannot be achieved. Yet, such strong incommensurability rarely obtains. It arises, not in 'normal' human rights conflicts, but in human rights dilemmas: particularly intense conflicts that involve an element of tragedy and for which the structured balancing test fails to provide a solution. Such human rights dilemmas can only be resolved by way of an arational choice. Because arational choices are by definition subjective, they should arguably be left to the legislator, who enjoys – in principle – greater democratic legitimacy than unelected judges.

The framework proposed in this book, as just sketched, is built on three foundational premises: (1) a conception of relative human rights as *pro tanto* rights; (2) the idea that human rights carry special normative force over the public interest; and (3) the concomitant proposition that human rights conflicts pose particular challenges for human rights adjudication. In this book, I have treated human rights conflicts as a special category of hard cases in law, distinct from 'traditional' human rights cases, in which human rights are opposed by the public interest (or private interests that are not protected by way of human rights). A core argument of this book has been that 'traditional' human rights cases and human rights conflicts should be tackled through distinct tests or resolution frameworks. This has important repercussions for the value of the framework proposed in this book to judicial practice across the globe.

The proposed framework for the adjudication of human rights conflicts is directly inspired by the case law of the ECtHR, the world's foremost and most influential human rights court. The Court's case law forms the analytical backdrop against which the book's theoretical framework is developed. The framework thus does not represent a drastic overhaul of the Court's judicial practice. Rather, it systematises and structures a myriad of elements already present within its case law. As such, the framework is fully consonant with the ECtHR's approach to human rights conflicts. The framework is, by extension, of immediate salience to other jurisdictions in which courts employ a 'priority of rights' model of proportionality, as the ECtHR does. The framework is, thus, relevant to the other two regional human rights courts: the Inter-American Court of Human Rights and the African Court on Human and Peoples' Rights. But it is also of immediate value to several constitutional courts, such as the Constitutional Court of South Africa and the Supreme Court of Israel, which have likewise adopted a 'priority of rights' model of proportionality analysis.

The framework is *prima facie* less congenial to courts that rely (in part) on an absolute conception of rights, as the US Supreme Court does. It is also less obviously suited to courts that favour a conception of rights as optimisation requirements, as the German Constitutional Court does. Whereas the former courts would take issue with the conception of human rights as *pro tanto* rights on which this book's framework is built, the latter would fail to see the need for a distinct resolution framework for human rights conflicts. Nevertheless, a few remarks are in order.

The first step of this book's framework is arguably of immediate value to *any* court. Judges the world over are likely to be attracted to solutions that defuse legal disputes, regardless of the specific features of the jurisdiction in which they adjudicate such disputes. If conflicts in law can be removed, while keeping the rights implied within them entirely intact, judges would presumably hesitate to reject such a solution out of hand. Instead, they would in all likelihood welcome it. Take the example of fair trial rights I discussed in Chapter 3. No matter in which jurisdiction judges adjudicate cases, they are bound to favour court proceedings that *simultaneously* respect equality of arms *and* ensure expedience of proceedings, instead of sacrificing one to safeguard the other.

The second and third steps of the framework, however, will not appeal to courts that rely on a 'specificationist' conception of rights as absolute rules. Yet, few courts rely on such an absolutist conception of rights. Within US constitutional law, for instance, even the absolute status of free speech is open to reasonable debate. Outside the specific domain of free speech, moreover, the second and third steps of the framework might very well prove of value to US constitutional law. In the area of privacy rights, for example, US constitutional law is more congenial to the underlying conception of human rights as *pro tanto* rights that informs this book's framework. In the final analysis, whether the framework may prove relevant to US constitutional adjudication depends not, I venture, on the conception of rights that underpins it. Rather, the pertinent question is whether the balancing approach of the third step of the framework, in particular, is sufficiently congenial to the current state of US constitutional law. The answer to that question I leave to US constitutional scholars and judges.

Switching to the perspective of courts that rely on a conception of rights as optimisation requirements, such as the German Constitutional Court, the second and third steps of this book's framework are not principally objectionable. The question that confronts these courts, rather, concerns the need for *distinct* resolution frameworks for 'traditional' cases and conflicting rights cases. Presumably, the German Constitutional Court and other courts that reject the special normative force of human (or constitutional) rights will fail to see such a need. This, however, does not *ipso facto* imply rejection of the framework proposed in this book. Judges at the Constitutional Court of Germany, for instance, may very well consider the framework not to be a *genuine alternative* to proportionality analysis. They might, rather, see it as a *refined version* of the proportionality test. As such, they might find great value in the framework after all, particularly in its balancing test.

The final court to briefly consider is the Court of Justice of the European Union (CJEU). In its fundamental rights adjudication under the Charter of Fundamental Rights of the EU, the CJEU often resorts to proportionality analysis. The Luxembourg Court does not, however, appear to conceive of fundamental rights as holding special normative force over the public interest. Nevertheless, the CJEU's case law is arguably congenial to some of the core arguments presented in this book. A full analysis cannot be provided here. Instead, I will discuss one particular example to illustrate – rather than demonstrate – the salience of this book's framework to the judicial practice of the CJEU. In its intermediary liability case law, the CJEU has ruled that a 'fair balance' must be struck between the fundamental rights of intermediaries, internet users and copyright holders.[1] Importantly, the CJEU does *not* favour a solution in which one of these parties' rights prevails over the others. Instead, the Court arguably seeks an equilibrium between the fundamental rights in conflict. Here, the second step of my resolution framework – on compromises – is of immediate salience. What I have proposed in Chapter 3 in relation to the ECtHR's *Delfi* case, in particular, could easily be extended to the intermediary liability case law of the CJEU. Indeed, a compromise solution to the intermediary liability conundrum would be fully consonant with the CJEU's view on the matter.

To conclude this book, I will return to its opening pages. In the Introduction, I put forth three core aims: (1) to debunk the scholarly argument that human rights conflicts do not pose distinct challenges for adjudication; (2) to propose a theoretically sound and practically useful framework for judicial practice, which currently struggles to adequately conceptualise and resolve human rights conflicts; and (3) to develop an alternative to – or refined account of – the proportionality test in the specific domain of conflicts between human rights. In developing a distinct framework for the adjudication of human rights conflicts throughout this book, I hope to have gone some way towards reaching these objectives. How far – if anywhere at all – the framework will travel depends on how it is received by judges and courts the world over, starting with the ECtHR in Europe. Proposing frameworks, after all, is relatively easy. The *real* task, which is far more daunting, belongs to the judges who have to tackle the dilemmas inherent in the adjudication of human rights conflicts in their daily judicial practice.

1 *Promusicae* [2007] EUECJ C-275/06; *Netlog* [2012] EUECJ C-360/10; *Scarlet Extended* [2011] EUECJ C-70/10; *UPC Telekabel Wien* [2014] EUECJ C-314/12.

Index

FSC
www.fsc.org
MIX
Papier | Fördert
gute Waldnutzung
FSC® C083411

Kolibri 360 GmbH
Ferdinand-Jühlke-Straße 7
99095 Erfurt, Deutschland
produktsicherheit@kolibri360.de